DEATH IS AN ILLUSION

A LOGICAL EXPLANATION BASED ON
MARTINUS' WORLDVIEW

ELSE BYSKOV

PARAGON HOUSE
St. Paul, Minnesota

112

First Edition, 2002

Published in the United States by
Paragon House
2700 University Avenue West
St. Paul, MN 55114

Manufactured in the United States of America.

Library of Congress Cataloging-in-Publishing data

Byskov, Else, 1950-
   Death is an illusion : a logical explanation based on Martinus' worldview /
by Else Byskov.-- 1st ed.
     p. cm.
Includes bibliographical references.
   ISBN 1-55778-813-8 (pbk. : alk. paper)
   1. Martinus. I. Title.
   BX9998.M37 B97 2002
   299'.93--dc21

                                                                  2002012091

                          10 9 8 7 6 5 4 3 2 1

         For current information about all releases from Paragon House,
             visit the web site at http://www.paragonhouse.com

"Where ignorance is removed, the so-called evil ceases to exist."
Martinus

Contents

Acknowledgments

My first profound thanks go to Martinus, who is the original source of this book. This book could never have been written if Martinus had not dedicated his life to revealing his world picture. Martinus has provided most of the material for this book. I have only presented it in English.

Next I thank my husband and life companion Erik Gadegaard, who has been my first reader and my first critic and whose love and support have been indispensable. I also thank my stepdaughter Ditte Brandt Gadegaard for reading the manuscript critically and suggesting many valuable changes.

A warm thanks goes to my editor Richard Laws for many good suggestions for changes to the original manuscript and for smoothing out creases in my English.

I am indebted to the following persons at the Martinus Institute who have helped me answer tricky questions: Ole Therkelsen, Hans Wittendorff, Mary McGovern, and Willy Kuipert.

I deeply thank Tessa McPherson, who has patiently listened to my explanations about the spiritual world and whose kindness, support, and willingness to help have been of great value.

I also send a warm thanks to my "computer wizards" Klaus Byskov Pedersen (my son), Klaus Langelund Larsen (his friend), and Mikkel Brandt Gadegaard (my stepson) for saving the manuscript at many occasions when its life was in danger because of my own computer ignorance.

Finally I thank my former business partner Jens Peter Dige for understanding my need to drop out of business and letting me go.

Dedication

I dedicate this book to the many people in the world, who through their research or work or through incidents in their lives, have come across aspects of life that they were unable to explain with the existing theories at hand. These people have uncovered features of the true nature of the world, but they had no comprehensive explanation for their findings.

Let me just mention a few a those who have sought and found,

- Ian Stevenson, who researched thousands of cases of reincarnation and laid the first stone to proving that reincarnation is a fact.

- Brian Weiss, who regressed people to health through their re-experiencing traumatic incidents in their past lives.

- Roger Woolger, who did the same without apparently believing in reincarnation.

- Carol Bowman, who found out how much past lives influence our children.

- Raymond Moody, who collected hundreds of cases of near-death experiences.

- Elisabeth Kübler Ross, who studied the process of dying and helped many people through the gates of death.

- Edith Fiore, who pointed out the role that spirit possessions play as a type of mental disturbance.

- Helen Wambach, who collected more than a thousand cases of past life recall and matched these to historical periods.

- Kenneth Ring, who studied what happens at death.

- Joel L. Whitton, who sought to map what happens between incarnations.

- James Lovelock who fathered the Gaia theory about the Earth being a living being.[1]

These people have looked to Buddhism or Hinduism or Gnosticism or to the Bible and found only bits and pieces. However, a complete comprehensive philosophy comprising both the physical and the spiritual levels of our world exists, it is new and not yet well known. Martinus presents a holistic world picture and with this it is possible to explain a whole number of phenomena that have otherwise been inexplicable.

Martinus' explanations confirm almost everything that the people mentioned above have found and vice versa—their findings demonstrate that Martinus' explanations are correct.

As Martinus' work is of great importance for our understanding of the world in which we live, it is desirable that its ideas be known to a growing number of people. Martinus' work is important because it constitutes one of the best keys available to opening the door to the vast sea of knowledge that lies beyond the physical world. The work is a key to the metaphysical level of existence and offers a completely new way of looking at the world.

The knowledge Martinus reveals cannot be accessed through the study of our earthly sciences. Through an initiation Martinus was linked up to a universal divine bank of data to which he had unlimited access. Through this he became a modern mystic—a person who has his knowledge from within. His inner source of knowledge and wisdom brought immense understanding, which he freely made available to all through his writings.

Martinus' world picture is original and unique and provides us with an opportunity to understand why the world situation is as it is and to grasp some of the means to greater happiness and contentment. The world is so full of questions and so short of lasting solutions to the many obvious problems and difficulties that are spread throughout our global community. All who are genuine seekers of answers to the big questions are invited to read these pages. They offer opportunities for deep contemplation and a means to solutions. And as the individual comes to more understanding and knowledge, so does the world.

Wohin soll es gehen?
Wohin es dir gefällt.
Wir sehen zuerst die kleine,
Dann die grosse Welt.

Where are we going?
Where ever you want,
First we see the small,
And then the big world.

Göethe, Faust[2]

1

Introduction

My Own Quest

My own quest for a logical explanation to the meaning of life started long ago when I was still a girl in Denmark. At a very early age I remember looking out of my window into the night sky and asking myself the question: "What is out there and who am I really? Am I really just this girl living in this house and born to these parents, or is there more to it?"

My parents didn't see eye to eye on the subject of religion or the meaning of life.

My father did not practice any religion, whereas my mother's side of the family was very traditional in their Christian faith. My mother's religious conviction was wavering, but my maternal grandmother held the evangelical banner high. She made it abundantly clear that we were not here to have fun, but were here for some obscure reason related to atoning our sins. The way she looked upon life had a funny, rather unsavory taste. It conveyed a feeling of not being allowed to have what you wanted. Everything that was nice was somehow forbidden, and nearly everything you did was a sin. The impression given by this kind of religion was that you could only be safe from sin if you led a joyless life. Joy and laughter were the forerunners of sin and they would lead you onto the smutty road of indulgence and carnal lust, which would eventually take you to the very gates of hell itself. I kept a secure

1

distance from this joyless attitude and my maternal grandmother viewed me with suspicion as a potential black sheep.

It didn't help that my father went into show business the same year I was born and established a variety theater in the building where we lived. From all over the world acrobats, performers, trapeze artists, dancers, magicians, jugglers, performing dogs, and even stripteasers came to perform in our house every night throughout the summer months. Every night I watched the show from my chair on the balcony. The variety theater showed a much happier side to life, there was always fun and laughter; every night was a ball and every night I fell asleep to the notes of "There's No Business Like Show Business." My father never mentioned the subject of sin. He was clearly here to enjoy himself.

My maternal grandmother correctly concluded that my father was a lost cause, but she still had some hopes of saving her daughter and granddaughter from eternal hell. She tried as best she could to exert her influence from a distance, but all her efforts fell on stony ground. Her daughter and granddaughter were, after all, living in a house of sin and could not be easily saved. For many years she refused to come and see the show, which had actually become quite successful. When she finally did, my father had to take out all the juicy bits and tell the performers to omit the dirty jokes because his mother-in-law was coming. Unamused and unrelenting, she watched the show and finally turned her thumbs down. My poor mother had to perform an intense diplomatic Ping-Pong service between my grandmother and my father, and she was under a lot of pressure from both sides. My grandmother was facing the famous choice between pest and cholera. She could not tell her daughter to get a divorce (which was a scandal and a sin) and she could not tell my father to close down the show, as it was our livelihood. Finally a kind of unresolved truce was reached, but my grandmother's resentment toward our whole way of living was always there as an unspoken reproach.

The whole thing was a farce, and no wonder I was a bit confused about what to think. In general, though, I supported my father's happy attitude to life and disregarded my grandmother's warnings about sin and hell.

I can still clearly remember the day at school, I was about ten, when our teacher told us about other religions. He said there were some religions that believed in reincarnation, but that "we" did not. To me the idea of reincarnation immediately sounded right and I wondered why "we" did not accept this idea. I remember thinking that if I, for instance, during an operation and due to some mistake on the surgeon's part, were to die, it seemed so unjust and illogical that I, through no mistake of my own, should lose my only life and that was it. It didn't seem logical that life could be so unjust.

At about the same time I felt that I could pray and relate to God and that I could do this directly. I didn't need the Church of Denmark or my grandmother's ministers to do this. The church seemed to impose a barrier between God and me with its rituals and solemnity and chanting of hymns. The churches were cold and smelled musty and the ministers in their imposing robes seemed to indicate that God was a very remote being who was not to be disturbed in his heaven. He could only be contacted occasionally through the mediation of the ministers, as they held some special position with him. The impression the ministers gave was that God could not be bothered by anybody as insignificant as me and that he was anyway angry with me because of my sins. After some stock-taking of my sins, which were fairly insignificant as I was only ten, I decided that God had no reason to be angry. I concluded that the ministerial barrier was not necessary, that God was all right, and that he did not mind that I skipped the middleman and went direct.

As I grew into womanhood and during my years at university, in spite of my faith in God as a child, I became an atheist and left the People's Church of Denmark of which one automatically becomes a member when baptized. To leave the established church you have to go to talk to the minister of your parish and tell him that you want to leave. He will, of course, try to dissuade you from doing this, saying that you have to stay if you believe in God, if you want to get married in a church, if you want to have your children baptized or if you want to be buried in holy ground. Not feeling deterred by this, I signed my resignation and was later married at the town hall and my two children were never baptized.

I became a searching soul, looking everywhere for some deeper meaning of the hardship and suffering that I saw in the world. However, for many years I remained an atheist and I was sure that there was no God and nothing on the other side of death. Death was the end and that was that. I had long ago abandoned my childhood belief in God and was convinced that we had only one life.

In 1990, when I was close to forty, my husband and I decided to emigrate from Denmark to see if we could establish a life in Spain. On cold and rainy days in Denmark I had often dreamed of the Spanish sun, of the blue Mediterranean, of the blooming bougainvilleas and warm velvety nights. I had majored in Spanish in the university and had taught the language plus English, in which I also have a degree, for eleven years before we emigrated. Spain exerted a strong pull on me, and when the country opened its borders to dentists from other EU countries in 1991, my husband was among the first to apply for a license to practice dentistry.

The decision to emigrate and the turmoil and hardship that came from leaving behind the security of the Danish welfare society only to live by our own devices in the Spanish post-Franco society served only to accelerate my quest. Because life was hard those first years in Spain, we became more aware of the fundamentals of existence, and I am sure that this emphasized my need to know the meaning of it all.

Around 1993 I remember reading *Life and How to Survive It* by John Skynner and John Cleese.[1] At a certain point in the book John Skynner says that the happiest people are those who have some kind of spirituality, who believe in something higher, something beyond the physical world. This really surprised me, because I thought that all intellectual people had the same attitude as I had myself, viz., that there was nothing beyond the physical world and nothing beyond death.

Not long after this I remember sitting on my terrace reading the newspaper *The European*. In this issue there was an article about a Dutch scientific research project, which had aimed to find out if there was anything beyond death.[2] As I was reading, I was sure that the conclusion of this would be that, of course, there was nothing, but to my great surprise the conclusion was quite the opposite. The Dutch scientists presented substantiated evidence showing that death was not the end and that life continued after death in some other form. This was really a revolutionary thought. I was surprised and overwhelmed and curious to know more.

Not long after reading this article a friend of ours came down from Denmark with nine boxes of our books, which had been stored in his house until we had made enough money to buy our own house in Spain. We had now been able to buy a house, and naturally we wanted to have our books with us.

I now know (I certainly didn't know it then) that nothing happens by chance. So it was no chance that on top in one of the boxes lay a book called *The Intuitive Thought* by John Engelbrecht.[3] My husband had bought the book at a sale a few years before, but neither of us had read it, but now it was on top in one of the boxes attracting our attention. In this book John Engelbrecht writes a short introduction to the thoughts and world picture of Martinus,[4] the Danish philosopher and mystic. As soon as I had read this, I knew that I had found at last what I had been looking for.

I read the three thousand pages of Martinus' *Livets Bog* (*The Book of Life*)[5] in a feverish rush, shouting out with joy and laughter as I progressed in my reading. Here it all was: a logical explanation of what life was all about. Every word rang true to me. I was convinced beyond a shadow of a doubt that this was the truth about our existence, about our planet and the universe, about our bodies and the microcosmos, about reincarnation and the nonexistence of death. This was in 1995.

This led us to buy the rest of Martinus' publications: *The Eternal World Picture* (four volumes), *Logic, Funeral Rites*, and twenty-eight smaller books. When I had read it all, the magnitude of what I had found gradually dawned on me. What Martinus presents is a world picture based on logic, a world picture meant for those who have outgrown the ability to believe in the religions, a world picture for the intellectual person. It is a world picture based not on faith but on logic and knowledge. He who has read it no longer has to believe, he knows.

But let me not anticipate these revelations, because these are what this book is all about.

Let me just say that after reading Martinus' books my appetite was whetted, and I started reading every book that I could get hold of on the subject of reincarnation, near-death experiences, regression therapy, deathbed visions, and the process of dying. This let me to read all attainable books by the people to whom I dedicate this book and many more.

As I read, the more depressed I became because all these good people had found aspects of the true nature of existence, but they did not have a satisfactory explanation. They were looking to Hinduism and Buddhism and the Bible to find explanations of the idea of reincarnation and the nonexistence of death, but none of these were satisfactory, as they did not offer a full comprehensive philosophy.

Ever since I read Martinus' books and the works of the people mentioned in the dedication, I have felt a very strong urge to write an introduction to Martinus' world picture in English, so that his extraordinary work can be known to the people in the English-speaking world and to those who are researching reincarnation, death, and the spiritual world. That is why I dedicate this book to all those who sought and found aspects of the truth, but who had no explanation to what they found. The explanation is there, in Martinus' work. The logic that governs the universe has been revealed to us, not as a new religion, but as a science of spirituality. This book is not about faith or belief. This book is about logic and knowledge.

2

The Changing World Pictures

The Old World Pictures

Before I start introducing Martinus' world picture, I would like briefly to mention how our concept of the world has changed down through history, as I think it is important to remember that our view of the world has never been constant. Our way of defining the world has been changing in tune with the discoveries made by explorers and scientists. Every time a revolutionary new discovery about the natural world was made, the world picture had to be adapted to incorporate the new findings.

Around the year 140 BC the Greek astronomer, philosopher, and mathematician Ptolemæus presented his view of the world in his work *Almagest*. According to this theory the Earth is the center of the universe; it is flat and stationary. The Sun, the Moon, the planets, and the stars pass over the Earth on the dome of the sky. Ptolemæus' view of the world is called the geocentric theory.

This way of envisaging the world and the universe survived for more than a thousand years, and even though Copernicus[1] in 1543 put forward his heliocentric theory in which the Sun was considered the center of the universe around which the Earth and the other planets circled, the old geocentric theory was still stubbornly adhered to by the majority of people on Earth up through the Middle Ages and fervently supported by the Catholic Church.

It is thought-provoking to remember that when Christopher Columbus sailed west in an attempt to reach "the Indies" in 1492, the general concept was still that the Earth was flat and that the ships would eventually fall over the edge, where they were likely to be swallowed by dragons or just simply fall straight into the flames of hell. Columbus himself had, during his years in Lisbon, belonged to a small group of geographers who were convinced that the Earth was round and that, consequently, Zipangu (Japan) could be reached by sailing west. Only he and his followers had miscalculated the circumference of the Earth by one-third, thus believing that the Earth was much smaller than it actually is. An imagined Earth of this size did not allow for any space for a continent the size of America, so Columbus died believing that he had reached "the Indies."

The role of the established Catholic Church is noteworthy in this connection, as it stubbornly and ignorantly stuck to the old Ptolemaic world picture and did everything in its power to prevent the Catholic queen and king of Spain, Isabel and Ferdinand, from granting Columbus the financial means to go through with his expedition. The priests said that it was heresy to believe that the Earth was round. God had created the Earth flat and they, the priests, knew better. Anyone who claimed that the Earth was round would pine eternally in hell for this heretic conviction.

However, in the course of the sixteenth century the old world picture was gradually abandoned and it became accepted among the intellectuals of the time (though not by the Church) that the Earth was, in fact, a sphere.

Galileo Galilei[2] made innumerable observations, that supported the heliocentric world picture. In 1610 he constructed the first telescope and through the invention of this he was able to observe many individual stars of the Milky Way and four of the moons of Jupiter. Through the observations of Galileo the established concept of the size of the universe was challenged, and again the role of the Catholic Church was far from supportive. In 1615 the

Pope created a council whose job it was to decide if Galileo's observations were correct. In 1616 the council decreed that Galileo's observations were heretic, that the heliocentric concept was absurd and that the Earth, according to the Bible, was flat. This was ratified by the Inquisition. Galileo's books were banned and he was summoned to Rome by the Inquisition. After a long process and possibly with the use of torture he was forced to renounce on oath that the Earth moves around the Sun. According to tradition Galileo is supposed to have whispered under his breath: "Eppur si muove" [It moves anyway]. The pope sentenced Galileo to lifelong imprisonment for his knowledge of the nature of the solar system. However, the pope pardoned him after some time and he was free to continue his scientific observations.

Later both Newton and Kepler[3] made important observations that supported and refined the heliocentric concept, but the idea that the Sun was the center of the universe was held until the 1800s. It was only then that it became clear that there were many celestial bodies of the same kind as the Sun, and that the Sun was indeed just another star.

With the building of large telescopes in the 1900s the heliocentric world picture was finally abandoned, as it was observed that the universe contains other galaxies than our own Milky Way and that our position in the universe is far from centric. Indeed, the center of the universe is still to be located.

When I went to primary school in Denmark in the 1950s we were taught that there were seven galaxies apart from our own Milky Way in the universe. According to the latest astrological observations[4] the number of galaxies is 100 billion. So in less than 50 years the number of galaxies has "grown" from 7 to 100,000,000,000. This is quite an increase, and this figure represents only what has been termed "the observable universe." Today we have come to understand that we can only observe galaxies and stars whose light has had time to travel to us. But for all we know there might be galaxies that are so far away that their light may only reach us in another million years or so. We do not know how large a part of the universe is observable to us. We still have no idea about the size of the universe, but one thing is certain: it grows as our cosmic horizon expands.

If we look only at the observable universe and say that this has 100,000,000,000 galaxies and when we know that in an average galaxy there are approximately 200 billion stars this gives an approximate total of 20,000,000,000,000,000,000,000,000 stars. We have figured so much out this far.

In 1995 a Swiss team of astronomers became the first to report a valid detection of a star similar to the Sun around which planets were observed to circle. This gave rise to the revolutionary new concept that if there were planets around other stars than the Sun, then there was also a possibility that there could be life on some of these planets. This did not, of course, prove that there was life beyond our solar system, but it opened the possibility that we were not alone in space. But if we were not alone in the universe, who were the others and how did they look? Were they friendly and could we contact them? As before, each new revelation gave rise to a number of questions.

Today the frontier of our scientific research is not only space (or our macrocosmos) but also to an ever-increasing degree life at the subatomic level, or our microcosmos. Many new discoveries are made within the fields of medicine, gene technology, particle physics, and biology. As the vast universe at subatomic level reveals itself to our scientists it is becoming increasingly clear that there are as many unanswered questions at the microcosmic level as there are at the macrocosmic level. Even though new knowledge is added almost every day about our physical world, it is becoming increasingly clear that we still do not have the definite answer to the fundamental question, "What is life, where does it come from, and why does it exist?"

The Materialistic World Picture

The predominant world picture in today's Western world could be called "the Materialistic World Picture." This is based on what we can observe when we weigh, measure and analyze the various forms of matter that we find in the physical world.

Our knowledge of the physical world is expanding as we uncover fact after fact. Every day we accumulate more facts. We know what the Earth weighs, how fast it moves, and where it moves. We know the position of the Earth, the Sun, and the planets, and we know which stars are our closest neighbors. We know the nature of all the different types of matter that exists on Earth and we know how to combine these types of matter in many different ways to suit our needs.

Through the advancements of scientific research into the gene and DNA we have found what is believed to be the very building stone of life, but all these observations both in macrocosmos and in microcosmos only bring us closer to knowing that we know very little. We have accumulated a huge sea of facts, but the why and the how are still unanswered. We do not know why we are here or how we came to be here. More facts of the same type as the ones we already have do not answer the questions of the why and how type. We stand as the illiterate in front of a very thick book. We can observe the letters and the full stops. We can measure the distances between the letters, we can count the number of lines, and we can weigh the pages of the book, but we cannot discern its meaning. We are still not able to read the text of the book of life. We still have not decoded this text. In order to decode this text we need to find the code.

Through the accumulation of facts the materialistic sciences have brought us close to the limit of our understanding. We have accumulated a huge amount of facts, but more facts about the physical world will not bring us any closer to the truth about our own existence and the meaning of it all. Although we know a lot, there are still many unanswered questions.

What we seem to have forgotten is that our materialistic world picture is based on assumptions and deductions, but we still do not know if what our scientists have arrived at are the right and final conclusions. We believe that they have and we believe that our sciences are very advanced and our scientists very clever, but whether they have arrived at the definite and final answers, we do not know.

For the last three centuries the basis of most of our earthly sciences has been the Cartesian/Newtonian[5] model, which views all living organisms as mechanical systems and attempts to reduce all aspects of living organisms to physical and chemical interactions of their smallest parts. The consequence of this concept of life is that all living organisms are viewed as machines that function like a clockwork. And just as a clock can be repaired by substituting a broken part with a new part, it is believed that all living beings can be repaired in exactly the same way. This reductionist view has been predominant within the field of medicine for centuries and is still predominant. Disease is seen as a malfunctioning of some biological mechanism and health is defined as an absence of illness. Death is seen as a system breakdown and its finality is unquestionable.

The reductionist view has also been predominant within the field of physics, as it was believed that there was a smallest building stone in the universe, the atom, of which all matter was constructed. But particle physics has shown that there is no such thing as a smallest building stone, and research on the subatomic level shows that all particles consist of even smaller particles and that indeed there is no substantial matter at subatomic level, only movement and energy. Even though the field of physics, which for centuries has been considered THE science par excellence, has long ago abandoned the reductionist view, many other sciences are still stuck with this philosophical basis. But the reductionist view is gradually revealing its flaws as it is becoming increasingly clear that a living being is much more than the mere sum of its parts and that the parts are not interchangeable. The more research is carried out at cell level it becomes clear that the interplay and interconnectedness of our cells are so complicated that they cannot be explained with the reductionist model. It is gradually becoming clear that the reductionist approach is only one of several possible approaches and that we need a holistic approach to reach an understanding of life. It is gradually becoming clear that all though we know a lot, there is even more that we do not know.

It is becoming clear that there is a limit to our understanding. At this limit it is getting a bit crowded.

The physicists are standing there. Through research into the atom they have found that all particles consist of even smaller particles and that at the subatomic level there is nothing but movement and energy. The observer somehow influences what happens at the subatomic level, but what this means they do not know.

The astronomers are standing there. They can now observe more and more galaxies and heavenly bodies, but 50,000 galaxies more or less do not explain what it is they see.

The microbiologists are also standing at the limit. They have found what is believed to be the very building stone of life, the DNA, but what this means and what regulates it, they do not know.

The people studying death and the near-death experience are standing at the limit. They seem to have found out that consciousness continues beyond death, but what happens beyond death, they do not know.

The regression therapists are standing at the limit. It seems that past lives have an influence in this life and that some traumas have their roots in former lives and that regression therapy can cure this, but how this works and whether reincarnation is a fact, they do not know.

The theologians are standing at the limit, or rather, they have sat down, because they have been at the limit for a long time and they were the first to reach it. They believe that there is a God, but if there is, whose God is it? Is it the Protestant God or the Catholic God, is it Allah, or is it Brahma, is it the God of the Jews or the God of the Mormons or Baptists? If God exists, who is he or she?

In many respects we have reached a point at which there is little more to learn about the physical world. We have been accumulating facts about the physical world for centuries now, and we really know a lot about it. We have accumulated a sea of facts about all matter to be found in the physical world.

In order to learn more we have to step up one level, i.e., to the nonphysical or metaphysical level. We have to look at what lies beyond the physical plane. Accepting that we have to move up one level can be hard, because it implies that we have to accept that there is more to the world than meets the eye. The hard-core materialistic scientist is not happy about this, because all his scientific research has been based on what was observable and measurable. Taking this step is like jumping out from an indeterminably high cliff without a parachute: No one knows where it will lead. But we have to jump, if we want to know more. We can only reach new insight if we have the courage to jump.

Our materialistic world picture has to be expanded, so that it includes the metaphysical level. As many times before we have to revise our world picture to adapt it to new findings. With the new world picture presented by Martinus we are handed a new key to understanding our world. With this key in our hand we will have to rethink our position in the universe, our own stage of development, our whole evolution, and our attitude to death. We will have to start looking at our planet and ourselves in a much larger perspective.

The Eternal World Picture

Martinus offers a complete world picture, which accounts for both the physical and the metaphysical or spiritual levels of existence. Martinus reveals the natural laws that govern life on both the physical and the spiritual levels. Martinus calls his world picture "the Eternal World Picture" and through this he reveals a holistic concept of the world in which all details fit in and he offers a complete explanation of the meaning of our existence. The explanation of the nature of the universe that Martinus puts forward is based on logic and it satisfies our intellect.

Martinus does not ask us to believe in what he reveals. He simply asks us to go out into the world and see if what he says does not coincide with what we can observe out there. Once we start this type of observation, we start looking at the world in a new way.

We now see the physical world as part of the much larger spiritual world beyond. We see that some of our ways of looking at our fate and at death have to be revised, because they were limited, as they did not take the spiritual level into consideration. Once we realize that there is a spiritual world beyond the physical world, we start opening a whole new field of science—the science of spirituality.

As just mentioned, Martinus calls his world picture "the Eternal World Picture." This world picture accounts for the existence of the many different life forms we see on Earth and it forms a whole. It is the first time in the history of mankind that a complete holistic world picture has been presented in which the meaning of all life forms from atoms via plants and mammals to stars has been explained. In Martinus' world picture everything fits and tallies. The world picture forms a logical whole.

Martinus calls his complete works *The Third Testament*. *The Third Testament* is a sequel to the New Testament, but it is not a basis for a new religion. *The Third Testament* has nothing to do with faith. It is a revelation of the logic that lies behind all creative processes in the universe, such as Martinus was able to see them with his cosmic consciousness[6]. *The Third Testament* is based on knowledge and on logic. It is a complete explanation of the structure of the universe, about the microcosmos (our cells), mesocosmos (ourselves and the living beings around us), and macrocosmos (our planet, the solar system, and the universe). Martinus explains in a logical way who we are, where we come from, and where we are going. He explains why we are here and how we came to be here. He explains our connection with the life force that is God and what the meaning of life is. He explains why we reincarnate and why there is no absolute death. He reveals how we can shape our fate ourselves through our knowledge of the law of karma, so that we can create happiness. He discloses why our family structure is in dissolution and why homosexuality is on the rise. He explains the reason for wars and assaults and unrest. He explains why many people are unhappy or ill or mentally disordered.

The Third Testament has been written for the intellectual person, the person who has outlived the ability to believe in the religions. It has been written for those who can no longer believe, but who have a need to know. *The Third Testament* constitutes a basis for a merging of science and spirituality in the way that spirituality becomes an intricate part of all science. There can be no conclusive science without spirituality. It is only when our sciences include the spiritual level that definite and final knowledge about the nature of the universe and our own existence can be obtained. The materialistic sciences will have to merge with spiritual science so that the two become one. Once we start this merging the book of life will gradually reveal its secrets.

What you are about to read is a summary of some of the most important aspects of *The Third Testament* written by Martinus. The complete works of Martinus comprise more than seven thousand pages, so only a part can be presented here.

I find that the most important aspects of Martinus' work at our present stage of evolution are those that help us understand the situation in the world today and our own role in this. So in this book I have concentrated on these aspects. Other people may have concentrated on other aspects of Martinus' work. This is my personal selection.

I have explained Martinus' world picture in my own words and such as I have understood it. So this book reflects my own understanding of Martinus' work. Apart from a whole article by Martinus in the conclusive chapter you will find only few quotations from him in this book. This is how Martinus wanted it to be. He encouraged us to write about his world picture in our own words and not to quote him excessively.

Throughout the book I mention examples from the latest research into death, reincarnation, regression therapy, etc., and compare these scientific advances with Martinus' world picture. Such as I see it, the latest scientific advances support what Martinus says. In my opinion we are in a process where our sciences are gradually beginning to reveal the existence of a world beyond the physical world. This is perhaps best seen in the study of the near-death experience where the experiencers all say that they have visited an otherworldly realm. As you shall see, this otherworldly realm is, according to Martinus, our primary level of existence and this is an example of how our research confirms aspects of Martinus' revelations.

Throughout his life Martinus produced a large number of symbols, which is what he called the drawings that support the texts. I have chosen to include six of these symbols in this book. The symbols are accompanied by the Martinus Institute's short standard explanation as well as my own explanation.

Until Martinus' world picture has been proven true by our earthly sciences, it can still be looked upon as a theory, although Martinus himself certainly did not consider his work to be a theory. Martinus would not call his work *The Third Testament* if he considered it to be a theory. However, if one is skeptical, one can look upon Martinus' world picture as a theory and start comparing it to the empirical world and see if the two do not coincide. This is indeed what Martinus himself asks us to do. He does not ask us to believe in what he says but he asks us to test his world picture against what we can observe "out there." He calls his work a supplement to life's own speech. When you start to look around and test Martinus' world picture against the empirical world, you have started a very interesting exercise. I have been doing this for several years now and every day I notice things that fit perfectly into Martinus' world picture. It is a matter of tuning in to seeing things from a new angle. I have not yet found a single aspect of Martinus' world picture that does not agree with what we can observe in the empirical world. There is not a shadow of a doubt in my mind that Martinus' world picture will one day replace all religions and with time be the foundation of all future science on this planet. There is not a shadow of a doubt in my mind that Martinus reveals The Truth.

But to come to this conclusion you may have to read the whole of Martinus' work. So it is my hope that this book will encourage you to read Martinus' original works. These are now in the process of being translated into English from Danish and many volumes have already been translated.[7]

Due to the nature of the reality that Martinus describes, he very often lacked words that could sufficiently cover the concepts, which he wanted to describe. As the concepts were completely new, there were no known words for them. The needed concepts were simply missing from the existing vocabulary. Consequently, Martinus had to explain new concepts using existing words. The concepts explained by Martinus in Danish have been translated into English in such a way that they best preserve their original flavor. An example of this could be "Den højeste ild," which in English is "The highest fire." This concept denominates the experience of the culmination of divine love.

I hope that you will put away your preconceived ideas and read the following with an open mind. Martinus' world picture redefines our whole world, so please be prepared to make a few mental somersaults. We now have to see ourselves as very small entities on a never-ending journey of evolution through physical and spiritual worlds in a universe that is teeming with life. I hope you will enjoy the journey.

3

Who Was Martinus?

Childhood and Youth

Martinus was born on August 11, 1890, in the vicinity of Sindal, a small town in the north of Jutland, Denmark. His mother was Else Christine Mikkelsen, and she was unmarried and forty-two years of age when she gave birth to Martinus. She was the housekeeper at a manor house called Christianshede and the proprietor was Lars Larsen. This Lars Larsen was most likely Martinus' father as he was known to be fond of Else Christine Mikkelsen and as Martinus resembled him quite a lot as he grew up. But due to the fear of a scandal, it was the foreman of Christianshede, Mikael Thomsen, who was proclaimed Martinus' father. Thus Martinus' full name came to be Martinus Thomsen.

His mother could not have her illegitimate child living with her at Christianshede, so she made arrangements before the birth to have the child adopted by her half brother and his wife, who agreed to bring it up in spite of the fact that they were very poor and already had eleven children. However, most of these eleven children had already left home to serve on other farms and there were only two children living at home, two boys of three and five respectively.

The adoptive parents owned a small holding called Moskildvad, and it was in this humble place that Martinus was born around midnight between the tenth and eleventh of August 1890. The clock on the wall struck twelve and just after the last stroke

Martinus was born. And then something strange happened: The clock on the wall fell to the ground with a big bang. This has later been interpreted to mean that an old epoch had ended and a new one begun.

Moskildvad, Martinus' childhood home, drawn by Martinus himself.

Martinus grew up in these humble surroundings. The adoptive parents were simple but good people and they could neither read nor write. The house had only one room in which the family both ate and slept. There were two beds and the three boys slept in one and the adoptive parents in the other. From the room a door led to a small kitchen and from there you entered the stable. Today Martinus' childhood home has been opened as a museum, which can be visited during the summer months.

Martinus had only a very basic education at the local school, where he was taught the fundamentals of Christian religion, a bit of history, some geography, arithmetic, and Danish. At the age of twelve he was sent to neighboring farms to shepherd cows, and the only teaching he received after this was when he was preparing to be "confirmed in the Christian faith." The minister was very strictly evangelical and threatened everybody with hell if they did not behave. He said that a child that died before it was baptized would forever burn in the flames of hell and furthermore that children born outside marriage were doomed likewise. On hearing this, Martinus started doubting the truth of what the minister said, as he was sure that God did not have a grudge against him for being born outside marriage. Why would God be angry with an unbaptized or illegitimate child? The child could not help it. Martinus began to be very skeptical about the teachings of the Church at a very early age. Although he was only a child, he intuitively felt that there was something very wrong with the way the established religion looked at life. Another peculiarity was that on many occasions during his childhood, when he was faced with a problem to which he had no answer, he would ask, "What would Jesus have done in this case?" And straightaway he had the answer.

Martinus age 11.

Martinus had several odd jobs at neighboring farms up through his teens and in 1907 he decided that he wanted to become a dairyman.

For the next ten years he worked at various dairies all over Denmark and his spare time was spent on his hobby of photography. In 1913 he was drafted to the navy and was assigned as an officer's servant. He was in the navy for only eight months and never carried arms.

In 1917, Martinus moved to Copenhagen where he was employed at a major dairy. Afterward he worked as a night watchman for a wealthy family there and following this as a postman.

While a postman, he moved into a small room at Jagtvej 52A, at Frederiksberg, Copenhagen, and he had his meals at a boarding-house near by.

In March 1920 he returned to work at a dairy, this time at Enigheden, a very big dairy. Martinus was now close to thirty and although his friends and colleagues dated girls and got married, he never had any inclination toward marriage. The thought of belonging to another person appalled him, and although Martinus did not at the time know his reasons for not wanting to marry, it later became clear why this was so. At this time Martinus was a kind but naïve young man. He had had no formal education after he left school in his early teens, and his professional training was dairy production and a bit of bookkeeping. He had never studied anything.

He was not very happy about his job and resented the thought of doing the same job day in and day out. He strongly wanted to find employment where he could serve his fellow human beings and wondered if he could become a missionary, but as he did not subscribe to any of the established religions, he had to abandon this idea.

The Book

At the dairy Martinus became acquainted with a young man who had an extra job as a musician. One day this man showed Martinus a book, which he had borrowed from another musician, Lars Nibelvang. Lars Nibelvang was very interested in theosophy, and the book was about reincarnation and meditation. Martinus had never heard about reincarnation and he did not know the meaning of the word. His friend told him that reincarnation meant that we had lived before, and although this was a completely new thought for Martinus, he immediately accepted it and thought that it sounded logical. He asked if he could borrow the book and his friend told him that he would ask Lars Nibelvang. A few days later Martinus was told that it was okay for him to borrow the book and to go to Nibelvang's place to pick it up. This he did on March 21, 1921.

Lars Nibelvang received Martinus kindly and Martinus was impressed by the number of books that Nibelvang had in his house. Most books were about theosophy, anthroposophy and similar religious and philosophical subjects. Nibelvang was widely read and had been a searching soul all his life. He asked Martinus if he had any knowledge of new religious ideas and Martinus answered that he knew nothing about this, but that he was a religious man and that he had prayed to Providence every day as far back as he could remember. Nibelvang said that prayer formed a natural part of the new religious ideas and this comforted Martinus. He was now allowed to borrow the book and when he and Nibelvang parted, Nibelvang said: *"You shall see, before long you will be my teacher"*[1]. Martinus thought that this was a strange remark, as he had read nothing and knew nothing about religion apart from the basics that he was taught as a child.

The Initiation

Two days later, on March 23, 1921, Martinus sat down in his chair to read the book in his room at Jagtvej 52 A. In the book he found instructions on how to meditate. Following these instructions, he turned off the light, rolled down the blinds, blindfolded himself, and sat down in his chair. Now everything was dark. Suddenly something very extraordinary happened. A spot of light appeared to his inner eye. It came closer and closer and gradually took the shape of a human form. Martinus recognized this form. It was the sculpture of Christ by Thorvaldsen, the famous Danish sculptor. The form was alive and glowed a brilliant white with blue shadows. It was as if the substance were made of thousands of microscopic sparks. The form came closer and closer until it finally walked straight into Martinus' bodily form. A wonderful, elated feeling seized him and he felt that his existence was no longer limited to his physical body. The light that invaded him made him able to see all of the Earth from a position high above it. He could see how the Earth revolved and he could see horizons with mountains and valleys, continents and oceans. He felt weightless in the middle of a brilliant sky. Gradually the sky became more and more brilliant until he finally found himself in an all-pervading white light. He felt that he no longer had a body and that he was one with God's consciousness. The strong light was more than he could bear and he had to get up and pull off his blindfold. Now he was back in his own humble room, but the light that he had experienced was still sparkling in his mind.

The next day Martinus sat down in his chair again and the light reappeared, but this time it was golden. Again Martinus felt weightless and one with a supreme source of love in an immense radiance of golden light. He felt that his physical body and all physical things around him had ceased to be and that he was one with the divine life force. Again the pressure on his brain became unbearable and he had to pull off his blindfold.

After this extraordinary experience Martinus felt that he was no longer the same. His vision was no longer limited to the physical world, he could see beyond the physical level of existence. His consciousness had been expanded and later on, when he was faced with a question or problem, the answer presented itself immediately. He only had to think of a particular question and immediately he had the answer. It was as if he had known these answers all his life. Little by little he realized that his knowledge had no limits. There was no question that he could not answer. It was as if he had been linked up with an immense sea of knowledge, a divine bank of data.

Martinus had no idea about what had happened to him, but the experience had made a great impact. He tried to read the book that Nibelvang had lent him, but he now realized that he could not read any book. A few days later he went to give the book back to Nibelvang and told him what had happened. Nibelvang was astounded, but as he was widely read, he could explain to Martinus what had happened to him. He was sure that Martinus had had an initiation, a revelation and that he had achieved cosmic consciousness.

Martinus age 30. This photograph was taken a few months after his initiation.

Although Nibelvang was widely read, he still had many unanswered questions of a metaphysical nature, and he now asked Martinus for answers to these questions. Although Martinus was never in doubt about how to answer the questions, he lacked routine in expressing himself. The only things he had ever written were letters to his adoptive parents, and now he had to find the words to answer complicated and deep questions. Nibelvang wasn't always happy about Martinus' answers, as they did not coincide with what he already knew, but after having thought about the answer for a while, he would exclaim, *"Yes—now I can see it! You are right! Nobody has ever been able to see this as clearly before!"*[2] Nibelvang and Martinus were to become inseparable friends for many years.

The First Difficult Years

Now a difficult time started. In order to support himself Martinus had to continue working at the dairy, but his mind was not with it, as this was far away from his newfound understanding. Nibelvang was possibly the first to realize that Martinus had a mission and that his time had to be spent communicating his new knowledge about the nature of existence to the world. Nibelvang offered to support Martinus to enable him to concentrate on communicating his newfound insight. However, Nibelvang had only a very meager income and he now had to support both Martinus and himself.

Martinus bought a typewriter and started to write his "cosmic analyses" (as he called his writings), but as he had very little experience in writing, everything that he wrote during the first years had to be rewritten. The sentences were so long that they filled entire pages. It took seven years before Martinus was ready to start writing his chief work, *Livets Bog* (*The Book of Life*).

In those first difficult years there were several people who supported Martinus financially, but there were still periods in which he had to go back to work at the dairy as there was simply not enough money to make ends meet. But from the autumn of 1922 he was able to dedicate all his time to his writings.

In order to facilitate the explanations of his cosmic answers Martinus also started producing colored drawings, which he called symbols, that illustrated and supported the texts. One of the symbols that gave Martinus most difficulties was the main symbol, which was also called "the Basic Analysis of the Living Being." He had to make several drafts and sketches before all the details were right. One day while he was standing at his desk putting the final touches to the symbol, he realized that he was not alone. On either side of him was a white-clad spiritual being, a being from one of the nonphysical realms. (These realms will be described later in this book). Completely silent and passive, they were contemplating the symbol with arms crossed. Then they nodded and disappeared.

From that day on Martinus felt that he had the support and sympathy of the spiritual world.

Among those who supported Martinus financially was a wealthy former church bell manufacturer named Bernhard Løw. He was head of the Anthroposophical Society in Denmark and had all his life been a searching soul. He had been strongly interested in the works of Rudolf Steiner[3], who had founded anthroposophy in

1913, and Løw had even visited Steiner in Switzerland. Bernhard Løw had read Nostradamus[4] and had noticed that Nostradamus was talking about the coming world teacher "the man from the North" who was predicted to appear in the 1920s. Løw strongly wanted to meet this man and he had the idea that this man might be Steiner. So at the end of one of his long stays in Switzerland and while Løw was saying good-bye to Steiner, he asked if he, Steiner, was this man. And Steiner said that in a hundred years there would be no such thing as anthroposophy. *"I see an opening in the clouds above your own native country Denmark. In a few years a new world teacher will appear there. As he may need support, it would be nice if somebody would help him".*[5]

Bernhardt Løw's support became of great importance to Martinus and in 1929, Martinus was able to move into his own flat in Lykkesholms Allé at Frederiksberg, Copenhagen. In 1930, Martinus gave his first public lecture, in which he presented his world picture for the first time.

It soon became clear to Martinus that he needed a secretary because he could no longer cope with the growing amount of letters that he received every day with all sorts of questions from people who had read some of his articles or heard his lectures.

Through friends, Martinus came into contact with Erik Gerner Larsson, a young man who was educated as a gardener and had been seriously ill, so ill that he had been given up by the doctors. However, Gerner Larsson survived, and as soon as he and Martinus met, Martinus immediately knew that this young man was the person he had been looking for as his secretary. Gerner Larsson started working for Martinus, but in the beginning he had to continue working as a gardener to support himself. Later Bernhard Løw agreed to support them both. Through the study of cosmology, as Martinus called his teachings, Gerner Larsson also began to give lectures. In spite of the support from Løw, money was still very sparse, and during these first years Martinus and Gerner Larsson owned only one suit between them, so they could not go out to give lectures at the same time. Gerner Larsson was the first person to work for Martinus, which he did from 1929 until his death in 1973.

The titles of some of the first lectures were: "Through Eternal Zones," "The Creation of Fate," "The Basic Analysis of the Universe," "Through the Gates of Death."

In 1930, Martinus finished the first volume of *Livets Bog*. Bernhardt Løw had promised to finance the printing and he wanted no expense spared, but as the book contained several colored symbols the printing became a costly affair. The amount that Løw had set aside could only pay for a thousand copies, but it became possible to raise the first issue to two thousand copies through the support of other benefactors. However, Løw was never to see the book finished. He died at the age of eighty-eight in 1931. The book was published in July 1932. His widow, Augusta Løw, loyally kept her husband's promise about financing the printing.

Another seven years passed before the second volume of *Livets Bog* was published, but in the intervening years Martinus had written a number of small books: *Logic, The Ideal Food, Funeral Rites, Easter, On the Birth of My Mission, Gift Culture,* and others. These books were first published as continued articles in *Kosmos,* a monthly magazine started in April 1933 and which is still published today. Later the articles were published as individual books, and they were meant as material for beginners in cosmic thinking or Cosmology.

Klint

Up through the years Martinus had met with his friends and followers during the winter months to discuss cosmic questions, and with time a wish arose to have a place where they could continue the studies during the summer months. In 1934 there was an advertisement in a Danish newspaper announcing a large plot of land for sale at a very cheap price. The land was right on the beach in Odsherred close to the village of Klint on the north coast of Sealand. After some discussions this plot of land was purchased, and in the following years a number of small summerhouses were built. Later an assembly hall was erected where lectures could be held.

In the summer of 1936 the Kosmos Vacation Colony, as it was then called, got its own flag. Martinus had designed the flag at the beginning of the year and the flag had the colors of the six basic energies plus the mother energy of which the universe is composed. Also the flag had the white pyramid or triangle, which expresses the living being. Permission was obtained from the prime minister to display the flag, as the general rule was that it was only the national flag, that could be displayed in public. Martinus himself raised the flag and among other things he said: "*Where this symbol of light sways in the wind all war, brutality and strife must be banned. And likewise a mental copy of this must sway in our hearts. Here it is also true that it must not be rent apart by the strong storms of passion and that it must forever sway and shine in an atmosphere of forgiveness and the fresh breeze of love.*" (*Kosmos*, 1936, page 90)[6]

In the beginning there was a vacation colony at Klint where people who were interested in cosmology could come and spend their summers. Today the main outgoing activity of the Martinus Institute takes place at Klint, where the Martinus Center is housed. A large lecture hall has been built together with a number of pavilions where people can be housed. At the Martinus Center, lectures and courses are held throughout most of the year. In August of each year, international weeks are held where people from all over the world come to be taught about Martinus' teachings in English and other languages.

Martinus Institute

The Cause, as Martinus called his mission, needed a place in Copenhagen where people could assemble to hear lectures, and in 1943, Martinus was able to move into the premises at Mariendalsvej 94–96, Frederiksberg, Copenhagen, where the Martinus Institute is still housed today. This stately building held a few flats and a fairly large assembly hall. Martinus himself moved into the flat on the first floor and lived there until his death in 1981.

Martinus Institute, Copenhagen.

Up through the years Martinus was incredibly diligent, and his complete works include more than seven thousand pages. Some of these are still unpublished and some of the symbols are also unpublished because he never had time to explain them. Martinus worked on his typewriter every day from four in the morning till late in the afternoon. He would then go for a walk or for a drive into the country with his friends. He needed very little sleep and normally slept only four hours.

Martinus' living room at Martinus Institute.

Up through the forties and fifties Martinus worked on his chief work *Livets Bog* and the seventh and last volume was published in 1960. He later wrote the four volumes of *The Eternal World Picture* plus several small books. He kept giving lectures both at the Martinus Institute in Copenhagen and at the Martinus Center at Klint, where he spent all his summers.

Martinus also found time to travel, and he traveled as far as Japan and India. He mostly traveled to where he was invited to give lectures, and in Japan he was invited by the Ananai-Kyo organization, whose main aim is the foundation of world peace through religion. In this organization they had heard about Martinus and they wanted him to speak at their world congress and to broadcast his speech on the radio. The trip to Japan took place in 1954 and on his way back from Japan, Martinus visited India where he stayed with friends for three months and where there was also a great interest in his work.

The Martinus Institute was founded in 1956 as a private foundation and is housed at the premises at Mariendalsvej 94–96, Frederiksberg, Copenhagen. The main object of the institute is to keep the works of Martinus intact and unchanged for future generations and to inform the public about the work. Also the institute has to make the works available for those who are interested in publishing and translating the works from Danish into other languages.[7] A council of five members governs the institute, and the institute is the sole owner of the copyrights. However, there is no membership and no organization. The access to study Martinus' books is free for everybody as the works of Martinus belong to all of mankind.

Martinus age 68.

The Third Testament

In the 1970s Martinus expressed the wish that all of his books, his work as a whole, be published with the general title *The Third Tes-*

tament. It was also in the 1970s that he declared that his mission was complete and that he had given mankind enough material to reach cosmic consciousness through the study of his works. He denominated the whole of his mission "the Cause."

On the eleventh of August 1980, Martinus celebrated his ninetieth birthday at Falkonercenteret in Copenhagen. Twelve hundred followers from Denmark and abroad came to celebrate this birthday, which was to be his last. Several people made speeches, and finally Martinus himself made his last public speech, in which he thanked everybody for the homage he had received, but that the homage was not owing to him, it was owing to God. The "analyses" (as he called his work) that he had been able to pass on to mankind were eternal realities. He himself had reached a stage at which he had the ability to manifest these analyses and he had made it his job to communicate these eternal truths to man. He was happy that so many people took interest in his work. He underlined that "the Cause" was neither a sect nor an organization. It was neutral and open to everybody. You could not become a member of "the Cause" and you could not be thrown out. Everybody was free to study the analyses and to form study groups or centers as long as they were loyal to the analyses. The access to these thoughts is as free as it is to the Sun in the sky. He also said that people who belonged to different religions and were happy with that should not leave these religions if they gained inspiration there.

Martinus underlined that his work, which constituted the Third Testament, had a center, which was a private foundation, and this was a guard to protect the work from being modified. The importance of his work was that his cosmic analyses formed a logical world picture.

In spite of his age Martinus spoke for fifty minutes and went through the main points in his world picture. The most important point was that the development was to lead the human being to become "man in the image and likeness of God" as it had been told in the Bible. One had to understand that this development could not take place within one life, but many lives were needed to reach this high degree of perfection. He also said that his mission was a continuation of the mission of Christ. He reminded the audience that Christ had announced that his mission would be continued, when he said to his disciples that he had many more things to tell them, but that they could not bear it now, "*but the spokesman, the Holy Spirit, which the Father will send in my name, he shall teach you everything and remind you of the things that I have said.*" (non-verbatim quotation from John 16: 12–16).[8] Martinus made it clear that this "spokesman" was not a man. It was not another Christ who came to preach, it was not a new world redeemer who came in person, but it was the writings and the books that were to give mankind the final solution to the mystery of life. The thoughts expressed in the books were the Holy Spirit. The spiritual science had been born.

Martinus finished his speech with the words, "*Even when I am dead, you can be sure that I shall be with you, but in a different way. And then I thank you for coming.*"[9]

Everybody in the hall applauded Martinus, and for most of them it was the last glimpse they had of him.

The Death of Martinus

During his last years on the physical plane Martinus was very tired and realized that he did not have much time left. However, he still worked a few hours a day on the computer that he had acquired, and not many months before he died he said to his housekeeper Mischa: "*I think that one day I shall fall out of bed*".[10] He must have had a premonition about how his physical life would end. On the fifth of March 1981 Martinus fell out of bed and broke his femur. He was taken to Frederiksberg Hospital where he died peacefully on March 8, 1981.

Martinus' passing was announced by the Martinus Institute in all major newspapers in Denmark, Norway, and Sweden and his funeral ceremony took place on March 29 in Tivoli's concert hall in Copenhagen. His coffin was covered with the flag of "the Cause."

Several speakers underlined that his death was no cause for

mourning. Martinus had fulfilled his mission on the physical plane and had returned to his own kingdom, the kingdom of light. He had fertilized this world with the wisdom of this kingdom of light.

Martinus is buried at Frederiksberg Kirkegaard, Copenhagen, but Martinus himself prophesied that his earthly remains would later be transferred to a mausoleum at Klint, where the Martinus Center still is today.

Martinus' Mission

Martinus was often asked why Denmark had been chosen as the place to continue the mission of Christ, and Martinus gave an answer that was not exactly flattering to the Danes. He said that the Danes were so far away from having any idea of a spiritual reality that he was sure to be left in peace there. As Martinus' mission was solely to write his cosmic analyses, he needed to be left alone to concentrate on his work. Had he been born in a country that had a higher level of interest in spirituality, he would have been too much in the limelight and would not have had the necessary peace and quiet to work. In Denmark he was tucked securely away.

As it was, in Denmark he was surrounded by a number of followers who supported him and helped him, but apart from that the news about his existence was never published. Martinus shunned all publicity around his person. All through his most productive years public interest in his work was very limited. When *Livets Bog* came out it got only a minimum of attention in the Danish press, and the general reaction was that it was not to be taken seriously. Martinus was not at all disappointed by this reaction, as he knew that it would take some time before people had reached a stage at which they could understand his work. He knew that his teaching would spread out over the world gradually over the next hundreds of years and he was in no hurry. He knew that his teachings would at times be met with intolerance and disbelief and that only time and man's growing intelligence and understanding of life would prove his teachings to be true.

4

The Being of Light

The Creator

Let us start the presentation of Martinus' world picture by stating that there is a creative force in the universe, a Creator. The Creator's existence is the prerequisite for the existence of everything else. The Creator was there before anything else.

Whether we call this creative force Creator or Being of Light or Divinity or Deity or God is of no importance. Martinus mostly uses the Danish word *Guddom* instead of "just" God. But English has no equivalent to *Guddom*, so I will call this creative life force God, as it is the easiest and shortest word to use.

So we start by stating that there is a creative force in the universe that was there before anything else and we call this life force God.

However, it is also important to underline that the God that we speak about in this book is not the stern and fear-inspiring man with the long white beard that we may have learned about in school or heard about in church, who for some obscure reason was angry with us because of our sins. The God that we speak about in this book is not an angry God and not a God that punishes other beings and likes to see them suffer. Our God is an all-pervading consciousness of light and of the highest and most sublime, un-conditional and undiluted love. This sublime love of God flows through the whole universe. This divine love is the basic tone of the universe.

The universe is God's body. Everything that exists in the universe is a part of God. All living beings live within God and God lives within them. This means that we, the human beings of planet Earth, are a part of God, too. Not only us, but everything else such as atoms, molecules, cells, insects, plants, trees, worms, fish, mammals, rivers, seas, lakes, mountains, moons, planets, stars, solar systems and galaxies are part of God. Everything that exists on both the physical and the spiritual levels is contained within God. The universe with its innumerable galaxies is God's body.

When we read in the Bible that, "*The Spirit of God was moving over the face of the waters*" (Genesis 1:2),[1] this is indeed a reflection of a cosmic truth. As spirit is the same as consciousness, this means that a consciousness with intelligence and logic is "*moving over the face of the waters.*" This consciousness was there before anything else and everything has been created by this consciousness. This again means that there is consciousness behind all the creative processes in nature and indeed behind the manifold creative processes of the universe. All matter has been created by God and is thus a result of an inconceivably intelligent mind and an inconceivably intelligent creative process. No life forms on Earth or elsewhere have come into existence "by chance" or "on their own accord." Everything that exists has been conceived and made functional through God's supreme intelligence.

When we look at the very complicated system of cells and organs that our own body constitutes, when we consider how absolutely marvelously our body works, and when we admit that we, with our advanced sciences, cannot even find out *how* it works, then we have to admit that there must be a creative force with a superior intelligence behind this creation; a force full of wisdom and logic. Something that functions in a logical way has to have been created according to a plan. If there were no plan, it could not be a logical creation. In order for a plan to exist, there has to be somebody who has thought out the plan. A logical plan does not just crop up. Behind the plan there has to be a thinker, in other words there has to be a Creator. All logical creations have been created by somebody.

The more we dig into matter and the more understanding we reach of the processes of life, the more do we marvel. The bodily processes are the work of genius. When we really start to think about the wonder of life, we begin to question the assumption that life should have come into existence by accident. Albert Einstein expressed it like this: "*The probability of life originating from accident is comparable to the probability of the unabridged dictionary resulting from an explosion in a print shop.*"

Our body consists of 100 trillion cells. All these cells cooperate in a perfect way and in such complicated patterns that their functioning is beyond our comprehension. To think that something as complicated and perfect as our own body can have come into existence by mere coincidence or through chance mutations, by a mere chance combination of cells, is a thought as fantastic as believing that New York City could have come into existence all by itself. When we look around in our world at the things that we, the humans, have created, we have never yet seen a logical creation that has come into existence all by itself. The only things that come into existence all by themselves are tumbleweed and fluff under beds and those can hardly be said to be perfect or logical creations. We have never seen a car or a radio or a building that has come into existence all by itself.

There is no reason to believe that a principle that is valid for us humans should not also be valid on a bigger scale. If things in our world have to have an intelligent creative force behind them in order to exist and function in a logical way, there is no reason to believe that this principle does not also apply on a bigger scale. When Man's logical creations cannot come into existence without a creator how should the logical manifestations of Nature be able to do that? In Nature there is a perfect balance and all the processes are beneficial to living beings in their final analysis. How can such perfection have come about by mere chance? In order for something to function in a perfect and logical way there has to be some kind of consciousness or intelligence behind it.

We do not expect any kind of machine here on Earth to have

just "cropped up." We know that a machine has to have been created by an intelligent consciousness in order to work. In exactly the same way, all logical things that exist in nature have to have been created and designed by an intelligent consciousness. Otherwise they would not be able to function and work. The accepted idea today is that all the various plants, all the various insects, and all the various animals have just cropped up by a chance combination of cells or chance mutations. But when we really start to think about this, it does seem unlikely that all those logical creations in a huge variety of different designs and bodily systems should have just happened to come into existence by a chance combination of cells. It does seem more logical to assume that there is intelligent consciousness behind their design and functioning.

Martinus points out that everything in the universe has been created and designed through the use of intelligence and that believing otherwise is as illogical as believing that a dead thing can create a living being. We have never yet seen that the house made the bricklayer; that the shoe made the shoemaker; that the chest of drawers made the carpenter, or that the dress made the dressmaker. Yet when it comes to the processes that we witness around us in the natural world, we immediately assume that the trees, the plants, the flowers, the insects, the mammals, the birds, the fish, the whales, the planets, etc., and we the human beings have come into existence all alone and by mere chance.

We (or should I say science) believe that life in its vast variety of forms has developed from a single living cell that once happened to drop down on Earth from space. From this single cell and through chance mutations and evolution and natural selection all life forms on Earth are believed to have come into existence. Everything is believed to have come into existence through a cosmic game of dice completely governed by chance. But maybe the time has now come for a revision of this concept to be put at the top of our agenda.

If we take stock of the species known to be living on Earth today we reach the following impressive approximate figures:[2]

Known species:

Insects and myriapods (centipedes, millipedes):	963,000
Plants:	270,000
Fungi and lichens:	100,000
Protozoans and algae:	80,000
Chelicerates (spiders, scorpions):	75,000
Mollusks (cockles, mussels):	70,000
Crustaceans (shrimps, lobsters):	40,000
Nematode worms (hookworms, filarial worms):	25,000
Fish:	22,000
Flatworms (flukes, tapeworms):	20,000
Annelid worms (earthworms, leeches):	12,000
Reptiles and amphibians:	10,500
Birds:	10,000
Cnidarians (jellyfish, corals, anemones):	10,000
Sponges:	10,000
Mammals:	4,500
Bacteria and archaea:	4,000
Other organisms:	10,000

This gives a total of some 1,750,000 different known species.

Is it really logical to believe that this huge variety of life forms with their very different bodily systems should have come into existence from one single cell through chance mutations? Think of the difference in bodily form and breathing system and system of procreation of a fish and a human, of a bird and a mushroom. Is it really logical to assume that these very different, yet perfectly functioning systems should all have come into existence from a single cell through random luck and coincidence?

Our logic ought to tell us that this idea should be abandoned just as we once abandoned the idea that the Earth is flat. A creation so full of logic as our own body, a creation so complicated that we cannot even figure out how it works, has to have been created by a superior intelligence. Something this advanced and logical cannot have come into existence by chance. Believing this is as silly as believing that a complex system such as the Eiffel Tower could have come into existence on its own and by mere chance. This idea defies logic.

Martinus emphasizes that there is a creator behind every creation and just as we accept that there is a creator behind a house, a car, a machine, a computer, a telephone, etc., we have to accept that there is also a creator behind a beetle, a millipede, a fern, a carrot, a lion and a trout, indeed behind everything in nature and behind the bodies of all living beings.

Evolution

But creation is also a process. A process takes time. Many of the things that we see in the natural world are things that are now at a certain stage in the process of evolution toward perfection. The perfect stage has not been reached yet. The perfect stage is being developed. Because creation is also a process toward more advanced stages, evolution and creation walk hand in hand. The life forms that have been designed and made functional through God's creative ability can pass through various stages in their process of evolution toward perfection.

The process from imperfection to perfection can be seen *en miniature* in the ripening of, say, an apple. When the apple is not ripe it is still sour and not a perfect creation. But when enough time has passed and the apple is ripe, it is a perfect creation. Just as the apple should not be judged by its sour stage, so should we not judge the Earth by its present stage. Our planet is in the process of being developed into a perfect and peaceful place for living beings, but the perfect stage has not been reached yet. As long as there are wars, illnesses, poverty, and unrest, the perfect stage has not been reached. The planet is still evolving toward the perfect stage. The planet and everything on it is subject to evolution.

If we look at the history of man in the Western world during the last two thousand years we can see how we have evolved. We have gone from having a relatively primitive society to having a relatively advanced society. We have gone from having a relatively primitive mentality to having a relatively humane mentality. We have gone from having simple and inefficient means of transportation to having advanced means of transportation. We have gone from having simple and inefficient means of communication to having advanced means of communication. We have gone from having no or a very basic science to having a relatively advanced science. It is evident that we have evolved, that we are evolving, and it is logical to assume that we will go on evolving. When we can see how we have evolved up till now, what reason do we then have to believe that evolution should stop? Evolution will never stop, and this means that we will evolve toward higher levels of perfection, as we shall see later. Evolution is an ongoing process and is in effect a question of "lifting" the level of function and organization through the consumption of time.

We can also look at our bodily and mental development. We know that we, the human race, have developed from being apes to becoming man such as we are today. We know that our bodily shape and brain size have changed significantly during the last thousands of years. In general terms we can say that our mentality has developed significantly. If we look at what people have found pleasurable during the last two thousand years, we can see that our mentality has developed away from cruelty toward being more humane. In ancient Rome people took pleasure in watching slaves being torn to pieces and eaten by lions in the arenas. In the Middle Ages people took pleasure in watching public executions in the town squares. Today there would be very few people who would think that this was a pleasurable pastime. Our mentality has in general developed away from being able to watch or take pleasure in witnessing cruelty done to our fellow man. Both our bodily structure and our mentality have developed through time and it is under constant development. Development never stops. Everything is in evolution at the same time as everything has been created and made functional by God. One does not exclude the other. The beings created by God can evolve as they adapt to changing environments, to changing living conditions and as they accumulate experience. The beings created by God can pass through various stages of evolution in their development toward perfection. Creation and evolution walk hand in hand. Evolution is the perfection of creation through the consumption of time. The beings created by God evolve toward perfection and in this way they are in constant change, in constant movement.

Then why did God not "just" create a perfect world in the first place? This question will be answered in the course of the book.

Movement

We know that when we want to check if something is alive, we prod it to see if it moves. If it moves, it is alive. Movement is the most distinguished characteristic of life. We immediately accept that if a duck moves across the grass, it is alive. But we do not realize that all movement is an expression of life. We are not so used to thinking that the movement of the waves of the sea, or the movement of the clouds across the sky, or the movement of the Earth around the Sun or the movement of the galaxies also express life. However, Martinus points out that all movement expresses life as the movement has to have been initiated by somebody. A movement does not just start on its own. A movement has to be initiated by a living being. As everything in the universe is in movement, be it galaxies or atoms, everything is an expression of life. The whole universe is teeming with life in many different forms.

We Are Not Alone

Another completely fantastic idea that is predominant on Earth at this point in time is the idea that we, the human beings on Earth, are the peak of evolution and that we are the ONLY BEINGS ALIVE in the universe. We spend billions and billions of dollars to build huge observatories so that we can observe the universe. Our astronomers have now been able to establish that there are at least 100 billion galaxies like our own Milky Way, in which our Sun is just an ordinary star. In an average galaxy there are "*A few hundred billion stars.*"[3] Still with this incredibly vast panorama in front of our eyes, we think that we are alone in space. It is true that in recent years our scientists have become increasingly open to the idea that there might be life on other planets, but this is still not something that is generally accepted.

Martinus explains that life is teeming everywhere in the universe; around innumerable suns, planets like or unlike our Earth circulate, most of them the home of some form of life. On innumerable planets the living conditions and the life forms are exactly as they are here on Earth, so that these planets are populated by humans and animals exactly like the species known on Earth. However, Martinus says, there are also planets where the manifestations of life appear in structures and shapes that are completely different from here, as these life forms unfold in evolutionary paths that have been designed differently from the ones we know.

Martinus puts it like this: "*To believe that the universe is nothing but an infinite ocean of the chance play of dead forces and to believe that from this chance play the bit of micro life which the earthly humanity constitutes, that is the inhabitants on the speck of dust in the universe, which we call the Earth, should be the only and highest existing life is a gigantic, cosmic derailment of logical thinking. It is to live in death instead of in life.*" (*Livets Bog* VI, paragraph 2350).

"The Spirit of God over the Face of the Waters"

On symbol number 1,[4] which is called "*The Spirit of God over the Face of the Waters*" (Genesis 1:2), we see a center of light at the top of the symbol. This center of light represents the divine life force or God. The rays emanating from this center of light represent the all pervading creative spirit, consciousness, will, and omnipotence of God.

In the sea of rays we see bands that go from light to dark. These bands represent the world impulses that emanate from God. The circles in the symbol represent planets. The circle in the center of the symbol with the double rings symbolizes our planet Earth. We can see that our planet is influenced by three different world impulses.

Symbol number 1: The Spirit of God over the Face of the Waters.

The symbol shows that there is consciousness behind all creative processes of nature and of the universe.

1. The center of light at the top, from which the rays radiate, symbolizes the creative "Something," or God.

2. The cross of flames symbolizes the totally perfect manifestation or creation of God.

3. The sea of rays shows God's all-pervasive creative spirit, consciousness, will, and omnipotence.

4. In the sea of rays shaded fields of tones from dark to light are seen. These constitute the cosmic world impulses, which release and maintain the levels of experience and the planes of existence of the living beings.

5. The many circles symbolize the suns and planets of the universe and the consciousness of the living beings attached to them.

6. The double circle shows the Earth and its human population. This is in touch with three world impulses.

The one at the bottom shows the consciousness of "primitive" people.

The one in the middle shows the world impulse from which Christianity, Islam, and Buddhism have emerged.

The impulse at the top shows the new world impulse, which will with time make the various religions superfluous as it will reveal the religious or real side of life as absolute science.

At the bottom of the circle we see a very narrow band that is almost disappearing from Earth. This represents *"the ancient world impulse"* of the religions of the aboriginal or "primitive" tribes[5] that once lived on Earth and of which there are only very few left such as in the jungles of Sumatra or Brazil or in the center of Australia. These are tribes of hunters and gatherers who have no modern conveniences and who practice "primitive" religions. They live in complete harmony with nature and believe in pantheism,[6] although they do not know the word. They believe that God is present everywhere in nature and they see the storm, the cold, the heat, the water, the darkness, the light, the stones, the rocks, the mountains, the trees, the flowers, etc., as expressions coming from mystical living beings. Through their strong instinct they are still very much in contact with the divine consciousness.

Once our civilization has reached these tribes, their natural habitat is taken over by civilization and the Earth then no longer offers suitable living space for these people. They are then either "absorbed" into our society (usually unsuccessfully) or they "die out" and a lot of fuss is made about this. But this is a natural process in the evolution of the Earth. These "primitive" tribes do not die and are not lost. When their natural habitat on Earth is taken over by modern society, they simply reincarnate on other planets where living conditions are more suitable for them and continue their development there. As there are planets at all levels of development, there are planets where living conditions are much better for these tribes, and they will reincarnate there.

The reason why they can in general not be successfully incorporated into our societies is that they cannot "jump" or "skip" thousands or hundreds of years of development. They are not mentally ready to enter a relatively advanced civilization. Their traditional way of life and their particular energy combination predominated by instinct (to be explained later) determine their place on the ladder of evolution. We cannot uproot a pygmy from the jungle and replant him in New York City and expect him to thrive. He cannot catch up with hundreds of years of evolution in just a few months. He cannot understand the workings of a modern society and he will feel an outcast. He simply cannot adapt.

In the universe there are planets that have beings on all levels of development from the most primitive life forms to life forms that are much more advanced than our own. When a certain planet no longer offers suitable living conditions for a certain species, be it a bird, a horse or a man, this being will then, in his next incarnation, reincarnate on a planet where conditions are more suited to his present level of development and he will continue his evolution there.

If again we look at symbol number 1, we see a band that covers most of the planet. This band represents the world impulse that gave rise to the major religions such as Christianity, Islam, and Buddhism. Martinus calls this impulse "*the old world impulse*" and it is the predominant impulse on Earth today. The majority of people living on Earth today are influenced by one of these "old" religions. Where the "old world impulse" predominates, the instinct loses ground and the various human manifestations become more and more defined by intelligence. The growing intelligence is responsible for our present technological and scientific levels, which we have achieved through our study of physical matter. As instinct loses ground and intelligence grows, people also become more and more godless. They are no longer able to believe because the explanations offered by the religions do not satisfy their intellect. It is in the civilized societies of "the old world impulse" that we find the godless beings.

At the top of the circle we see a band of even more light and this represents "*the new world impulse.*" This new world impulse is a strong emanation of light and love from God and with time it will replace the various religions and reveal the real truth about life as a science of spirituality. It will reveal the solution to the mystery of life. This influence is strong today and we see it where peace and internationalism is promoted and where aspects of the true nature of life is revealed as in the works of the people mentioned in the dedication who are all bearers of the new world impulse. However, one of the most important representatives of the new world impulse was Martinus himself, as his reincarnation on Earth was prompted by this new world impulse, which will eventually reveal the true nature of our existence as fact.

On the symbol we also see many other circles that represent other planets. Some of these planets are already further up toward the light than the Earth and are consequently more influenced by the new world impulse. This means that on these planets civilization is much more advanced than on Earth. On some of these planets a great number of people have achieved cosmic consciousness and consequently these planets are completely free from wars, strife, unrest, etc. On these planets peace reigns.

On the symbol we also see planets that are further behind than we are. On these planets living conditions can be as they were for us thousands of years ago, with "primitive" tribes living there, or they can be as we experienced a thousand years ago, when we rode around on horses and fought battles with swords.

We, as present inhabitants of the Earth, have not always reincarnated on this planet; we may have lived on other planets with similar living conditions to the ones on Earth. We may have chosen to reincarnate on Earth in this life because for us the Earth now offers good possibilities for growth. The Earth is in an accelerated phase of its development at this moment in time, so many people have reincarnated here in order to benefit from this fast development, as it offers beneficial opportunities for growth. There is no need to worry that the Earth will be overpopulated. The size of the population of Earth is regulated by Providence.[7] Because of the beneficial opportunities for growth that the Earth offers at this moment we are many who have chosen to reincarnate here now in order to make the best of the accelerated development. As the population of the Earth is growing, it is logical that we cannot all have lived here before. A great number of us have lived on other planets in our last incarnation and then have chosen to reincarnate here now because there are lessons for us to learn here at this point in time.

Likewise many prominent "earthlings" who lived on this planet in the 1800s have now reincarnated on planets that are more advanced in development than Earth, because this planet had no more possibilities for growth to offer to these people.

About these interplanetary "travels" Martinus says: "*You have to understand that the development of the living beings cannot for any being eternally be linked to the planet on which they are at present experiencing life, but it has had a previous and will have a future development on completely different planets in the universe. Thus the development of the beings manifests itself in paths that go from planet to planet*" (*Livets Bog* I, paragraph 284).

This means that we may live several lives on the same planet, but we cannot forever go on living on one planet. We have to change planets when there are no more lessons to learn on a particular planet.

Again let me stress that there is no need to worry when certain species of animals become extinct on Earth. I am not saying that it is not deplorable that we lose certain species, but seen in a larger perspective there is a reason why certain species "die out." When a certain species "dies out" it means that the Earth is no longer the ideal place for these creatures to live. This is the case with, for instances, horses. Development on Earth has meant that cars and tractors have taken over the work once done by horses. The horses have, to a large extent, been made redundant. They will therefore reincarnate on planets where horses are still needed to do work and they continue their development there. So when a species dies out on Earth it goes to a place that is better for its development and that is not something that we should deplore. So *"extinct is forever"* is not true. We only have to see things in a larger perspective.

Because the spirit of God pervades everything in the universe, *"everything is very good"* (Genesis 1:31). That means that seen in a large perspective things are just as they should be. We do not have to worry about the extinction of mankind or whether our planet will be destroyed. We are not heading toward annihilation or autodestruction. Things on Earth may not be perfect, but that is because the perfect stage has not been reached yet. The planet is not "ripe" yet. There are still wars, upheavals, poverty, and injustice but with time these will be eliminated as the creation of the perfect stage is being carried out. Everything is happening according to a master plan. We will not be able to destroy our planet through nuclear war or pollution. There are benevolent forces at work that take care that this does not happen. Martinus points out that it is not within our ability to destroy the planet. Providence will interfere long before that can happen. We are being looked after and taken care of. We are in God's hand, so to speak.

God's Body and God's Consciousness

The universe is God's body and we live inside this body. This means that we are alive inside an incredibly huge living body. Nothing exists that is not contained within God's body. Consequently the universe is one giant organism in which all elements, all units, are alive and cooperate. As the whole universe is God's body this means that God is everywhere, he is present in every nook and cranny, and every speck of dust is part of his body. As we are all part of God, we are all one. But the one is formed by innumerable individuals just as our body is made up of innumerable cells. Just as there is no part of our body that is not alive, there is life everywhere in God's body, the universe.

God not only has a body, he (or should I say she? Actually God is neither he nor she, but double-poled as will be explained in chapter 14) also has a consciousness in exactly the same way as we have both a body and a consciousness. Just as the sum of all physical bodies in the universe is God's physical body, so is the sum of the consciousness of all beings in the universe God's consciousness. God's consciousness is all consciousness put together. It is this huge "sea" of consciousness to which a person with cosmic consciousness has access. This sea of consciousness is in Theosophy referred to as the Akashic Records.[8]

Like all other beings, God has a consciousness for being awake and a consciousness for being asleep. We, the humans, also have a day consciousness through which we experience our daily life when we are awake and a night consciousness through which we experience life while our body is asleep. As we shall see later, our consciousness does not cease when we sleep. Through our night consciousness we experience life on a nonphysical level while our body is resting. We are not so aware of our night consciousness, as we have generally forgotten what we experienced during the night when we wake up. We may remember some dreams, but we have no fully conscious remembrance of what we experience through our night consciousness.

Martinus calls day consciousness the primary consciousness and night consciousness the secondary consciousness. So God has a primary consciousness (day consciousness) and a secondary consciousness (night consciousness) just as we have. As God's consciousness is all consciousness put together, there have to be some smaller units that "carry" the day and the night consciousness respectively. Advanced spiritual beings and physical beings with cosmic consciousness are the bearers of God's primary or day consciousness. On the other hand all "ordinary" physical beings such as humans and animals are the bearers of God's secondary or night consciousness. As we, the humans on Earth, are physical beings without cosmic consciousness, we are bearers of God's secondary or night consciousness at this moment in time. But later, when we have evolved further, we shall become bearers of God's primary consciousness. This happens when we achieve cosmic consciousness, as I shall explain in a later chapter.

God and the Quantum of God

Our relationship to God can also be expressed as God and Son of God. The Son of God is also by Martinus called quantum of God. God is the sum of all the quanta. In exactly the same way as a newspaper photo is composed of a large number of dots to form a whole, so is both God's body and God's consciousness composed of all the dots that are the microbeings inside his body. We are the dots, but every one of us is important as a part of the whole. The whole universe is one huge organism in which all the units are interdependent.

God's body is the sum of all mineral, plant, animal, and human bodies of the universe, and God's consciousness is the sum of all the consciousness of all living creatures. As a consequence of this God's experience of life is also the sum of the experience of life of all the quanta. As we experience life, so does God. God is the only being alive that does not have a mesocosmos or macrocosmos to be alive in. God has no outer world because he IS the whole world, the whole universe. There is no one next to or above God. There is no "outside" for God to experience. So God has to experience life "within." God experiences life through the life experience of his microbeings, the cells of his body. The experience of life is very important in order to renew our consciousness, as we shall see later.

God and You

The fact that we are all part of God also means that we meet God in every being we encounter. To us every other being represents God. Our neighbor represents God to us; he is the instrument God uses to contact us. In the same way, we are also God's instrument toward our neighbor. There are only two players on the scene: God and you. Every being that we meet is God in some kind of disguise, be it a dog, a mosquito, a beggar, a king, a snail, or our spouse. Every living being represents God for us. This may be useful to remember the next time we meet a dirty beggar that we treat with disdain or when we kick a dog or crush a fly or show intolerance toward a fellow being. God is everywhere and in everybody. God is omniscient, omnipresent, and all-loving.

But the fact that there are only two players on the scene, God and you, also means that our whole life is one large communication and interplay with God. Every day God teaches us things through our interplay with God's representatives, the other human beings and animals. Everything that happens to us, everything that we experience is an expression of a lesson from God. Through our daily life and the things that we experience, God teaches us a lesson. If good things happen to us, God shows us that we have behaved in a cosmically correct way and consequently we get a good feedback. If we have behaved in a cosmically incorrect way, unpleasant things happen to us. We reap as we sow. This will be explained at length in chapter 13 about the law of karma.

What we might remember every morning when we get out of bed is that school has started again, the teacher (God) is already standing at the blackboard, and the lesson is about to begin. Throughout the day God will teach us. But until we are aware of this, we may not get a lot out of his lessons. We are not very good pupils as long as we do not realize that we are in a classroom. We are simply not paying attention. However, as soon as we realize that a lesson is going on, we start paying more attention and consequently we will learn more. Once we start every day asking ourselves, "What will he teach me today?" we have begun a constructive process.

Once we start thinking about what it is God is trying to tell us and we start acting according to God's instructions, we will soon be able to graduate ourselves out of the animal kingdom and into the real human kingdom of light and love. Our present position in the animal kingdom will be explained in a later chapter.

Concepts of God

So God is there and he always has been. He is teaching us and looking after us. He is constantly reminding us that we are part of him and that he loves us. If we have lost faith in him, he is patiently waiting for his lost sheep to return and he is more than happy to welcome us back whenever we choose to "come home." If we have never lost faith in him, he is there as he always has been, but maybe not in the way that has been preached in the churches.

The stern and angry God that I was presented with in my childhood from school and churches is a product of the limited perception of unfinished human beings. It is an image of God reflecting Man's concept of himself. It is God in the image and likeness of Man.

Down through history Man has mirrored God in his own image in many different ways. The Vikings believed that God (Odin) was a big, bearded man sitting in a large hall eating huge chunks of meat and drinking excessive amounts of ale from horns served by fair-haired damsels surrounded by his noisy friends. This vision of paradise the Vikings called Valhalla. This is a concept of God that fitted with what the Vikings found pleasurable. It is a concept of God in the image and likeness of the man that has created it.

In a similar way the Christian Church has created a concept of God that fitted Man's own limited perception. God was believed to be like a feudal king to whom one should give gifts in return for special favors. God was seen as someone who had to be mollified with tributes in order to be willing to give something in return. The crucifixion of Christ has been interpreted as a sacrifice to appease God so that he would forgive us our sins. Christ assumed all our sins and he was ready to die for all those sins, so that we could go free. And because of that blood-sacrifice God was mollified and he forgave us our sins. In this interpretation God is seen as someone who could not just forgive, he needed a blood sacrifice, an offering, in order to give something in return. Once he got this sacrifice from a completely innocent man, who had to endure a horrible death on the cross, he was willing to let the real culprits go free. This reflects a concept of God as some kind of despot, who doesn't care if it is a completely innocent man who has to suffer as long as he gets his blood sacrifice. Once he has his blood sacrifice, he is willing to let the real culprits go free. God is not seen as a loving and forgiving God, but as somebody who has to cash in (in blood) before he will give something in return.

In Christianity it has also been preached that an unbaptized child or a child born outside of marriage would forever burn in hell. But what kind of God would sentence an innocent child to eternal damnation because of some technicality for which the child itself was not responsible? Is God really no better than that? Is God really so petty that he would let an insignificant detail lead to eternal flames? Doesn't this sound more like the behavior of a fairly primitive man than the behavior of an all-loving God?

Martinus explains that such a concept of God is completely false, completely misinterpreted, and completely silly. God is not mirrored on Man; he is a good deal better than that. He is not petty and fussy and he needs no sacrifices. Christ knew his mission and had agreed to the crucifixion prior to his reincarnation on Earth. The mission of Christ culminated on the cross when he was able to show the "new" mentality that people were to learn, the mentality of forgiveness. With his famous words on the cross *"Father, forgive them, for they know not what they do"* (Luke 23: 34), Jesus demonstrated an attitude that was then completely new, the attitude of forgiveness. Thus Christ initiated the *"old world impulse"* in the Western world, the world impulse that during the last 2000 years has been teaching people on Earth to abstain from seeking revenge, to love their neighbor, and to forgive. The mission of Christ was to demonstrate this "new" attitude. It was not to assume the sins of innumerable sinners and murderers in order to please an angry God.

If we have such a concept of God, we can start looking upon God in a new light. God is all love. He is not angry and he is certainly not bloodthirsty. He does not need to be appeased with blood sacrifices and he takes no pleasure in sending children to hell. God is a good deal better than what many religions seem to think.

Martinus once said: "*It is impossible for me to explain to you how much love there is within the system.*" We have to understand that God's love is everywhere and that the amount of love is incomprehensible. Love is the basis of the whole universe. God's love, omnipotence, and ability to forgive are greater than we have ever imagined. God's consciousness of love pervades the whole universe and no evil exists in this perfect universe. But in order for there to be light, there also has to be darkness. Without contrast there can be no perception, no experience of life, as we shall soon see.

5

The Parent Principle

The parent principle or the principle of world redemption is a fundamental basis for prompting development on the various planets. It can be seen as an effect of the world impulses emanating from God.

Providence

Most living beings that are born on this planet have parents that take care of them until they can fend for themselves. The parents are there to protect, teach, help, and support the being, but until the being reaches a certain age, it is not aware that the parents are there. The baby cries and its needs are tended to from somewhere, care is provided, but the baby does not know from where. It just realizes that crying helps and that soon its needs are taken care of by somebody. The toddler walks along the pavement and does not notice the anxious parents who run behind it and prevent it from running into the street. A small child does not realize that there are parents who look after it and that these parents tend to its every need. The parents are there, they look after the child and care for it, they keep the child out of danger, but the child is completely unaware of this.

This is the parent principle.

In exactly the same way we, the living beings on Earth, are being looked after by Providence, and we are exactly as unaware of this as the child. At our present stage we have no idea that we are being looked after. We think that we are all alone in the universe, completely unprotected and left to fend for ourselves like "babes in the wood," but this is fortunately not so. Martinus explains that Providence is like our parents, it looks after us and takes care of us and keeps us out of danger. Providence works through a host of spiritual beings. Everywhere there are spiritual beings around us and each one of us has one or more guardian angels.

Providence sees to it that things on Earth do not go astray. We have a certain amount of free will, but there are things that we cannot do because Providence will interfere long before we can do them. For instance, many people think that we will be able to completely destroy our planet and wipe out all life on Earth through nuclear war or pollution. But this will never happen, because Providence will interfere and prevent this long before things get that far out of hand. It is simply not within our power to destroy our planet in any major way. Providence has plans for the planet and we, its microorganisms, will not be allowed to destroy it. There are benevolent forces at work and they oversee that things do not get out of hand.

Visitors from Higher Realms

Providence monitors the development on Earth and makes sure that things go as they should. At intervals Providence estimates that help is needed down here and a being from a higher realm is sent down to teach us and to get development on to the right track. The higher realms from which the advanced beings come are those that are further along in development than we are. They will be fully defined later in this book, but let me just say here that they are realms where full insight into the mystery of life has been achieved and where the beings are one with the basic tone of the universe, which is love. This higher being is someone further along in development than we are, he* is a being who has reached the stage at which he has become "Man in the image and likeness

* I use "he" throughout the book to denominate both sexes.

of God." We will all reach this stage eventually. Being "Man in the image and likeness of God" is not something that is reserved only for world redeemers such as Buddha or Jesus; it is a stage we will all reach. But we, the humans on planet Earth, have not reached this high stage of development yet. We are still not fully finished human beings, so we still need instructions from those who are more advanced. The being that is sent "down" by Providence is a being whose morals are much more advanced than ours, his insight, intelligence, and ability to love are far more advanced than ours. When help is needed such an advanced being then agrees to reincarnate in a human body here on Earth. The advanced beings are generally called world redeemers, and the "mechanism" of sending them "down" is called "the principle of world redemption" or "the parent principle." The principle of world redemption is a fundamental principle of love.

Mostly these visitors from higher realms come to teach us morals and through their insight some of them or their followers have founded the major religions such as Christianity, Buddhism, and Islam.

Cosmic Glimpses

These visitors from higher realms have incarnated in a human body on Earth and they look like any other "earthling." However, it is only in their looks that they resemble other earthlings; their mentality and morality are far from being similar to that of the people they have reincarnated among. It is their superior mentality and morals that make them "models" for other people to imitate. The insight they have has generally been revealed to them in their disguise as earthlings through cosmic glimpses, which means that at a certain point in their lives they experience a vision, a revelation, or initiation. This vision reveals the logic of the universe, the immortality of all living beings, and the consciousness of God in a short flash.

Martinus expresses the experience of a cosmic glimpse like

this: "*A cosmic glimpse is a momentary experience of a few seconds of the mental light which in the Bible is expressed as 'The Holy Spirit.' When this overshadowing of God's spirit is unadulterated and has not been provoked artificially, the being then experiences his own immortality in a glimpse, he experiences that the structure of the universe is perfect and that love is the basic tone of the universe. At the same time the being begins to understand that all creations of nature in their ultimate state of perfection are a blessing and a delight to living creatures*" (*Livets Bog* VI, paragraph 2139).

The beings in whose name some of the major religions were founded such as Buddha and Mohammed had cosmic glimpses. Through these cosmic glimpses they were able to form an idea of the spiritual world and the existence of a Creator, and they conveyed this idea to their contemporaries and followers. With time a cult arose around these beings and a new religion was founded.

Moses had a cosmic glimpse when he saw the radiant spirit in the burning thornbush and heard the voice, which told him to go to Egypt to free the people of Israel from its slavery.

The apostle Saul (later Paul) also had a cosmic glimpse when he, on the road to Damascus, was enveloped in a strong white light and heard a voice, which said: "*Saul, Saul, why do you persecute me?*" (Acts 9:4) This cosmic glimpse completely changed Saul and he became a great apostle for Christianity.

Jesus, too, had a cosmic glimpse when he was baptized by John the Baptist in the river Jordan. He then experienced a glimpse of God's spirit symbolized by the radiant dove and he heard the voice, which said: "*Thou art my beloved son; with thee I am well pleased*" (Luke 3:22). Shortly after this Jesus was again overshadowed by God's spirit when he experienced the "*transfiguration on the mount*" (Luke 9:28). On this occasion Jesus did not only experience a cosmic glimpse, but permanent cosmic consciousness was opened in his mind.

It is certainly so that many more persons on Earth have experienced cosmic glimpses, but they were not world redeemers. Let me just mention some of these: Plato, Dante, Bartolomé de las

Casas, Santa Teresa de Jesus, San Juan de la Cruz, Francis Bacon, William Blake, Walt Whitman, Honoré de Balzac, Richard Bucke, and Rudolf Steiner.[1] The writings of these people show that they have experienced something unique, something that transcends the physical existence and that has given them an extraordinary insight.

Today we have reached the point at which a number of people are beginning to experience cosmic glimpses. A woman in Sweden experienced a cosmic glimpse while looking at a snowflake, a woman in Denmark experienced a cosmic glimpse during meditation, a woman in the USA experienced a cosmic glimpse while picking flowers in a field.[2]

I think that also Carol Bowman, author of *Children's Past Lives,* experienced a cosmic glimpse at the beach in her youth. After a long night of fun with her friends in the dunes Carol Bowman went off on her own to watch the sun rise. She says:

"As I watched the first splinter of orange sun peek over the horizon, I noticed a strange buzzing sound in my ears, and everything I looked at started to sparkle and wink. The horizon began to shimmer. Then suddenly everything changed in a way I had never experienced before. My exhaustion, the hypnotic sound of the surf, the sparkle of the new sun on the water, and other forces unknown conspired in the moment to transport me to a different state of consciousness.

I wasn't just seeing with my eyes—I was perceiving everything around me. I was seeing, sensing, becoming, being the sand, the waves, the endless orange and pink sky. My body was still sitting on the dune, but I can't say 'I' was sitting on the dune because suddenly I was all energy, and everything around me was all the same energy, flowing within me and without me. What I normally thought of as solid matter was now a seamless reflection of all this golden energy. My body seemed to melt away totally. I became one with the sand and the surf—and then, for a moment, with all of creation. I felt tremendously expanded and alive. I was worlds more than the 'me' in my body, more than the 'Carol' personality that I had always thought was my limit. Joy and relief filled my mind as I understood—really understood—that I was a part of something greater than the finite me.

In a flash I realized that this energy I felt within myself could never be destroyed—it would always exist. Only the body dies, while this essence that was everywhere but somehow still centered in my body continues forever."[3]

What Carol Bowman experienced on the beach seems to fit the description that Martinus gives of a cosmic glimpse.

A cosmic glimpse occurs when the masculine and the feminine poles of the being momentarily reach a balance point. At this balance point a short contact is established with the sea of wisdom of the spiritual world, which is identical to God's primary consciousness or the Holy Spirit. The masculine and feminine poles will be explained in chapter 14.

The cosmic glimpses reveal certain aspects of the universal truth and leave the persons who have experienced them with a vision of the harmony of the universe and of their own immortality. These cosmic glimpses have then given rise to the many different religions that we know on Earth. But the source of all the different religions is one and the same: glimpses of God's primary consciousness. There is only one truth, and not a Catholic truth, a Muslim truth, a Buddhist truth, a Hindu truth, a Mormon truth, a Protestant truth, etc. All these different religions are interpretations of the universal truth made by imperfect beings that came after the founders and who, for different reasons, wanted to weave their own dogmas and superstitious beliefs into the universal vision of the founder.

Permanent Cosmic Consciousness and Its Forerunners

The cosmic glimpses, which have been experienced by a number of people, are forerunners of achieving permanent cosmic consciousness, which Martinus also calls "the great birth." Experiencing "the great birth" is the same as coming into full realization of our oneness with God or entering the realm of God's primary consciousness. This will be explained later.

Generally the first cosmic glimpse will come as a single glimpse in a lifetime. Then in the following lives we will get two or more cosmic glimpses and so on until we reach permanent cosmic consciousness or "the great birth."

So we start experiencing cosmic glimpses several lives before we reach permanent cosmic consciousness. To have permanent cosmic consciousness means that the being has the energy of intuition completely under the control of his will. The energy of intuition (cf. chapter 9), which is the energy that conveys all cosmic insight, obeys the will of the cosmic conscious being in the same way as our eyesight obeys our wills. In this way the being that has cosmic consciousness can "look" at any question and get an answer in the same way as we can look at any particular object with our eyes. The being with cosmic consciousness has the energy of intuition under the control of his will and he can access the answers to all questions by just thinking about a particular question.

According to Martinus, both Jesus and Martinus himself had permanent cosmic consciousness. They could both access the energy of intuition at will and did not "only" have access to the cosmic truths through cosmic glimpses.

The fact that it is not only world redeemers who have had cosmic glimpses shows us that we are progressing and that we have reached a point in development at which the spiritual reality is beginning to reveal itself to us. As we progress further, more and more people will have cosmic insight, and through this insight the truth about our existence will reveal itself. Man has now reached a point when the mystery of life is about to be revealed. This means that gradually over the next centuries and millennia, all the different religions will be abandoned and taken over, not by a new religion, but by a new knowledge based on a merger of science and spirituality.

The Bible

Providence sees to it that things on Earth go in the right direction and Providence also sees to it that man is provided with guidelines to his behavior and moral aims. The Bible is such a guideline, but the different testaments of the Bible have been given at different times in accordance with the different stages of development that Man has reached.

The Old Testament was given to Man some four thousand years ago or more[4] and the aim of this testament was to teach Man certain morals as in the ten Commandments. But also the Old Testament encouraged man to seek revenge, to pay "*an eye for an eye and a tooth for a tooth.*" In this way the Old Testament became a guideline for man into darkness, into misery and unhappiness, as revenge generates darkness, misery, and unhappiness. As we shall see later, darkness is as necessary as light for the experience of life of the living beings. This will be explained in chapter 11.

The Old Testament was meant as a guide for people who lived four thousand years ago, so generally speaking its value as a guide has to some extent outlived itself today.

Two thousand years ago a new morality was introduced on Earth through the teachings of Jesus Christ. His teachings went against the teachings of the Old Testament as he preached forgiveness and told people: "*But if any one strikes you on the right cheek, turn to him the other also*" (Matthew 4:39) and thus he went against the morality of revenge expressed in "*an eye for an eye and a tooth for a tooth.*" Jesus told people to love their neighbor, to put the sword away, to forgive the neighbor seven times seventy a day, and at the peak of his sufferings on the cross he was able to pray for his executioners and excuse their behavior through the words: "*Father, forgive them; for they know not what they do*" (Luke 23:34). In this way Jesus demonstrated a mentality that was completely superior to that of his executioners, and with these words he underlined the nature of his mission: To teach people on Earth to practice forgiveness. Jesus addressed these words to God ("*Father...*"), but God did not need to be reminded to forgive, as he IS all-forgiving. The words were expressed for the benefit of the people witnessing the crucifixion, so that they could see the mentality of forgiveness demonstrated, a mentality, that was to become the core of Christianity for the next thousands of years.

So, through his all-pervading attitude of forgiveness, Jesus created the foundation of a new religion, the religion of Christianity, in which we are told to *"love your God above all things and your neighbor as yourself."* In this way the teachings of Christ in the New Testament constituted a turning point. In the Old Testament there was no advocating love and forgiveness. The Old Testament offered directions to a "correct" behavior (the ten Commandments), but also advocated revenge (*"an eye for an eye"*). The teachings of Christ constituted completely new directions, directions contrary to the previous ones. These new directions came at exactly the time when some people on Earth were ready to understand them and accept them as a moral aim. In a cosmic sense the teachings of Christ constituted the showdown with the animal mentality in Man and pointed in the direction of the mentality of the real human being. Thus the mission of Christ constituted the birth of the human mentality of love and forgiveness if not all over the Earth, then in the Western world.

The impact of the teachings and sufferings of Jesus has been unparalleled on Earth, and innumerable churches have been built to worship Christ. The effects of the gospel of love have also been important and every child in the Western world has been taught to love his neighbor. However, this is easier said than done, and the century that we have just left has seen the worst wars the Earth has known to this date.

However, man has now reached a stage in his development where the teachings of Christ can no longer satisfy his intellect. The teachings of Christ were adapted to the mental stage of the people who lived on Earth two thousand years ago. But much has happened during the last two thousand years and Man has developed. Through the birth of science and research, Man's knowledge of the physical world has advanced enormously and his intellect has developed. Seen with the eyes of modern man the New Testament is no longer "new"; to a certain degree it has become outdated, not because of the truths it reveals, because they are eternal truths, but because these truths had to be told in ways so that the unintellectual beings of two thousand years ago could understand them. The teachings of Christ had to appeal more to people's feelings than to their intellects. Christ had to talk about sin, the Devil, and hell to make his contemporaries understand what was good and what was bad. In a cosmic sense there is no sin, no Devil, no hell, and no evil, but Jesus used these concepts to convince the people of his time that there were things that were desirable and things that were undesirable. He had to appeal to the feelings and instinct of his followers and not to their intellect. Two thousand years ago people were not very intellectual, but they could be molded when their instinct and feelings were appealed to. So instead of offering a logical explanation, Jesus had to use suggestive images and parables. People had to be scared away from evil because of their fear of hell. The intellect of the people living two thousand years ago was not yet very developed, so they would not have been able to understand what Jesus said if he had expressed his teachings in plain words. If Jesus had expressed his teachings in plain words, he would have given his followers stones for bread; his teachings would then have been as indigestible to their intellect as stones would be to their digestion. So we have to understand that the eternal truths revealed by Christ two thousand years ago had to be presented in a way that suited people then and therefore they do not necessarily suit people today. They simply have not been presented in a sufficiently intellectual way to suit us today. Jesus knew that his contemporaries were not ready to be told the solution to the mystery of life because their intellectual and humane abilities were not sufficiently developed. He knew that the final revelation had to wait until they had outgrown the major part of their animal mentality. That is why he could say, *"I have yet many things to say to you, but you cannot bear them now. When the Spirit of truth comes, he will guide you into all the truth"* (John 16:12–13).

Through science, investigation, and accumulation of experience, man has reached a point today at which his intellect has grown. Man has simply become more intelligent than he was two thousand years ago. Today Man needs a logical explanation to the things he sees. Man can no longer be satisfied with explanations that appeal solely to his feelings such as those offered by the Bible or the religions. The religions have revealed the eternal truths as myths, symbols, parables, and poetic images—the truths have been presented as suggestive metaphors, as concepts that could appeal to man's instinct and feelings and not to his intellect. The truths have been wrapped up in a thick layer of poetic paraphrases, symbolic circumlocutions, and obscure suggestive images. They had to be presented like that because that was the only way Man could understand them previously, because his intellect simply had not developed to the point at which he would understand the truths had they been explained as scientific facts. But at a certain point in time Man reaches an intellectual level at which he no longer needs paraphrases, images, and parables. At a certain point in time Man becomes so intelligent that he can understand the truths when they are explained to him in a straightforward way. That point in time is now. Man has now, to a very large extent, outgrown his ability to believe in the religions, his instinct has decreased, and his intelligence has grown. It is not that Man no longer wants to believe in the religions, he simply cannot. The religious dogmas are presented as postulates without a logical basis, and this molests his intelligence. His intellect tells him only to subscribe to explanations that have a logical and scientific foundation. This means that he is ready to be told the truth in a straightforward way, not as a new religion, but as scientific fact.

Therefore, Providence has sent another being down from the higher realms to quench mankind's thirst for knowledge about our existence and a solution to the mystery of life.

The Third Testament

Martinus is that being and his work is the promised " spirit of truth" or holy knowledge. His work is a revelation of the truth about our existence in plain words with no beating about the bush. But as "the spirit of truth" reveals some fairly complicated facts about basic energies, about the laws that govern both physical and spiritual matter, about the structure of both micro, meso, and macrocosmos, it is clear that the revelation of this had to wait until Man had reached a certain intellectual and scientific level. There would be as little point in telling Man these truths two thousand years ago as there would be teaching a dog mathematics. In order to be able to understand and accept the cosmic truths about our existence a certain intellectual level has to have been reached by the pupil. You do not start teaching theoretical physics to a child in the first grade. You start with the alphabet. In this way we have to understand that both the Old, the New and the Third Testaments have been given to Man at times when their contents could be understood and Man's emotional and intellectual levels matched the contents of the teachings.

Permanent cosmic consciousness was opened in Martinus' mind when he had his initiation at the age of thirty. This initiation has been explained in chapter 3. You can also read about Martinus' initiation in his book *On the Birth of my Mission.* It was through his cosmic consciousness that Martinus was able to reveal the truth about our existence. It is this truth that he reveals in *The Third Testament.* Jesus predicted his coming in the words: "*I have yet many things to say to you, but you cannot bear them now. When the spirit of truth comes, he will guide you into all the truth; for he will not speak on his own authority, but whatever he hears he will speak, and he will declare to you the things that are to come. He will glorify me, for he will take what is mine and declare it to you. All that the Father has is mine; therefore I said that he will take what is mine and declare it to you.*" (John 16:12–15).

Martinus' mission is a continuation of the mission of Christ, as Christ already announced his coming two thousand years ago when he promised that the father would send somebody "to guide you into all the truth." Consequently Martinus' work is called "The Third Testament." Throughout *The Third Testament,* Martinus ex-

plains many of the sayings of Jesus. He reveals how we can understand these today, how they can be understood when we "unpack"
the cosmic truths from their wrapping of poetic circumlocutions
and symbolism. This is what Jesus refers to when he says: "He will
glorify me, for he will take what is mine and declare it to you."
An example of this could be Martinus' explanation of the law of
karma (cf. chapter 13), which by Jesus was expressed through the
words. "Put your sword back into its place; for all who take the
sword will perish by the sword." (Matthew 26:52). More examples
of Martinus' interpretations of Jesus' words can be seen on pages:
79, 89, 142, 156, 157, 182, 192, 199, 200, 216, 219, 263, 292, 299,
309, 311, 312-15, 318, 322, 324-25, 327, 346-47.

The Third Testament offers a logical explanation to the mystery
of life and hinges this explanation on to the present level of our
materialistic sciences. The Third Testament points out the direction
our sciences can take to reach a new level of cognition, and it reveals the spiritual forces that lie behind the physical world and that
govern the physical world. The Third Testament satisfies the growing intellect of modern man and it is mostly intended to appeal to
our intellects and not so much to our feelings. Martinus' complete
works are The Third Testament, and as this testament is based on
logic it is not a basis for a new religion, as religion is based on faith
and not on logic. The Third Testament can and will put an end to
all religions over the next centuries. The Third Testament constitutes a basis for a merging of spirituality and science. Martinus
also calls his work cosmology.

The Third Testament will be the last to be revealed on this planet. It will be the last because no more testaments will be needed.
As more and more people on Earth reach the point at which they
have cosmic glimpses, the universal truths will become known by
a growing number of people. Once a number of people on Earth
have achieved cosmic insight, this insight will spread and with
time the cosmic truths will become general knowledge. Then we
will need no more teachers from higher realms, but we will be able
to teach ourselves.

We have now reached a point in time when a number of people on Earth have reached a sufficiently high moral standard to be candidates for cosmic glimpses. That is why it is necessary that the "spirit of truth" in the shape of *The Third Testament* should come now to reveal the mystery of existence, so that those who get cosmic glimpses know what they are experiencing.

The fact that an increasing number of people are getting cosmic glimpses also tells us that these people, within a number of lifetimes, will reach the point when they get permanent cosmic consciousness. This again means that every man and woman on Earth sooner or later will have cosmic consciousness and become "*Man in the image and likeness of God.*" However, we all stand on different levels of morality and love and it is only those who are furthest along in developments who are the present candidates. Until today it is only visitors from higher realms that have manifested permanent cosmic consciousness on Earth. No natural "earthling" has yet reached that point, but within the next thousand or two thousand years those that are furthest along in development will have reached "the great birth." But sooner or later we will all reach the point in which we achieve cosmic consciousness.

But how do we qualify to get cosmic glimpses and later cosmic consciousness? In general one can say that we become candidates for cosmic glimpses when we have no more animal mentality left, when our moral standard and capacity for universal love have become very high and when our masculine and feminine poles have reached a balance point. In order to understand why this is so, we have to climb up to a very high position from where we can get an overview of the whole of the spiral cycle, which we are at present going through. We have to look at the world from God's own viewpoint. This we will do in the following chapters.

6

The Structure of the Living Being

Physical and Spiritual Matter

Martinus says that beyond the physical world there is a spiritual world, a world beyond time and space, a world from which the physical world is created and governed, as it is this spiritual world that is the primary world. In order to understand how such a world can exist, we have to look at what matter is. Martinus makes a distinction between physical and spiritual matter, which means that we can talk of matter that is not physical.

We all know that physical matter exists, because we can see and touch it. We also know that physical matter has various stages: solid, liquid, and gaseous or vaporous.

We know these stages from the way water behaves. Water can be solid when frozen, liquid when between 0 and 100 degrees Celsius, and vaporous when over 100 degrees Celsius. When water boils it dematerializes, it is no longer tangible, but it still exists as vapor. We know that the water still exists although it is vaporous, because when the vapor hits the cold windowpane, the water materializes again and runs down the pane as droplets. So in the vaporous state water is mainly invisible and intangible, but its molecules are still there, they are only more dispersed.

However, according to Martinus there is yet a state to be added to the list, the ray-formed state. In the ray-formed state, matter is even more invisible than it is in the vaporous state, but it exists nevertheless. So according to Martinus all matter has four states: solid, liquid, gaseous, and ray-formed. Our sciences have not yet officially acknowledged the existence of ray-formed matter, but this is really illogical, because it is common knowledge that rays and waves exist. We know that radio waves, television waves, microwaves, infrared waves, ultraviolet waves, X-rays, and gamma waves exist. These rays and waves form what we have called the electromagnetic spectrum. We know that these rays and waves are not solid, not liquid, and not gaseous, indeed we know that they all move at light speed. As we know they exist, they have to exist in a state that is none of the three "known" states. So we can say that they exist in the ray-formed state. They have to exist in a state, otherwise they cannot exist. We operate with rays and waves every day when we watch television or listen to the radio, when we receive mobile phone calls, when we use the microwave oven, or when we use radar. We know that there are waves and rays all around us; we know they are there, even though they are invisible to our eyes. We operate with the existence of ray-formed matter every day and indeed a considerable part of our technological advances have been based on the existence of this type of matter. The existence of ray-formed matter is irrefutable; the question is just how we define it.

Martinus calls ray-formed matter spiritual matter. Ray-formed or spiritual matter is matter that exists on fine wavelengths, it is invisible and intangible, but it is matter nevertheless. Ray-formed matter is measurable and useful.

Martinus would define our thoughts, electricity, television and radio waves, magnetism, microwaves, infrared waves, X-rays, and gamma rays as spiritual matter. Spiritual matter is the first and primary type of matter, it is the matter that thoughts and consciousness consist of. Spiritual matter is the "Spirit of God that moves over the face of the waters," it is the thought matter that was there before anything else and from this matter all other matter has been created. The physical world has been created through a process of condensation of spiritual matter. This means that the physical world is condensed or "frozen" thoughts or consciousness matter.

Spiritual or ray-formed matter furthermore has the ability to penetrate physical matter. We know that radio and television waves are not stopped by walls, glass, metal, or flesh.

With the acknowledgment of the existence of ray-formed matter, we have already accepted that matter can exist in a state, that is not physical, because how can we call it physical when it is both invisible and intangible? If we agree to define matter that is invisible and intangible as nonphysical or metaphysical, we should have no problem accepting that a metaphysical level of existence can exist. We already know that this type of matter exists and we know some of the things it can do, such as send messages, which we do on radio, television, and with mobile phones. It is a well-known fact that rays and waves exist, and if we can agree to define this type of matter as nonphysical (as it is both invisible and intangible) or spiritual we have come a long way in accepting that a spiritual level of existence can be "out there."

We know some of the properties of ray-formed or spiritual matter, such as its ability to send information and pass through solid matter, but we may not know all its properties. The existence of ray-formed matter may mean that a whole world exists that consists of ray-formed matter. As ray-formed or spiritual matter is invisible and intangible, such a world can exist even though we cannot see and feel it. Our senses are simply not sophisticated enough to pick up this type of matter. We certainly cannot prove that such a world does not exist. According to Martinus such a world *does* exist beyond the physical world and in the following chapters we shall see what the characteristics of this world are. Martinus refers to this world as the spiritual world.

The "I" and Its Triune Structure

Just as there is a world of ray-formed matter beyond the physical world, there is a body of ray-formed matter beyond every physical body. This means that we have a body apart from our physical body, in other words our physical body is not the only body we have, we also have a body of ray-formed matter. Every living being alive in the universe has such a ray-formed body behind or in addition to its physical body. This ray-formed body is an energy field, so its existence can be measured. It can be measured in life monitoring devices, which will show a flat line when the energy field is no longer there, and it can be seen by those who can see auras. Our spiritual body can be seen in our aura. The aura is the electromagnetic field that surrounds all living beings. We can actually say that all living beings have a physical body and six spiritual bodies, a body for each basic energy plus the mother energy. The basic energies will be explained in chapter 9.

Behind our seven bodies there is a logical structure. This is the invisible structure of the "I," the core of who we are. This structure is the same for every living creature.

Now, what does this structure of the "I" consist of? As a concept, the "I" and its bodies is a triune principle consisting of three interdependent factors that Martinus calls X 1, X 2, and X 3.

X 1 is the eternally existing core of every being. X 1 is defined as "something that is." X 1 can have no analysis apart from "something that is," because you cannot say that it is good or bad, black or white, pretty or ugly, big or small. It is all of these things or none of these things. X 1 has no characteristics apart from "something that is."

X 2 is X 1's eternal ability to create. X 2 is the ability of creation of all beings. In X 2 lies stored the "know-how" of creation particular to the individual such as its talents (abilities, dispositions, character traits), its fate element, its pole structure, and its consciousness, which are all eternal entities that accompany the being from life to life.

X 3 is the result of the two first Xs or something that has been created by X 1 through the use of X 2. X 3 is the created body or everything that has been created. So our physical body is X 3. The body of a dog is X 3, the body of a bird, a fish, a spider, a planet, a sunflower, a cell, a tree, a mouse, etc., are all X 3s.

X 1 and X 2 are eternal entities. They have no beginning and no end. Something that is eternal cannot have begun at a certain point, nor can it ever cease to exist. If it does, it is not eternal. So X1 and X2, which constitute our essential being, are eternal. The most essential part of who we are is eternal.

Now, the X 1 can through its X 2 (its ability to create) create X 3, which are all things created. As X 3 is something that has been created, it is not eternal; it has a beginning and an end. In the physical world we see all the X 3s, all the created things. All created things are subject to the process of aging; as soon as they have reached their peak manifestation, they start to degenerate. Everything in the physical world is subject to this process of degeneration or gradual dissolution. Our bodies are X 3s, as they are physical tools of manifestation that the X 1, the core of the "I," has created through the use of the X 2, its creative ability.

Every living being has this triune structure and this structure is in fact the same as what has been symbolically expressed in the Bible as the Father (X 1), the Son (X 2), and the Holy Spirit (X 3).

The structure of the living being can be illustrated like this:

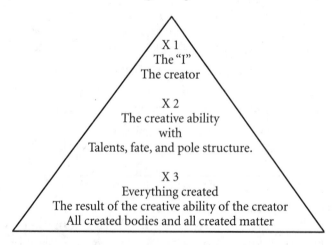

When we say that every living being has this structure, there is no exception. The fly has this structure, the sea anemone has this structure, the eagle, the mouse, the whale, the kangaroo, the syca-more tree, the crocodile, the mosquito, the blood cell, the Earth, the lily, the Sun, the sperm, the solar system, the galaxy, and even God has this structure. God has this structure because God's "I" is the sum of all the existing "I"s or all X 1s, just as God's body is the sum of all existing bodies or all X 3s, which have been created through the X 2s, or the eternal ability to create of all living beings.

Every living being has its eternal X 1, its eternal ability to cre-ate, X 2, and something that it has created, X 3, in either physical or spiritual matter. As we shall see later, X 3 varies as we pass through the spiral cycle. This means that the "I" makes use of a variety of different bodies as it moves through eternity.

We have not always manifested our "I" through a human body as the one we have now, but we have manifested our "I" in many, many different bodies, as we shall see later. Our bodies or X 3s are subject to evolution. Our eternal X 1 through the use of our eter-nal X 2 enables us to manifest ourselves in innumerable ways and through this we experience life eternally in endless varieties.

A Physical and a Spiritual Body

Through this look at the structure of the living being it was point-ed out that we are more than our physical body. Behind or beyond the physical body we have an eternal structure, which creates and defines our manifestations in matter. Through the use of X 2 we can create bodies in both physical and spiritual (ray-formed) mat-ter. Apart from a physical body all living beings have a body of ray-formed matter. This body of ray-formed matter is an electri-cal field or an energy field. This electrical field can be seen in our aura.

It is this energy field that makes a body come alive. The presence of the energy field in a body is what makes the difference between a living body and a corpse. If we look at a corpse and a sleeping body, there is little difference apart from a bit of pallor. The physical in-gredients are exactly the same: heart, liver, kidneys, lungs, brain, skeleton, muscles, skin, hair, nails, blood, etc. The only thing that the corpse does not have is the energy field.[1] When the energy field of the "I" leaves the body, an electrocardiograph will show a flat line. When there is a flat line there is no longer any electric current running through the body on the mesocosmic level, there is no life force. When there is no electric current running through the body, we say that the body is dead. It is the electric current consisting of ray-formed matter that makes the body come alive.

This is really very much the same as in any electric appliance. When we plug the mixer in, it becomes alive and whips our cream. If we do not plug it in, it is as dead as a pickled herring. It is the current that makes the appliance work. In principle there is no difference between the current in our bodies and the current supplied by the power company. Martinus explains that all electricity is life force on either micro-, meso- or macrocosmic levels.

We can measure that there is a field of energy behind or around the physical body. Those who can see auras can confirm the existence of such a field. Martinus says that this energy field is eternal. How close are our sciences to confirming this? In order to answer this question we can look at what the science of physics says about energy. The first law of thermodynamics tells us that the sum of energy is always constant. According to this law energy cannot be destroyed and it cannot dissolve. It may take on a new form, but it does not disappear. Something that cannot disappear and that cannot be destroyed can be said to be eternal. If it cannot be destroyed, it cannot cease to exist and consequently it is eternal. If we say that our core being, the electromagnetic field, is the same as what has traditionally been called the soul, we have established a sound basis for saying that the soul is eternal. There is something behind the body that is of an electrical nature, and as electricity is energy and as energy cannot be destroyed this something is eternal. The first law of thermodynamics confirms this. The electromagnetic field or the soul does not simply cease to exist when we die. The electromagnetic field leaves the body at death, but it does not disappear or cease to exist. The electromagnetic field "moves on" to a new location after its severance from the physical body at death, it moves into the spiritual world, which is a world consisting of ray-formed matter. We shall look at where the electrical field goes in chapter 15.

Consciousness

X 1 and X 2 are referred to as "supraconsciousness." Our supraconsciousness is electrical in its nature and it is eternal. Our thoughts and thought function, our gifts, knowledge, intelligence, morals, manner, tastes, and dispositions, all our talents, our fate element, and our pole structure are embedded in our supraconsciousness. All these elements form the basis for our physical manifestations. We create our physical and ray-formed bodies from the information we have stored in our X 2. More about this in chapter 12. Part of the information we have stored in our X 2 is a result of experience accumulated during many lives. This information is the same as our consciousness. We create our consciousness through the accumulation of experiences and talents that we reap and refine as we live life after life. In this way we add new elements to our consciousness all the time, and because it forms part of X 2 it is eternal.

Because all the elements that form our consciousness are of an electrical nature and are eternal, our consciousness does not cease when we die. This has been confirmed by the people who have had near-death experiences.[2] They all say that their consciousness did not cease even though they no longer had a physical body. They were feeling fine without the physical body; they were still basically the same. Not having a physical body made no difference to their sense of who they were. Our electrical field with our consciousness is who we are and we have our consciousness whether we have a physical body or not, as our consciousness forms an intricate part of our eternal structure. Our consciousness is who we *really* are, it accompanies us after death, and it accompanies us from life to life. During each physical life we add new talents, knowledge, and morals. In this way we evolve. Our whole nonphysical structure (X 1 and X 2) is eternal. It is only the physical body (X 3), the vehicle for the supra consciousness on the physical plane, that is not eternal. It is only the physical body that we shed at death. Our supraconsciousness accompanies us from life to life. I shall explain talent kernels in chapter 12 and the pole structure in chapter 14.

Time and Eternity

We saw that all created things were called X 3. Everything that we find in the physical world is X 3. It is something that has been created and as it has been created, it has a beginning and an end. Even time is X 3. Time is something that has been created and linear time only exists on the physical plane. Time marks the two points of creation and extinction. Between these two points there is a distance. We call this distance time and we can say that this distance creates a "room." But this room is not a physical room and time is not a physical distance. When time is not a physical distance, it can only be a spiritual distance. So even in our physical world we operate with a nonphysical dimension, the fourth dimension, that of time. Even though time can be measured, it is not physical; we cannot see or grab time. Still, time is X 3, it is something created and it only exists on the physical plane.

When we shed our physical body we enter the spiritual level where time, as we know it, is nonexistent. This has been confirmed by people who have had near-death experiences. The near-death experiencers were momentarily severed from their physical body and in their energy body they entered the spiritual realms. Raymond Moody relates how several of the people he interviewed about their near-death experience told how their perception of time completely changed once they had left their physical body. What was only five minutes in earthly time seemed like years on the spiritual plane. One woman said that her near-death experience lasted one minute or ten thousand years. The concept of time is completely different on the spiritual level. In fact there is no time on the spiritual level, only "now." This aspect of time is mentioned by Jesus when he says, *"But do not ignore this one fact, beloved, that with the Lord one day is as a thousand years, and a thousand years as one day."* (2 Peter 3:8). The spiritual plane is what Jesus refers to as *"with the Lord."*

Time is a phenomenon that exists only on the physical plane; time is X 3. This may lead us to think that eternity belongs solely to the spiritual plane and is not present in the physical world. But this is not so. Eternity and infinity are present in every object and in every unit of time.

Let us look at a pea, for instance. We can cut the pea in half. Then again we can cut the half in half. And again we can cut this bit in half. Every bit, no matter how small, can be cut in half. There is no limit to when we can cut the bit in half. We may reach a point at which our instruments are not fine enough to cut the bit in half, but that only means that we have to get finer instruments. We will always be able to cut the bit in half, if not physically then mentally. No object is so small that it cannot be divided. In this way we see that eternity is present in every object.

In the same way we can divide a second into half a second and then divide this half-second into another half and so on endlessly. No time unit is so small that it cannot be divided. Eternity is also present in all measurement of time.

The principle works in the same way if we double. There is no size and no number that we cannot double. If we cannot do it physically, we can always do it mentally. In fact our numeric system illustrates this perfectly. We can always double a number, no matter how big it is. Martinus explains at the end of the third volume of *Livets Bog* that our numeric system is perfect. Martinus offers a number of reasons for this, one of them being that the numeric system illustrates infinity. We cannot mention a number to which we cannot add another number. Thus our numeric system illustrates infinity. It has no end and no beginning.

Linear time is an aspect of eternity, something that has been created. It is X 3 in the same way as our body is X 3. But if we are eternal beings with a ray-formed eternal body, why do we need to enter linear time and physical space in a perishable body? Why we need linear time, physical space, and physical bodies shall be explained in the following chapters.

7

The Principle of Life Units

The Outer World

As we saw in the previous chapter, the "I" (X 1) has the ability to create (X 2), and the created physical bodies (X 3) are its manifestations on the physical plane. The idea of having a physical body is that through this, we can create an interchange with the outside world. What would there be for the "I" to experience if this outer world did not exist?

What would there be to see, hear, smell, feel, and touch if there were no outer world that could provide the things to see, hear, smell, feel, and touch? What would there be to experience if there were no outer world?

In order to maintain the body as a fit instrument for the experience of life, the body has to be provided with food and water. What would there be to feed the body with, if food and water were not available in the outer world?

How would the "I" be able to create anything, if there were no materials in the outer world from which it could create? The "I" is dependent on the outer world for its manifestations. The planet Earth and its surroundings constitute our present outer world, and the planet provides us with everything that we need to feed ourselves, to protect ourselves from the elements, to manifest ourselves, to create, and to experience. The planet Earth provides us with things to see, hear, feel, touch, smell, eat, and drink, etc. The planet Earth provides us with everything we need to maintain our physical existence.

The Inner World

But at the same time as the "I" is dependent on the outer world for its experience of life, it is also dependent on its interior world or organs and cells or microcosmos for its manifestation. How would the "I" be able to lift its arm if not for the interplay between its brain, its nerve cells, and its muscle cells? A great number of cells have to be put to work in order for the "I" to lift its arm. If the "I" could not depend on the work of these cells, no arm lifting could take place.

Nor could the "I" blink its eyes, or taste the wine, or digest a banana, or move its bowels, or look into a microscope, or have an orgasm if not for the innumerable cells in its body, which do the jobs that they have been put there to do.

All the different cells in the body have a job to do. Their place of work is our body. If our body is their place of work, this means that our body constitutes the outer world of these cells. Our body is the universe of our cells, their outer world. They are born there, they communicate with other cells there, they live and work there, and they die there. Our body is their outer world, the world that provides them with everything they need for their life sustenance, the place where they experience life in exactly the same way, as the Earth is our outer world.

When we hear a very loud noise like an angry dog barking or when we watch a scary movie, the cells get afraid and we feel it like a rush of anxiety through our whole body. When we are happy or when we laugh, we send waves of sunshine through our body and our cells react to this by paying us back with good health. When we are tired we yawn and this is a collective cry for help from our cells telling us they need a rest. When we are hungry, our cells convey to us that there is nothing there to fuel the furnace and that if we don't supply them with food soon, they will go to the depots (the fat cells) and get their supplies from there. We know when they have done that, because then we no longer feel hungry. The cells feed themselves from the nutrition that we supply them with. Without the complicated interplay of our cells, our body could not be alive. We are dependent on our cells for the functioning of our body and at the same time our cells are dependent on our body, as it constitutes their outer world, their universe.

Just as our cells cannot be alive if there is not a body for them to be alive in, we, the human beings of the Earth, cannot be alive if we do not have a body to be alive in. The planet Earth is the body in which we are alive. And just as our body is alive so that it can provide food and oxygen for our cells, so is the Earth alive, so that it can provide food and oxygen for us. The Earth is a living being. We cannot experience life if the planet does not cater for us and provide us with food, heat, oxygen, etc. The planet Earth is as alive as we are. We are the microbeings of the Earth together with all the other living beings that we see in our mesocosmos in exactly the same way as our cells are our microorganisms. At our present stage we, the humans, are the brain cells of the planet, says Martinus.

The Earth

The planet Earth is a living organism. The globe, the planet itself, is the body of this giant being. The rivers are the bloodstreams of the Earth, the mountains and mineral matter constitute its skeleton; the soil and soft layers of rocks are its muscle structure and the cycle of water, the evaporation and condensation of water, is its huge breathing. The weather is a reflection of its mental state, its thought climate. The Earth also eats, it eats all day. Its food is the particles of light matter that are ejected from the Sun in huge amounts at all times.

James Lovelock, who has presented the Gaia theory, is right.[1] The planet is a living being and it regulates its bodily functions in an automatic way in exactly the same way as we regulate our bodily functions automatically. Temperature control, control of oxygen and carbon dioxide levels, and salinity of the seas are just a few of the functions that the giant Earth-being regulates. We experience these bodily regulations as climatic changes. Many of the phenomena that we witness these days such as holes in the ozone layer or floods or global warming and which we believe are solely due to our interference with nature or pollution can "just" be the Earth-being regulating its bodily functions. We know that the climate has never been completely constant and this ought to tell us that regulations have always taken place. We do not know how our pollution affects the body of the Earth-being, if at all. The climatic changes that we see today may be solely due to natural bodily regulations of the Earth or the Sun. We should probably also allow for the possibility that the Earth can compensate for our pollution somehow by taking measures that counteract our activities in exactly the same way as our body takes measures through temperature control (fever) during illness. We have no idea today how this works, but the fact that the Earth is a living being certainly means that we are not solely responsible for all the changes that are taking place. Not only these bodily functions, but also what happens on Earth such as natural disasters are regulated by the Earth-being.

The Moon

Those who have had the privilege to look at Earth from space say that the planet looks alive and very inviting. You can practically see that it is a living being. On the contrary the Moon looks very dead. When man visited the Moon in 1969 it was also revealed that there were no living creatures there, no life whatsoever, not even on a microorganic level. Martinus explains that the Moon is in fact a planet corpse, the physical remains of a being that was once alive. The Moon was once a living planet with living microorganisms on it just like the Earth, but it then had another position. During some major outbreak of force on the macrocosmic level the Moon was forced out of its orbit and was made unable to sustain life. The "I" of the Moon-being left the planet to reincarnate on another planet and gradually all life forms on the micro level died. At a certain point in time the Moon was attracted by the gravitational field of the Earth, so today the Moon is our satellite, a dead planet, a planet corpse.

The "I" of the Earth-Being

The Earth has an "I" just like all other living beings have an "I." The electromagnetic field that surrounds the Earth is the life force of this "I" in exactly the same way as our electromagnetic field, our aura, is our life force. Just as our "I" is the highest authority in our body, the "I" of the Earth-being is the highest authority on this planet. There is no need to think that it is the president of the USA or the general secretary of the United Nations that is the highest authority on Earth. The "I" of the earth being is the one who makes the final decisions here. Just imagine if one of our brain cells got the crazy idea that it was the highest authority in our body. This idea is as silly as the idea that one of us should be the highest authority on Earth.

No, we are microbeings and at our present stage we are, as already mentioned, the brain cells of the Earth-being. All the other living beings carry out other functions in the Earth's body and our joint effort keeps the planet alive. But this is, as we saw in the case of our bodies, a mutually beneficial arrangement, as the Earth also keeps us alive. The Earth feeds us, clothes us, and provides us with shelter, heating, water, and material with which to create.

It is also the "I" of the Earth-being that is responsible for gravity. The "I" is an electromagnetic field, and the Earth has an electromagnetic field just as we have one. Logically the Earth's electromagnetic field is much stronger than ours, but the principle is the same. The cells in our body also have an electromagnetic field, but this field is very weak compared to ours. All "I"s on the micro, meso, or macrocosmic level are electromagnetic fields. This electromagnetic field exerts a gravitational pull on things it gets in contact with. This means it holds things together. That is the reason why a body starts to disintegrate once the "I" has left at death. There is no longer an electromagnetic field to keep the various parts together, so the body starts to dissolve. Because the Moon is a planet corpse it has no "I" and as a consequence its gravitational pull is very weak, so weak that it cannot hold onto an atmosphere.

Martinus goes as far as saying that nothing in the physical world is what it seems to be. We see things from our local perspective, but from a cosmic perspective everything is different. The cells in our body may think that their world is the only existing world, as this is all they can experience. Our situation is exactly the same. From our perspective we are the only beings alive in the Universe, but we are as wrong as our own cells are.

Everything Is Life Inside Life

Symbol number 7 shows the principle of life units. We see a circle with a triangle in the center. The triangle symbolizes the "I" and the circle symbolizes the body. Inside the body there are other circles with a triangle or an "I" in the center, and inside this body there are other circles with triangles or "I"s in the center and so on. There is a living being inside a living being on all levels.

Let us say that the big circle is our body. Then the smaller circles would be our organs such as heart, liver, lungs, brain, kidneys, uterus, etc. Inside these organs there are heart cells, liver cells, lung cells, brain cells, kidney cells, uterus cells, etc. Inside these cells there are smaller cells such as molecules and atoms, and inside the atoms there are neutrons, electrons, etc.

We can also say that the big circle symbolizes our galaxy. Then the smaller circles would represent solar systems, the even smaller ones planets, the even smaller ones us, the living beings on the planets and so on.

In this way we see that also the solar system is a living being in which the Earth is an organ and again the galaxy is a living being in which the solar system is an organ, etc.

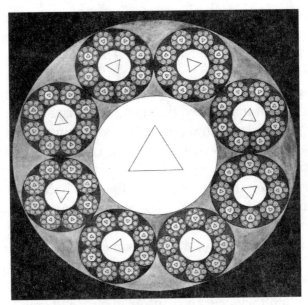

Symbol number 7.
The Principle of Life Units.
© Martinus Institute

The symbol shows that the universe is one organism consisting of living beings inside living beings. This construction means that all beings are micro and macrobeings at the same time. The universe is an all-inclusive ocean of life and consciousness.

1. The triangle with the white field in the middle symbolizes the "I" and its supra consciousness, the field around it is its physical organism.

2. The repetition of the symbol in many smaller sizes shows that the living beings exist inside each other.

Our physical organism is living space for our organs, which again are living space for our cells and even smaller microbeings and so on infinitely in the microcosmos.

In the same way, Man is a being in the organism of the Earth, which is an organ in the solar system, and so on infinitely in the macrocosmos.

Everything alive is contained inside another living being. This principle is the same on all levels of size, endlessly into the macrocosmos and endlessly into the microcosmos. There is life both "up" and "down" as far as the eye can see, and even further. Thus the universe is teeming with life. The universe is one giant being with life forms on all levels of size. Life is present on all levels. This all-pervading principle of life makes the whole universe one inseparable unit maintained through the "I"s and bodies of all living beings. All living beings play a role and cooperate in the maintenance of the giant body that the universe constitutes. It is this giant being that we call God.

Because everything is life inside life, and because the pattern is the same "upward" into the macrocosmos and "downward" into microcosmos, we can find the answer to a multitude of questions by studying ourselves. We are at the same time micro beings in the body of the Earth and macro beings of the cells in our body. We are, ourselves, a whole universe. Billions of beings are alive inside our body, and they depend on us for their well-being and we depend on them for our well-being.

As the principle of life is the same on all size levels, there is no need to look further into space or into the microscope for an answer to the mystery of life. The answer is right here, in our own bodies, and the principle of life is the same both on macro and on microcosmic levels. Particle physics has shown that matter on the subatomic level consists of a nucleus around which electrons move at very high speed. Between the nucleus and the electrons there is a vast empty space. It is the incredible speed of the electrons that constitutes (or should I say simulates) "solid matter." The further we look into microcosmos we see that there is no solid matter, only particle movement at incredible speed. The mass of the atom is actually energy. This structure is exactly the same at all size levels. We are ourselves microorganisms living on an electron (the Earth) that is moving at incredible speed around a nucleus (the Sun). In between the electron and the nucleus there is a vast empty space (the distance from the Earth to the Sun). Thus we form solid matter at a much higher level. This may not be very easy to grasp and it does, indeed, make us very insignificant, but there it is. For all we know we may be the cells in the little finger of some giant be-ing. If we want to know how the universe is constructed we can "just" look at our own body. Our various organs are galaxies in the universe that our body constitutes. We are ourselves a whole universe *en miniature*. This realization makes space travel super-fluous. There is nothing out there that we cannot observe within ourselves. The principle is exactly the same on all levels.

The expansion of the universe is "only" a macrocosmic breath or a pulsation on the macrocosmic level in exactly the same way as our body pulsates. Our body is a universe in exactly the same way as God's body is a universe. In this sense we are "Man in the image and likeness of God." We are copies of God. The body of every living being is a universe—there are as many universes as there are living beings.

The Universe Is God

The giant being that has the whole Universe as its body can only be the divine being, God. And through this we see the truth in what the Bible says: "*In him we live, move and have our being*" (Acts 17:28).

God is the only being alive that is not alive inside another being. This again means that God does not have an outer world, there is nobody next to or above God. Consequently there is nothing "out there" for God to experience. God's experience of life has to take place within his own body, his X 3. God experiences life through us, his cells. When we renew our life experience, God also renews his. We shall see how our life experience is constantly renewed in the following chapters.

The Meaning of Life

Because God does not have a meso or macrocosmos to be alive in, he has no outer experience of life. There is no "out there" for him, only an "in there." God has only an inner experience of life. God can only experience life through us, his microorganisms. Be-cause of that the overall meaning of life is to experience it. If we do not have a life experience, neither will God. The experience of life is the meaning of life in a cosmic sense as this is the only way in which God can renew his consciousness. When we experience new things we renew our consciousness. We are here to experience life. Because the experience of life is fundamental, our experience of life has to vary. If our life experience were always the same, no renewal of consciousness could take place. If we don't renew our experience of life, God does not renew his. In order to renew our experience of life, we move through eternity in a spiral cycle in a variety of different bodies, as shall soon be explained.

Although the overall meaning of life is to experience it, there are many smaller and more "local" meanings of life depending on the stage of development we stand on.

Our "local" meaning of life right now is to outlive and "unlearn" our animal mentality (to be explained shortly) and become 100 percent human. Once we have become 100 percent human, everybody will help everybody and peace will reign on the planet. Helping each other, showing forgiveness and love, promoting the shedding of our animal mentality, and creating peace on the planet is our "local" aim, our "local" meaning of life.

Relativity

The fact that everything is life inside life also confirms that everything is relative. We think that we are fairly big, but when we look at the galaxies we are very small in comparison. To us an elephant is big and a mouse is small, but to an ant the mouse is huge. We think a year is a long time, but when we look at the mayfly that lives only a few days, we realize that time is also relative. The mayfly experiences a whole life in what for us is only a few days. What we experience as a year is probably just "a day" for the Earth-being. Both time and space are relative, and whether they are perceived as long or short, big or small depends entirely on the being who experiences them. There is no absolute time and no absolute space. Everything is relative.

8

The Cyclic Principle

The Various Cycles

We know from our school days that there is no such thing in the universe as a straight line. What looks as a straight line is really just a segment of a circle. The circle may be so big that a segment of it looks like a straight line, but it is not so. Everything in the natural world goes in cycles.

Some of these cycles are well known to us such as the cycle of night and day and the cycle of the seasons. We also know the cycle of matter in which all dead matter is broken down in order to be reabsorbed in plants, be eaten by animals, or wither only to return to the Earth from which it will again be "recycled." Furthermore we are familiar with the cycle of water in which the water on the surface of the Earth evaporates when heated, is condensed when cooled, and falls as rain.

The cyclic principle is a universal one and there are many cycles that we do not yet know about, because they are not as immediately evident as those mentioned above.

A person's average life span is around seventy-five years. In these seventy-five years the person goes through childhood, puberty, youth, man- or womanhood, and old age. Sooner or later the person dies and after a rest in the spiritual realms he or she reincarnates again in a new physical body and starts the cycle all over again. We all know the stages of human life, but it has generally been assumed that it was new souls that were born in the new babies. However, the souls that reincarnate in the new babies are "old" souls, so we can really talk about "soul recycling." Without the concept of reincarnation we cannot see Man's life as a cycle.

Life is eternal and we are reborn again and again onto the physical plane (to be fully explained in chapter 12). In this eternal wandering we also move in a cycle. This cycle is obviously a very big one, so big that we cannot overview it ourselves; we need someone with cosmic consciousness to tell us about this huge cycle. This huge cycle is part of a spiral, which we are at present passing through. In order to understand the spiral cycle and our present position in this it is necessary first to explain the basic principle for all perception and experience: *contrast*.

The Basis of All Perception Is Contrast

The basis of all perception is contrast. We can only perceive black on a background of white or some other contrasting color. When we put black on black or white on white we cannot perceive anything. We cannot paint a picture using only white paint on a white canvas. There would be nothing to see. In order to paint a picture we need contrasting colors. The same principle applies here as in photography: If a photo is overexposed the film becomes dark and as there are no contrasts, there is nothing to see. Likewise if the photo is underexposed, the film is too light and again there is nothing to see because of the lack of contrast.

All pleasurable things in life are only pleasurable because they constitute a contrast to what we experienced before. We cannot experience beauty without ugliness, good without evil, hard without soft, sweet without sour, etc. When we have worked hard for a long time, it is a great experience to be allowed to take a few weeks off and go on holiday. But when we are unemployed and have no job to go to, it is boring to have all that time off, and we wish that we had a job.

Winter is nice in contrast to the heat of summer, but an eternal winter would be horrible. The darkness of the night is pleasurable in contrast to the light of day, but an eternal night or an eternal day would be equally horrible. Contrast is fundamental for our perception and life experience.

This principle is the same as the principle of hunger and satiation. When we are hungry we have a great desire to eat, but then when we have eaten and are full, we cannot bear to think about more food. The wonderful dish that we longed for while we were hungry makes us nauseous when we are full. The things that we have had enough of simply no longer have an appeal, on the contrary, they make us sick. Nobody can go on enjoying the same thing without eventually becoming satiated by this thing. Satiation gives rise to hunger for a new thing and so on. Our whole life experience is based on this principle. The contrast of hunger and satiation is absolutely fundamental to our experience of life. It is the basic law for all motivation. We cannot renew our experience of life without the motivation for experiencing contrast. We have to know the opposite of love in order to know what love is.

Enfolding and Unfolding

As we move through our eternal existence we move in circles. In each circle there is contrast. We can say that in the upper part of the circle there is light and in the lower part there is darkness. This is in principle exactly the same as what we experience during the twenty-four hours of the circadian rhythm where we experience the contrasts of night and day. We experience contrast in each cyclical movement that we undertake.

We can say that we eternally move between two extremes: light and darkness. The light is represented by the spiritual worlds and the darkness by the physical world. Once we have become satiated with the light, we get hungry for the darkness and we move toward it. Once we have become satiated with the darkness we get hungry for the light and move back toward it. In this way our eternal existence is a constant process of enfolding and unfolding. Enfolding can be seen as the process away from the light, the process in which the living being that is satiated with the light and wisdom of the spiritual world moves toward darkness and ignorance. This process of enfolding is a process of immersing oneself into physical matter. In this process the being gradually "forgets" his eternal link to God. Once he has completely forgotten about his link to God and believes that he is one with his physical body and lives in a godless universe, he has reached the bottom of darkness. When the being has become completely satiated by darkness the process of unfolding begins. The being then moves toward the light and he gradually overcomes his ignorance about the natural laws of life and he "remembers" his eternal link to God. In the process of unfolding he moves away from physical matter, he realizes the existence of a spiritual world and enters the spiritual realms. In this way we move eternally between the two extremes of darkness/ignorance and light/wisdom. If we did not do that, all experience of life would be impossible. We cannot eternally experience the same thing—in the end this experience would become devoid of meaning. As the universe has been designed to exist eternally it has to have a structure that can provide its microbeings with the possibility to experience contrast. That is the reason why God did not "just" create a "perfect" world from the beginning. If he had created a "perfect" world where there was no darkness and no ignorance, it would have been an imperfect world because all perception would be impossible as there would be no contrast. In this way we see that God did create a perfect world, because he created a world with both light and darkness. Because of the existence of these two extremes the universe can exist eternally. Were it not for the existence of the two extremes, the universe could not exist eternally. It would have to end when one extreme had been reached and there was nothing more to experience. The world can only be perfect when the contrasts of light and darkness are there to be experienced by the living beings. As we enfold and unfold both darkness/ignorance and light/wisdom are created as an ongoing process and it is this process of creation of the two extremes that we perceive as evolution.

The Spiral

In our eternal existence we move in a spiral. Each time we have completed a cyclical movement of the spiral we move one step up. This means that we move in a spiraling motion, around and around and up and up. If we did not move one step up, we would repeat the same cycle time after time, and no renewal would take place of our experience of life.

The spiral is illustrated in the following drawing:

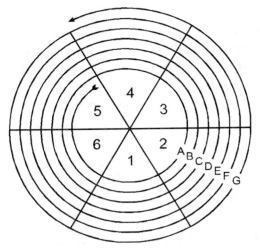

The Spiral.

The drawing shows seven cyclical passages: A, B, C, D, E, F, and G. Each letter represents one cycle. Once a cycle has been completed we step up one level, so that we do not repeat the same cycle again. The drawing represents a section of the spiral that we are now passing. Our present cyclic passage is the one called "D." This is the cycle in which we appear as animals and later as humans. This cycle will be explained in chapter 11. "Below" us we have three cyclic passages:

A. This is the cycle of molecules.

B. This is the cycle of cells.

C. This is the cycle of organs in a body like our own, such as heart, liver, kidneys, etc.

These three cycles represent our microcosmos. Our microcosmos consists of all molecules, cells, and organs in our own body. All these are living beings.

D. This is our present cycle in which we manifest ourselves as animals and later as humans.

This cycle represents our mesocosmos. The term mesocosmos expresses all the beings that we experience in our surroundings and whose sizes are at level with our own such as all other human beings and all plants, insects, and animals.

"Above" us there are three cycles depicted:

E. This is the cycle of planets.

F. This is the cycle of solar systems.

G. This is the cycle of galaxies.

These three cycles represent our macrocosmos. Our macrocosmos consists of all heavenly bodies, planets, suns, asteroids, comets, galaxies, etc.

All beings in microcosmos, mesocosmos, and macrocosmos are living beings within living beings as has been explained in chapter 7. The seven cycles illustrated here are only our immediate "neighbors" and they represent only a section of the spiral. The spiral is never-ending both downward and upward as we are eternal beings and our existence has no beginning and no end.

The Basic Energies and the Corresponding Realms

On the spiral figure we also see the numbers from 1—6. The numbers from 1 to 6 represent a different basic energy. There are six basic energies in the universe and each passing of the cycle is divided into sections, which constitute one-sixth of the cycle. In this one-sixth of the cycle one of the six basic energies is predominant. These six energies will be explained in the next chapter, but let me just say here that "1" is the energy of gravity, "2" is the energy of feeling, "3" is the energy of intelligence, "4" is the energy of intuition, "5" is the energy of memory, and "6" is the energy of instinct.

Everything is a combination of the six basic energies. Everything that exists is a result of a combination of these six energies and the seventh energy, the mother energy. Out of these six energies everything that exists is created.

We can also put it like this: There are "only" six basic energies plus the mother energy in the universe, but all matter is a result of a combination of these energies and a result of their level of condensation. Depending on the level of condensation, all matter manifests itself as solid, liquid, vaporous, or ray-formed. The physical world is "only" more condensed than the spiritual world, but both worlds consist in their final analysis of the same six energies. The energies are primarily energies of consciousness or thought, which means that the ray-formed state is their primary state. Through a process of condensation this thought matter can be transformed into physical matter. This means that the physical world is condensed or "frozen" consciousness matter or thoughts.

The six energies can be combined in innumerable ways to give rise to all the various types of matter that we know. These different types of matter have reactivity. All matter has its own specific reactivity, which means that it will react with other matter. This is valid whether it is physical or ray-formed (spiritual) matter that we are talking about. Spiritual energies react in specific ways in exactly the same way as physical energies do. More about this in chapter 13.

In the passing of one cycle of the spiral, each of the six basic energies has a peak manifestation. This means that in the course of passing through a cycle we pass through a realm or section in which the energy of instinct is predominant, after that we pass through a realm in which the energy of gravity predominates, then a realm in which the energy of feeling is predominant, then a realm in which the energy of intelligence is predominant, then a realm in which the energy of intuition dominates, and finally a realm in which the energy of memory prevails. But all energies are always present at the same time only in varying degrees of unfolding. It is the degree of unfolding of the basic energies that constitutes the basis for our life experience. We experience life differently when for instance the energy of gravity is predominant, as when the energy of memory is predominant. It is through the varying degrees of unfolding of the basic energies in the passing of the cycle that we experience contrast.

To each basic energy there is attributed a realm or "kingdom." The realm corresponds to one-sixth of the cycle in which a particular basic energy is predominant.

Energy	"Kingdom"
instinct	plant
gravity	animal
feeling	human (the real human kindom)
intelligence	wisdom
intuition	divinity (the divine world)
memory	bliss

This means that when for instance the energy of instinct is predominant, we are in the plant kingdom and when the energy of gravity is predominant we are in the animal kingdom, etc.

Let me mention that Martinus chose the names of the energies and the corresponding kingdoms. Undoubtedly, Martinus has chosen the names carefully and has given much thought to which word could best cover the concept at hand. The translation of the concepts into English is the closest we can get to the words Martinus chose in Danish. The different energies are concepts. If the name of an energy does not correspond to the concept generally understood by the chosen word, the reader is asked to disregard the connotations that are normally conveyed by the chosen word and see the chosen word as an expression of a new concept. For instance the expression "energy of feeling" has been translated from the Danish *følelsesenergi*. In English "feeling" conveys connotations of warmth, whereas in Danish the word is more neutral. *Følelse* in Danish can be both warm and cold. So please do not be surprised that the "energy of feeling" conveys coldness. The "energy of feeling" is what Martinus has chosen to call the third basic energy. Please look at this as a concept, as an expression of a general principle.

All basic energies are present in every "kingdom" but at different levels of manifestation or unfolding, as we shall see on symbol number 12 called "the Combination of the Basic Energies."

Symbol number 12 shows the six basic energies and the proportions in which they unfold in each realm. The six full bands represent a cycle. In "reading" the symbol we start at the bottom and "move" upward.

The color	red	is for the	plant kingdom (instinct).
The color	orange	is for the	animal kingdom (gravity).
The color	yellow	is for the	real human kingdom (feeling).
The color	green	is for the	kingdom of wisdom (intelligence)
The color	blue	is for the	divine world (intuition).
The color	indigo	is for the	kingdom of bliss (memory).

If we look at the symbol on page 100 we see colored horizontal bands in the six colors of the spectrum. Each of these represents a plane of existence or kingdom as indicated above. At the top and at the bottom there is a half band, and this only means that the pattern continues in both directions, that is "down" toward microcosmos and "up" toward macrocosmos. The six full-colored bands represent one cyclic movement of the spiral as illustrated on the drawing of the spiral on page 95.

The full squares to the left and the right indicate the various kingdoms, and one full square corresponds to one-sixth of a cyclic movement. The bands that vary in size indicate the level of un-folding of the various energies in the different kingdoms and they show how the energies are combined in each realm. We see that the level of unfolding of the six basic energies varies from a latent stage (a line) to a culminating stage (a hexagon) with increasing and decreasing intermediate stages.

If we look at the red figure symbolizing the energy of instinct and trace it upward from its culminating stage at the bottom of the symbol next to the full red square to the left we can see how its un-folding culminates in the plant kingdom only to decrease through the animal kingdom (orange) and real human kingdom (yellow). It reaches its lowest level of unfolding or latent stage in the king-dom of wisdom (green), but starts increasing again in the divine world (blue) and through the kingdom of bliss (indigo) only to culminate again in a new plant kingdom (red).

Now if we place a ruler horizontally in the middle of the or-ange field (which represents the animal kingdom) and "read" to-wards the right we first come to a red field after the orange square. We see that the red field,

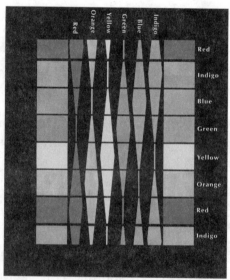

The Combinations of the Basic Energies.
(Color version on cover)
© Martinus Institute

The symbol shows the six planes of existence and at the same time it symbolizes a continuous cosmic cycle.

In each plane there are six basic energies present in a certain combination in the consciousness of the living being. The various planes of existence are characterized by one energy culminating.

1.   The square fields symbolize the six planes of existence.

The plant kingdom	red
The animal kingdom	orange
The real human kingdom	yellow
The kingdom of wisdom	green
The divine world	blue
The kingdom of bliss	indigo

2.   The six vertical figures show the level of unfolding of the basic energies. This takes place as an eternal rhythmic unfolding from the latent to the culminating state.

3.   In each plane of existence one basic energy is culminating and one is latent. Two are increasing and two are decreasing in the first and the second stages respectively. The combinations of the basic energies depicted here are the eternal foundations of life and the basis for the experience of life for all living beings.

representing the energy of instinct, is quite predominant, but on the decrease when we "read" toward the top. The orange field, representing the energy of gravity, is at its peak manifestation. The yellow field, the energy of feeling, is also quite predominant and on the increase. The green field, the energy of intelligence, has a rather weak manifestation, but it is also on the increase. The blue, representing the energy of intuition, is only a line, which means that this energy is at its minimum unfolding or latent in the animal kingdom. Finally, the energy of memory also has a rather weak manifestation and is decreasing in the animal kingdom.

The combinations of energies that we get at this particular place where the ruler is placed is the combination of energies that defines an animal. That means that an animal consists of the six energies in the proportions indicated on the figure.

If the ruler is placed in the middle of the red field and we "read" across, the combination of energies that defines a plant is revealed.

The characteristics of each of the six energies will be explained in the next chapter. In general we can say that the energies of instinct, gravity, and feeling are energies for physical creation. They are the "main ingredients" of physical matter. The energies of intelligence, intuition, and memory have finer vibrations and are mainly energies for the creation of spiritual or ray-formed matter.

In order to complete a cycle of the spiral we pass through six kingdoms each predominated by one of the six basic energies.

9

The Basic Energies

As mentioned in the previous chapter, each cycle of the spiral consists of six realms or kingdoms in which one basic energy is predominant. This is illustrated on the drawing of the spiral on page 95 and on symbol number 12 "The Combinations of the Basic Energies." We can also express it like this: in order to complete a cyclic movement we pass through six different realms, in each of which one basic energy is predominant. For instance, in the animal kingdom the energy of gravity is predominant, the energy of intuition is latent, the energies of instinct and memory are decreasing, and the energies of feeling and intelligence are increasing. The typical characteristics of each kingdom are a consequence of the mutual reactions of the six energies. Logically the predominant energy is the one that plays the major role in the kingdom that it defines and the other energies play minor roles according to their degree of unfolding.

How life unfolds in each of the six kingdoms is defined by the effects that the particular combination of energies has on the living being. The energies are first and foremost energies of consciousness or thought which, through a process of condensation, manifest as physical matter. Physical matter is condensed consciousness.

Let us take a closer look at each basic energy.

The Energy of Instinct (Red)

The energy of instinct is responsible for all physical growth. In the plant kingdom, in which the energy of instinct is predominant, we see how all plant forms automatically grow. The physical bodies of other life forms such as animals and humans also grow. This growth is conveyed by the energy of instinct.

The energy of instinct not only regulates the organic function of growth, but it is also an energy of consciousness or thought. However, as an energy of consciousness the energy of instinct is fairly weak. It can only convey a vague sensing. We see this clearly in the plants. A plant can vaguely sense what goes on in its surroundings. It can sense heat and cold, light and darkness, and it can react to these sensations. In cold and darkness the plant closes itself and in heat and light it opens up. The plant has a vague experience of its surroundings, but nothing more. It does not "know" what is going on "out there." It can sense what is pleasant and what is unpleasant in a very vague way, that is all. The plant body cannot offer its originator or "I" (X 1) a complete experience of its surroundings. Everything that is a vague sensation is conveyed by the energy of instinct.

The energy of instinct is also quite predominant in the animal kingdom as instinct plays an important part in the behavior of animals. The energy of instinct tells the animal what to do, so the behavior of the animal is generally defined by its instinct. The instinct is actually remnants of the cosmic consciousness the being had in its previous cycle, now transformed into an automatic and unconscious function. The animal instinctively knows how to hunt, how to mate, how to take care of its young, in other words its instinct makes it survive. In the beginning of the animal kingdom the energy of intelligence has not reached a very high degree of unfolding, so the animal is not able to analyze what happens. The animal behaves in certain appropriate ways, but it does not know why. Were it not for its instinct, the animal would not be able to survive.

We, the humans, still belong to the animal kingdom, so in us the energy of instinct also plays a part, but as the influence of this energy is decreasing as we approach the real human kingdom (the yellow field), the role of the energy of instinct becomes weaker and weaker.

It is the energy of instinct that is responsible for our religious beliefs. A religious belief is not based on facts or on knowledge but on vague sensations. The energy of instinct conveys us with a vague sensation of the existence of a Creator or God. We believe there is a Creator, but we do not know why nor do we ask why, we only have a vague sensation that it is so. This vague sensation about the existence of God has then been dressed up by the religious authorities with words, fine robes, ceremonies, incense, candles, and singing of psalms and these ceremonies give support to the belief in a creator. But as long as the energy of instinct is still strong in our mentality, we do not question the teachings of the religions. We just accept a given religion without asking why. This acceptance is conveyed by the energy of instinct. We can see that the energy of instinct is still quite predominant today, as many people on Earth still subscribe to the various religions.

As an energy for physical perception the energy of instinct is a weak and vague energy that can only convey an unspecified and undefined sensation to the "I."

The Energy of Gravity (Orange)

The energy of gravity is identical with heat and fire. The characteristics of fire are that it heats, expands, dissolves, and dematerializes. We clearly see this when we heat water. First the water gets warm and as it gets warm it expands. When the water boils it evaporates and thus dematerializes. After a certain time of boiling there is no water left. The water has dematerialized. In the same way a fire dematerializes all physical things that come into contact with it, when allowed to unfold freely.

The energy of gravity conveys the heat of the sun and the heat in our own organisms. Every type of heat and combustion (sunshine, fever, burning wood or gas, electrical appliances giving off heat, hot springs, etc.) is conveyed by the energy of gravity. A fire is an expression of energy of gravity unfolding freely.

On a consciousness level this energy gives rise to all mental explosions such as rage or extreme anger. When we experience anger, the energy of gravity has taken the upper hand in our mentality and we are carried along on a wave of furious energy. Once the energy of gravity has taken hold of us, it can be difficult to get this energy under control. We may then do or say things that we later regret. When we are in the grip of the energy of gravity, we may yell at people or verbally abuse them, or even hit or kill them. We feel that we are not really in control of what we are doing, as indeed we are not, as the energy of gravity has taken control of what we do. Everybody who has experienced extreme anger will recognize this. This has been called "to act in passion."

It is also the energy of gravity that enables the animal to produce the display of force that makes it capable of killing its prey. When a lioness makes her final spurt towards the gazelle, this violent effort is conveyed by the energy of gravity. The energy of gravity carries her along on a wave of ferocious strength and enables her to accelerate and finally "explode" in the attack on the prey and the act of killing. It is consequently this energy that conveys the killing principle. All killing, rage, anger, and violence are conveyed by the energy of gravity. As the capacity to kill is vital in the animal kingdom, it is the energy of gravity that is predominant in this kingdom. The animal kingdom is characterized by the killing principle. Where the energy of gravity has the upper hand, intolerance, destruction, devastation, war, murder, killings, and bloodshed prevail.

The Energy of Feeling (Yellow)

The energy of feeling keeps the fiery energy of gravity at bay. The energy of gravity and the energy of feeling are almost always present at the same time in all physical matter, as the two energies balance each other. We saw that the energy of gravity conveyed heat and fire. To counterbalance this heat and fire the energy of feeling conveys coldness. In order for there to be neither extreme heat nor extreme cold the two energies have to mix. To create a "normal" temperature there have to be approximately equal amounts of energy of gravity and energy of feeling. Our body temperature of approximately 37 degrees Celsius is a result of an appropriate mixture of the two energies.

So the energy of feeling is characterized by coldness. The coldness of the universe is conveyed by the energy of feeling. Coldness has the ability to freeze, condense, crystallize, and materialize. Again we can witness this process if we look at how water reacts. The water that was dematerialized when exposed to the energy of gravity through boiling is materialized again in our freezer. We know that if we have not de-iced our freezer for some time, a thick layer of ice accumulates on all sides of the freezer. This is the dematerialized water molecules invisibly present in the air that materialize when exposed to subzero temperatures or when exposed to the energy of feeling. So the energy of feeling is cold and as such it is an energy that counterbalances the energy of gravity. Where the two energies of gravity and feeling coexist, they create a mutual tension. The whole physical world is based on the interplay between coldness and fire. The body temperature of all living beings is an expression of the balance point between these two energies.

The tension that arises between these two energies is identical with all types of power or force. Without force no movement would be able to take place. The great creative processes of nature are conveyed by the force or tension that arises from the counterposition of these two energies. This tension is identical to our life force, but also the manifestations of the planets, suns, and galaxies, their movements and paths are based on the balance of these two energies.

The energy of feeling curbs the fiery and dangerous energy of gravity. Wherever the energy of feeling gets the upper hand, calm and quiet reign. In our mentality the energy of feeling is experienced as a soothing tendency. In a calm and quiet person the energy of feeling has the upper hand and such a person is generally difficult to arouse. He will remain calm even in the most turbulent situations. The calming and soothing effects of the energy of feeling counterbalance a hot temper. A hot-tempered person has too little energy of feeling. If a hot-tempered person experiences a burst of anger, he only has to put his hands in ice-cold water or take a cold shower. The cold from the water, which is the same as energy of feeling, is then transferred to the person's body and calm and quiet returns to the mentality of the angry person. The energy of feeling is essential if a person wants to get rid of hot temper, and getting rid of hot temper, or the dominance of the energy of gravity in one's mentality, is what conditions a person to be a recipient for even higher mental energies.

It is the energy of feeling that conveys all manifestations of harmony, beauty, peace, and happiness. But these positive manifestations can only become perfect when the energy of feeling is mixed with the next energy, the energy of intelligence.

The Energy of Intelligence (Green)

The energy of intelligence conveys logic and analytical ability. It conveys our ability to understand the world that surrounds us. Consequently our materialistic sciences are founded on the energy of intelligence. It is through the growing influence of the energy of intelligence in our mentality that our materialistic sciences were born. With the growth of the energy of intelligence in our mentality our manifestations become more and more logical. All logical creations of Man, be it houses, tools, machines, means of transportation, means of communication, or works of art originate in the energy of intelligence. Our intelligence is growing. We become smarter and smarter and better and better at controlling and analyzing the processes of nature. With our machines we can make the forces of nature work for us. Our understanding of the natural world becomes greater and greater. Our sciences become more and more sophisticated. Each day we know more about our natural world and the universe that surrounds us. All our knowledge and all our sciences and all our analytical abilities are conveyed by the energy of intelligence.

At the point of evolution to which we have arrived today (upper part of the orange field) our energy of intelligence is quite developed, so the energy of intelligence begins to take over the roles formerly played by the energy of instinct, which is decreasing. Our instinct tells us how to mate and how to care for our young, but these functions are also now being intellectualized in the sense that if our instinct has become too weak to tell us what to do, we can simply buy a book and read what other people say about it. In this way we see that the instinctive processes have been intellectualized. With our intelligence we have analyzed what we instinctively do. If our instinct no longer tells us how to take care of a newborn baby, we can go and buy one of the hundreds of books that have been published about this topic. Through our intelligence we can then get access to the instinctive knowledge that has left us because of the decrease of the energy of instinct.

Our experiences can be intellectually understood with the energy of intelligence. With intelligence we can explore and observe and analyze the nature of our experiences in the physical world. We can understand how the physical processes work. In this way we are able to acquire knowledge about these as facts. Through this energy we are able to think logically and consequently to create logically. Through this energy combined with the other energies we are capable of acquiring considerable knowledge about the physical reality.

Love is intellectualized feeling. In order to manifest universal love we need a balanced amount of the energies of feeling and intelligence. The energy of feeling alone will not convey love, but sentimentality. Love is a consequence of a balance of the energies of feeling and intelligence. This again means that we can only manifest universal love when we have evolved to a point at which an appropriate balance of the two energies has been reached. An animal in its pure manifestation cannot demonstrate love. The energies of feeling and intelligence have not yet reached a sufficient level of development for love to unfold. It is only with the growth of the energies of feeling and intelligence and the decrease of the energies of instinct and gravity that universal love will unfold in human beings.

With the energy of intelligence alone the living being cannot perceive anything that is beyond the physical world, as the energy of intelligence can only convey information about things that are time and space dimensional, things that can be weighed and measured. As mentioned before, many of our materialistic sciences such as astronomy and microbiology have reached the limit of what can be grasped with the energy of intelligence alone. The materialistic sciences have been expanded and refined to a very high degree, but in order to understand the logic that lies behind the physical manifestations, we need to take the materialistic sciences up to a new level of cognition: the spiritual level. Knowledge of the spiritual plane is conveyed by the energy of intuition, so in order to perceive beyond the physical plane we need the next energy: the energy of intuition.

The Energy of Intuition (Blue)

This energy is the one through which all facts beyond the time and space dimensions are revealed. The revelation of the eternal facts about living beings such as the solution to the mystery of life, the immortality of living beings, love as being the basic tone of the universe, and the existence of God can only come about through the presence of the energy of intuition in the mentality. The energy of intuition is the finest consciousness matter that exists, it is identical with "the holy spirit" or the matter of which the very consciousness of God is created.

The energy of intuition begins to develop in strength in the mentality of the being when the results of its sufferings begin to be fundamental. It is through our sufferings and consequential development of compassion that our humanity is born. With the development of compassion and humanity, the energy of intuition enters our mentality. It is the first weak manifestations of this energy that we find among great artists and scientists. These great artists and scientists have flashes of intuition, which they experience as flashes of inspiration. A flash of inspiration is a finished idea, a revelation in your mind of a universal fact, a glimpse of truth, a vision of logic, an answer to a difficult problem. Great scientists have in some cases found the answers to difficult problems with which they have been struggling in such a flash of inspiration. Great artists such as composers and painters have had ideas for works of art revealed to them through such flashes of inspiration. These flashes of inspiration are conveyed by the energy of intuition.

Very few people on Earth have had cosmic glimpses as described in the chapter about the Parent Principle. However, these cosmic glimpses are short manifestations of the energy of intuition in the mentality. In such a cosmic glimpse the logic of the universe and our own immortality is revealed in a short flash.

World redeemers such as Jesus and Martinus had permanent cosmic consciousness. This means that they had the energy of intuition completely under the control of their wills. Whenever they want to they can make the energy of intuition obey their wills. The stronger the energy of intuition is in the mentality of the being, the more complete and perfect are the cosmic answers that the being has access to. The person who has the energy of intuition completely under the control of his will has access to all answers to all questions by just thinking about them. When he thinks about a question, the answer immediately presents itself. He does not have to wait to get a flash of intuition as an answer to his questions such as, for instance, great scientists. He can control the energy of intuition with his wills, so that this energy obeys him 100 percent; the energy of intuition flows to him at his beck and call. The question of whether you can make the energy of intuition obey your will is "only" a question of the strength of the energy of intuition in your bodily structure. Once we all reach the real human kingdom, we will all have the energy of intuition under the control of our wills and consequently we will all have access to the answers to all questions.

Having the answers to all questions is having cosmic consciousness. When one has cosmic consciousness, the mystery of life ceases to be a mystery. Then one knows all there is to know. When one knows all there is to know, one has become part of God's primary consciousness.

Intuition is a higher form of experience, which differs from the physical experience because it is of an inner nature. Intuition is something that is experienced from within. It is not something that you experience through your physical senses.

The Energy of Memory or Bliss (Indigo)

Without this energy, all recall of things past would be impossible. The importance of this energy is best seen in cases of amnesia. In such cases the person does not know who he is, what he is called, where he belongs, where he is going, and who his family is. Without the energy of memory, all recall of the past would be impossible. The person would have to live in the "now." All experiences would be forgotten as soon as they had passed the "now."

But then nobody would be able to learn anything, because learning is adding fact to fact and memorizing these facts. Without the ability to learn, no creation of consciousness would be possible, as our consciousness is created through our interplay with the world. When we interact with the world, we reap a lot of experiences. Through the reaping of experiences we grow wiser. But we can only grow wiser if we are able to remember the effects of our acts. It is through our ability to memorize the experiences and the effects of our acts that our consciousness is created. The more we learn, the more experiences we reap, the more does our consciousness grow. Without the presence of the energy of memory, no accumulation of experience would take place.

The energy of memory conveys the ability to remember our own past and through this energy we are able to create mental "copies" of our experiences. With time we get a whole collection of these "copies." It is these "copies" that we call memories. These memories constitute a whole little world of their own. We can mentally go into this world and for a time dwell in this world of our own memories. We can move through this mental world and relive different moods; we can relive sad or happy moments. In this inner world the details of the past are kept. Our ability to recall the details depends on the strength of the energy of memory in our mental setup.

Through the ability to move in and out of memories, we are able to guide and direct ourselves in the decisions we have to make in the "now." Through the experiences of the past an important basis for our future is formed, as it is on the basis of past experiences and the knowledge we have gathered that we make the decisions that point toward the future.

The energy of memory furthermore has the ability to ripen the "copies" of our past. Through this process of ripening, the memories become more positive; they become happier and more valued. Martinus calls these "gold copies" and with this he stresses the fact that with time the memories grow into something very precious. We all know this is so when we for instance think of our memories of a summer holiday. After some time has passed, the memory of the summer holiday shines and lights in our mentality and the things that we experienced seem much happier than at the time when we actually experienced them. We also know that many old people rejoice in their childhood memories that now, as "gold copies," appear much happier than at the time they were experienced. Because the energy of memory conveys happiness through the remembrance of things past as "gold copies," this energy is also called the energy of bliss.

The Mother Energy (Purple)

Whereas the six energies just mentioned form the material for the creation of all timely matter and all timely organisms (X 3) the seventh energy forms material for all the eternal characteristics of the living beings. The eternal X 2 is created from the seventh basic energy. In this energy talents, abilities, and our sense of self are embedded and as these are formed from the eternally existing mother energy they accompany us from life to life. All the other energies are embedded in the mother energy and it is this energy that releases the fluctuations of the six basic energies as illustrated on symbol number 12. It is the mother energy that is responsible for releasing the arches of karma that will be explained in chapter 13 and it is responsible for the fluctuations of the pole structure that will be explained in chapter 14. The mother energy is the most fundamental energy, the primary energy. The mother energy is represented by the color purple on Martinus' symbols.

10

The Human Being of Today

The Energies that Form the Human Being at its Present Stage

When we look at symbol number 12 we can find our own position in the cycle. We, as the human beings we are today, are placed in the upper part of the orange field, quite close to the yellow field. We are still in the animal kingdom but we have passed its peak manifestation. However, we have not yet reached the yellow field, which represents the real human kingdom. In this sense we are still animals and not yet real human beings. We are in fact part animals and part humans. In the words of Martinus we are "*wounded fugitives between two kingdoms.*"

Now let us look at how we, the human beings at our present stage, are characterized by the combination of the six basic energies. It is important to underline, however, that no two persons on Earth stand on exactly the same stage in development, so the exact combination of energies is not the same in anybody. Every single being has a unique combination of energies. Those who can see auras can confirm this. No two auras are alike and the different colors of each individual person's aura reflect the energy combination.

But the overall degree of unfolding of the energies is the same for beings of the same species. That means that, for instance, all lions have the same general combination of energies, with only very small individual variations. What characterizes the human being at its present stage has to be seen as an analysis of what is valid for the majority. The combination of energies that is predominant at this stage can be seen in symbol number 12 if we place a ruler in the orange field one-fifth of the way down from the yellow field.

We see that the energy of instinct (red) is still quite predominant. This energy conveys physical growth and it gives us the "vague sensation." It gives us a vague sensation that there is a God and a meaning somewhere. It enables us to believe in the different religions. We also see that this energy is on the decrease as we move upward toward the yellow field, and this means that many people today have outgrown the ability to believe in religion. When the energy of instinct has decreased sufficiently, the person loses the ability to believe in religion. He will then no longer subscribe to any religion and becomes an atheist. Because the energy of intelligence increases at the same time, he will "believe" in science instead. He will be convinced that science will "save the day." However, the energy of instinct is still important inasmuch as it controls many organic processes.

The energy of gravity (orange) is the most predominant energy in the human being at our present stage. It is this energy that on the mental level conveys explosions such as anger and hot temper and this energy also conveys the animal thought climates such as greed, envy, selfishness, intolerance, etc. Violent and aggressive people are very much under the influence of the energy of gravity. The energy of gravity also conveys killings, wars, and unrest. The energy of feeling (yellow) is needed to keep the energy of gravity at bay. We can see that at the point we are today the energies of gravity and feeling are almost at the same level of unfolding. The energy of gravity is decreasing and the energy of feeling is increasing, but at the point where we are today they are almost level.

A very hot-tempered person lacks energy of feeling. Calm people have enough energy of feeling to counterbalance the fiery energy of gravity. These people have a calming and soothing effect on their surroundings and they are generally difficult to arouse. We can see that the energy of feeling is increasing as we approach the yellow field, the real human kingdom. This means that our mentality will develop toward being kinder, more loving, more tolerant, and more forgiving as these milder mentality traits are conveyed by the energy of feeling.

We also see that the energy of intelligence is at a fairly low stage but increasing, and it has almost reached the level of unfolding of the energy of instinct. So we are close to the point in time when the energy of intelligence will overtake the energy of instinct. This means that our behavior will be less defined by instinct and more defined by intelligence. Our present level of intelligence is such that it enables us to observe and analyze the things that we find in our physical surroundings. These observations are what form the basis of our present materialistic sciences, which are based on what can be measured and weighed and analyzed. As the energy of intelligence is increasing as we move up toward the yellow field, we will become more and more intelligent. This again means that more and more of our unused brain capacity will be deployed to "house" the growing intelligence. According to Martinus we only employ 5 to10 percent of our brain's capacity at our present stage, so there is plenty of unused potential in our brain.

Once an appropriate mixture of the energies of feeling and intelligence has been reached, we begin to be able to manifest universal love, love toward all beings. The ability to manifest universal love is only obtained when the energies of feeling and intelligence have reached a level of unfolding at which they are in harmony. The animal in its pure manifestation has no ability to love, only an instinct of how to mate and care for its offspring. The energy combination of the animal has not yet reached a level at which the manifestation of love is possible. It simply does not have enough of the two energies of feeling and intelligence.

As the energy of intuition (blue) is latent at this stage, we are unable to access facts of life beyond what is physically observable. We have no perception of the spiritual world that surrounds us.

We have no idea about the metaphysical level of existence and we think that we are one with our physical body. We can find no solution to the mystery of life or its meaning, nor do we have any idea about our own immortality. We think that our life ends when our physical body is worn out. We believe in death. We are cosmic illiterates, due to the latent character of the energy of intuition at this stage. However, as we approach the yellow field, the energy of intuition will start to stir. With the growing influence of the energy of intuition, people will start to have cosmic glimpses, and with the growth of the energy of intuition the mystery of life will be a mystery no longer. Those who have experienced cosmic glimpses are probably very close to the yellow field and consequently about to exit the animal kingdom.

The energy of memory (indigo) is quite weak at this stage and decreasing, and it will reach its latent stage in the next kingdom, the real human kingdom. However, it is still strong enough to enable us to "travel" through our memories and to draw on these memories when decisions have to be made. Still, many people are experiencing the low level of unfolding of the energy of memory at this point. They forget. They have trouble remembering the most basic things, some cannot even remember what they did or said yesterday, not to mention where they put the keys, left the purse, parked the car, etc. This is all an effect of the low level of unfolding of the energy of memory at our present stage.

Everything that we are today, what we can do and what we cannot do, what we know and what we do not know, what we believe and what we do not believe, our ability to love and our whole level of development is an immediate result of the combination of the basic energies in our bodily and mental structure at our present stage of evolution.

The Animal and Human Thought Climates

We saw that we are still in the animal kingdom, that we are still part animals. This should come as no surprise, as our sciences have long ago established that we have evolved from the big primates. Still many people may not like to hear this and may think that we are real humans, because we are much more intelligent than animals and our societies are much more advanced than those of animals. However, when we analyze what is meant by our still being part animals, we may be willing to agree that we have still not completely left the animal kingdom. We still have thought climates that are characteristic of the animal kingdom such as: greed, revenge, intolerance, envy, possessiveness, harshness, selfishness, jealousy, anger, irritation, hatred, etc., all conveyed by the basic energy of gravity.

The thought climates just mentioned are called animal thought climates because they are founded in the selfishness that is fundamental for the animal in its pure stage as predator to survive. Selfishness is fundamental for survival in the animal kingdom. If the predator were not driven by pure selfishness, it would not be able to survive. This display of selfishness is conveyed by the energy of gravity. Through thousands of lives we have been animals and have been driven by a strong sense of self-preservation founded in selfishness. Seen in a cosmic perspective it is not very long ago that we were real animals. We have developed away from the animal and we have a body that is different from that of the animal, but not all that different. Our way of procreation is exactly the same as that of all other mammals and our bodily structure is very much like that of other mammals. Indeed our DNA is almost identical to that of certain mammals. But in comparison to other mammals our bodily structure is finer, our intelligence is higher, and our mentality has developed away from that of the animal.

In the animal kingdom (central part of the orange field) the manifestations of the animal are prompted by a strong sense of self preservation conveyed by the energies of instinct and gravity. By animal is understood wild animals such as predators, not domestic animals. Instinctively the animal fights for its own preservation and that of its offspring. Egoism and selfishness rule. In order to maintain its own existence the animal has to manifest selfishness.

In the animal kingdom it is kill or be killed. In order to survive, the animal has to be extremely selfish. All the animal thought climates that will be mentioned later have their roots in the self-preservation and selfishness that predominate in the animal kingdom. Anger is an example. In order to defend itself against a potential killer the animal has to show aggression and anger. It has to bare its teeth and growl. It is no use smiling and being friendly—this would land the animal right on the dinner table. In order to preserve its own life, the animal has to manifest an aggressive attitude. It is from the necessary selfishness of the animal kingdom that all the animal thought climates have evolved.

On the other hand we, the humans of today, also have thought climates that are typical of the real human kingdom towards which we are traveling. These humane thought climates are compassion, tolerance, mildness, understanding, affection, self-sacrifice, forgiveness, devotion, and love. We develop human thought climates through the sufferings that the animal experiences as a consequence of its selfish actions, because we reap as we sow. I shall explain this at length in chapter 13.

As the animal and human thought climates will be referred to many times in the following chapters, it is useful to define these thought climates:

Animal	**Human**
Greed	Self-sacrifice
Envy	Devotion
Dishonesty	Honesty
Jealousy	Dedication
Intolerance	Tolerance
Harshness	Lenience
Revenge	Forgiveness
Cruelty	Kindness
Possessiveness	Consecration
Anger	Mildness
Negativity	Positivism
Scorn	Clemency
Selfishness	Altruism
Irritability	Understanding
Vanity	Acceptance

Conceit	Comfort
Judgment	Pardon
Punishment	Compassion
Ambition	Pity
Pride	Mercy
Haughtiness	Helpfulness
Arrogance	Humility
Jingoism	Internationalism
Damnation	Humor
Hatred	Love

To the degree that our manifestations are defined by the animal thought climates, we are still animals. The more our manifestations are defined by the human thought climates, the more human are we.

The Sphinx

As we are still very much under the influence of both animal and human thought climates we are in fact like the sphinx, which is part man, part animal, or a lion with a human face. To the degree that we are still influenced by the animal thought climates, based in selfishness, we are still animals. The more we manifest the animal thought climates, the more animal are we. The more we make use of the human thought climates, the more humane are we. It is only when we can honestly and truthfully say that we have none of the animal thought climates left that we are real human beings. Most of us are under the influence of both animal and human thought climates. In this sense we are like the sphinx.

Martinus explains that the sphinx was built together with the pyramids approximately eighty to ninety thousand years ago, which makes them much older than is generally believed. The pyramids and sphinx were built by initiated beings with cosmic consciousness who were sent down from higher realms to establish a settlement of humans on Earth. The sphinx is our likeness and it was placed there to tell us who or what we are. The sphinx is the key to understanding who we are.

Both the sphinx and the pyramids were built using the methods of materialization and dematerialization. All initiated beings, i.e., beings with cosmic consciousness, have the ability to materialize and dematerialize physical matter. So in the building of the pyramids, no huge hordes of slaves were employed such as it is generally believed. As a matter of fact nobody has yet been able to explain how the pyramids were built, as the huge hordes of slaves could not really have done it after all. How the pyramids were built has remained a mystery. This is no wonder as they were built using mental forces. As very few people on Earth have any knowledge of the use of mental forces, it is no wonder that the question about the building of the pyramids has remained a mystery. I shall explain the process of materialization and dematerialization in chapter 14.

Martinus explains that just as the sphinx and pyramids are physical ruins from the settlement of the initiated people who were sent "down" to establish a human settlement on Earth, there are also spiritual ruins from this settlement. The spiritual ruins are the Eastern religions that support beliefs in reincarnation such as Hinduism and Buddhism. Martinus calls these religions ruins, not in any way to denigrate them, but only to say that they still contain some elements of the original insight of the initiated people or cosmic truths, but some of this insight has been lost over the centuries. Still, some central concepts have survived. As it is only a part of the original insight that has survived in the Eastern religions, Martinus calls them "spiritual ruins." To the north and the west of the pyramids the insight of the initiated people was completely lost, and consequently these parts of the world were submerged in almost total cosmic or spiritual darkness. This is the spiritual darkness that we have experienced in the Western world during the last thousands of years, but which is now in the process of lifting as we approach the real human kingdom. The closer we get to the real human kingdom, the effect of the influence of the new world impulse will manifest itself more and more on our planet and we will gradually be able to put our animal patterns of behavior behind us.

11

Our Present Spiral Cycle

In order to fully reveal the characteristics of the huge cycle that we are now passing, the cycle that was denominated "D" on the drawing of the spiral, Martinus has made a symbol that explains our present spiral cycle. We shall now look at this symbol called:

The Eternal, Cosmic, Organic Connection Between God and Son of God

Symbol number 22 is a visual representation of the cyclical passage of the spiral that we are moving through at this point in time. Martinus calls this symbol "*The eternal, cosmic, organic connection between God and Son of God.*" When we move in a spiral it means that when we complete one cycle we step up one level and pass through a new cycle consisting of the six basic energies again but at another level of manifestation. Symbol number 22 illustrates such a cyclic motion at the same time as it illustrates the cycle that we are now passing: our present spiral cycle. Martinus does not say how long it takes to pass our present spiral cycle, but it is logical to assume that we are talking about millions of years.

We saw in symbol number 7 that everything in the universe is life inside life inside life.

There is nothing that is alive that is not dependent on macro or microorganisms in order to sustain its life. Only God has no meso or macrocosmos, God has only a micro organism. In our eternal wanderings we are now micro organisms in the body of planet Earth. In a former cycle we were organs in a body like our own, and before that we were cells in a body like our own. Once we have finished this cycle we will enter the cycle of planets and after that the cycle of solar systems. For each cyclic passing we step up one level in size, so to speak. On each level life manifests itself in a variety of different life forms, so each passing of a spiral cyclic movement offers new experiences and new aspects of the unfolding of life.

On symbol number 22 we see a visual representation of our present cycle, the one we are passing through at this very point in time. Our exact position right now will be pointed out later. We can see the colors of the six basic energies and we can see that each basic energy defines or dominates one-sixth of the circle. We all stand at a specific point in the passing of the cycle and in front of us we have all the beings that are further evolved than we are, and behind us we have the beings that are less evolved.

We know from symbol number 12 how the six sections are denominated: The plant kingdom (red), the animal kingdom (orange), the real human kingdom (yellow), the kingdom of wisdom (green), the divine world (blue), and finally the kingdom of memory or bliss (indigo).

In order to complete the cycle, our eternal "I" manifests itself in both physical and spiritual matter. In a cyclic passage there is a peak manifestation of light and a peak manifestation of darkness. The peak manifestation of light is in the spiritual realm of the divine world (blue) and the peak manifestation of darkness is in the physical realm of the animal kingdom (orange). So during a cyclic passage the being will experience the two contrasts of light and darkness and through these contrasting experiences it will renew its consciousness. The experience of light takes place on the spiritual level (upper part) and the experience of darkness takes place on the physical level (lower part).

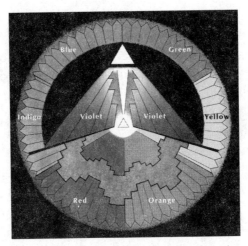

Symbol number 22.
The eternal, cosmic, organic connection between God and Son of God.
(Color version on cover) © Martinus Institute

The symbol shows the cosmic connection of every living being with God.

The white and violet-colored pyramid-shaped figure symbolizes the organic structure of the already mentioned cosmic connection. This structure exists between all living beings and God. This connection is expressed by the concept of God and Son of God.

The triangular figure in the middle of the symbol shows the "I" of the Son of God. The colored fields attached to this symbolize the physical bodies of the Son of God.

The two dark stripes that run across divide the symbol in two. Of these the lower part constitutes the physical world, whereas the upper part constitutes the spiritual world.

The consciousness and knowledge of the materialistic or godless Son of God embraces only the lower part. The physical world consists of mineral (indigo color), plant (red color), animal (orange), and a small part of the real human kingdom (yellow color).

From the short triangular shapes in the animal kingdom and until the yellow triangular shapes we find the unfinished humans of Earth.

The triangular figure that is half orange and half yellow symbolizes the humanely developed human beings. They have passed the major part of the culmination of darkness and begin to understand that the solution to the mystery of life does not exist on the physical plane. Their cosmic organic connection to God begins to stir again and they discover the strength of prayer. Gradually they will become susceptible to the great analyses of life and they will experience cosmic glimpses.

On the physical level the being manifests itself in mineral matter (indigo part), later it manifests itself in plant bodies (red part), later again in animal bodies (orange part), then in real human bodies (yellow part). After its exit of the physical realms it manifests itself in spiritual bodies in the spiritual part of the real human kingdom (yellow part), in the kingdom of wisdom (green part), the divine world (blue part), and the kingdom of memory or bliss (indigo part).

During its passage of the physical part of the cycle it is so that each time the eternal "I" loses a physical body through injury and death, it enters the spiritual realms. It stays there for a relatively short period only to reincarnate fairly quickly again into a new physical body. With each new physical body the bodily structure of the being evolves slightly, so that no two bodies are exactly the same even though they follow a logical line of evolution. With each physical life the bodily and mental structure of the being evolve slightly in tune with the changing combinations of the basic energies. In this way our life experience changes constantly and consequently our eternal voyage is anything but dull.

When we look at symbol number 22 we see two white triangles, one at the center of the symbol and one at the top. The one at the top represents the "I" of God and the one at the center represents the living being (us). We see that a ray of light goes from God's "I" to our "I." This ray represents the cosmic link that exists between God and the living being. This link between God and the living being can also be expressed through the concept of God and Son of God.

We, the living beings, are organically linked to God as our physical body is a part of God's physical body and as our consciousness is a part of God's consciousness. This link or organic connection between God and the living being can never be severed. No living being is "lost" or forgotten by God, but in a certain section of the cycle, which is the passing of the animal kingdom (the orange section) where darkness reigns, the living being can be so far away from God that it has lost the knowledge of the eternal link. The living being then no longer believes in God's existence, it thinks it is one with its physical body and that it lives only one life. At a certain point in the passing of the cycle the being becomes godless. It has come as far away from God as it is mentally possible. It has lost the knowledge that it is organically and spiritually a part of God. It has forgotten about its eternal link to God. It is experiencing its cosmic death.

On the symbol we see that two black lines, radiating from the center, cut the circle. These black lines constitute the boundary between the physical world and the spiritual world. The physical world is everything that lies below the two black lines and consequently the spiritual world is everything that lies above the two black lines. The section that lies above the two black lines is slightly bigger than the section that lies below the two black lines. This means that through the passing of a cycle our sojourn in the spiritual realms is longer than our sojourn in the physical realms. As the spiritual realms constitute the world of light and love and the physical realms constitute the world of darkness, it can serve as comfort to us, the living beings that are passing through this cycle, that the period of darkness is shorter than the period of light. We live more time in the light than we do in the darkness.

But the godless human being that is passing the animal kingdom, which constitutes the peak of darkness, has no knowledge about the existence of an eternal link with God, nor does he have any idea about the existence of the part of the cycle that lies above the two black lines. He is completely ignorant about the existence of the spiritual world, of the existence of his own eternal "I." He thinks that only the physical reality exists, he has nothing but the physical world and physical matter to cling to. He thinks he is one with his physical body. The godless person is a being for whom physical matter is the primary and only existing reality. He has forgotten about his eternal link to God. This constitutes the culmination of his experience of darkness. The being experiences the culmination of darkness when he thinks he lives in a godless universe governed by chance, anarchy, and chaos. But once he has culminated in the dark experience of being godless, he begins the process of remembering his link with God. In this way he then begins to move toward the light. Actually it is only in a very small segment of the circle that the being is ignorant about his own immortality.

The outer circle with the colors of the six basic energies represents the six realms or kingdoms; each dominated by one of the basic energies. Each pointed section of the outer circle represents a living being at a certain point in its development. In the lower part of the cycle, the part that represents the physical world, we see that the outer band with the pointed sections waves up and down and that the pointed sections are either short or long. The difference in length of the pointed sections illustrates that the fate of the beings varies within the same kingdom, meaning that, for instance, in the animal kingdom the being can have various bodily manifestations and thus different ways to experience life.

However, no matter how the being manifests itself, no matter if the being is a plant, an animal, a godless human being, an atheist, an agnostic, or a believer in God, there is no real distance between the being and God. The gray band on the lower part of the symbol illustrates this. If the gray band illustrates the imagined distance between God and the living being, we see that the gray band is always equally thick no matter if the pointed sections are long or short. The gray band waves up and down according to the length of the pointed sections. This again means that God's nearness to the being is the same whether the being is a plant, an animal, or a human being. God's nearness to the being is always constant whether the being is aware of this or not. In exactly the same way that parents look after the young child, so does God look after the living beings. He is there whether we are aware of this or not. God is not further away from or closer to the ant or the snail than he is to the priest or the atheist. The atheist believes that he lives in a godless universe, but even so God is no further away from him than he is from the most pious monk. It makes no difference if the being is aware of God's existence or not. God is as close to the cosmic illiterate as to the cosmic conscious being. To God all living creatures are equally important. Nobody is lost or forgotten by God.

On symbol number 12 we saw how the energies are composed differently in each realm. On symbol no. 22 only the predominant energy is depicted in the outer circle, but this does not, of course, mean that the other energies are not present as well. In each realm the energies are present in the proportions depicted on symbol number 12.

Because the combination of the basic energies is different in each realm, the life forms or manifestations of life are consequently also different in each realm. So the eternal "I" or X 1 creates various bodies or X 3s through its ability to create, X 2, as it passes the cycle according to the combination of the basic energies that are at its disposal in the different realms. One combination gives one life form and another combination gives another life form. But still the living being behind these life forms, the "I," is the same. The passing through the different realms of the basic energies and the dressing of oneself in a variety of different bodies constitutes the renovation of the experience of life for each living being or "I." Thus the living being perceives the contrasts that are fundamental for its life experience. In this way not only the experience of life of the being but also God's experience of life is renewed. Because of the huge variety of bodies the "I" makes use of during the passage, there is never a dull moment on this voyage.

Let us now look at how life unfolds for the beings that live in the six different kingdoms or realms. We will start our voyage through the circle at the point where the living being comes into the physical world, that is at the black line on the left. In "reading" the symbol we move counterclockwise.

The Plant Kingdom (Red Section)

We will start our voyage through the cycle in the plant kingdom (the red section) below the black line at the left and leave the 2½ indigo shapes to be explained under the kingdom of memory to where they belong. This voyage through the cycle is what every living being experiences as an individual at our present stage. So in our present cycle we were first plants, later we became animals, at our present position we are part animals, part humans, later we will become real humans and then, as spiritual beings, we will pass the nonphysical realms.

The plant is a being in which the energy of instinct is predominant. The energy of gravity is on the increase and is quite predominant. After this comes the energy of feeling, which is also increasing. The energy of intelligence is latent or at its lowest degree of unfolding and the energy of intuition is at its lowest stage before the latent stage. Finally the energy of memory (or bliss) is still quite strong, as it is at its stage just after its culmination and it thus has a fairly predominant influence. Please refer to symbol number 12 to see the degrees of unfolding of the different energies.

The most important role in the constitution of the plant is played by the energy of instinct. This energy is so predominant that it automatically conveys the outer life functions of the plant such as its growth, its bodily shape and form, and it also conveys the plant with its ability to sense vaguely. The only perception of its surroundings that the plant has is a vague sensation of what is pleasant and what is unpleasant. As the energy of intelligence is at its latent stage, the plant has no means with which to analyze what it is sensing.

The day-consciousness of the plant is still on the spiritual plane, and this means that the consciousness of the plant is not with it on the physical plane; the plant is absent-minded, so to speak. The plant is still conscious in the realm of memory, which it has just left. In this way the plant is a being that is half-spiritual, half-physical. The realm of memory (or the realm of bliss) is where we experience the highest, the most brilliant sensation of light. The ecstasy or blissful joy that the plant experiences with its day-consciousness on the spiritual plane vibrates through to its physical body and creates the wonderful flowers with all their different shapes, colors, and perfumes. So when we look at a flower, it is really physical manifestations from the spiritual kingdom of memory or bliss that we are looking at. As the plant-being has relatively recently entered the physical plane from the kingdom of bliss, it is still glowing with a halo from this cosmic realm and this cosmic halo manifests itself through the energy of bliss in the physical world as the marvelously beautiful colors, shapes, and perfumes of the plants and their flowers. Wherever there is a display of flowers, it is memories from the kingdom of bliss that manifest themselves on the physical plane. The beautiful flowers and their perfumes are the result of the cosmic consciousness of a former spiral cycle transformed into an automatic function. It is no wonder that a display of flowers conveys us with an elated feeling, conveys us with a feeling that a higher world exists. It is impossible to look at a beautiful flower and at the same time be angry or depressed. This is the reason why a light depression will lift when we go into nature. The energy of bliss, which is present in all plants, will transport the depressed person onto another state of mind, it will lift the depression.

Through its presence in the physical world and the growing influences of the energies of gravity and feeling, from where the plant gets its life force, the plant becomes increasingly physical. Through thousands of years of influence from the physical forces such as heat and cold, rain and sunshine, and the damaging of its physical bodies by animals and humans, the plant organism becomes more and more physical and consequently increasingly conscious on the physical plane. No being on the physical plane is more damaged and injured than the plant. The flowers are picked, the grass is cut, the trees are felled and roots, leaves and stalks are eaten by animals and humans. In this connection it is a divine measure that the plant can experience the injuries from the outer world to its physical body only as vague sensations. The plant cannot experience real physical pain. Because the plant has recently come from the spiritual worlds and through its own longing has entered the physical plane, the plant experiences all physical contact such as injuries to its body as a pleasant experience, as it constitutes a contrast to the spiritual plane. The plant came into the physical world to experience contrast to the spiritual plane, so everything that makes the plant sense this contrast is experienced as pleasant.

It is a divine arrangement that the plant can feel the various attacks from animals and humans on its physical body only as vague sensations, or even as pleasure, as plants are meant as the main source of food for a large section of other beings. The plant cannot feel pain and it cannot suffer to any great extent no matter how much we injure its physical body.

As we have seen, the many influences from the outside world on its body mean that the plant becomes more and more conscious on the physical plane and at the same time its body gets more and more life force through the growing influences of the energies of gravity and feeling. At a certain point the plant develops a primitive digestive system as we see in the insectivorous plants, which represent a being at a stage between a plant and an animal.

Logically the development from plant to animal has a multitude of transitory stages in a huge variation of physical bodies each representing a step in development and each defined by a specific combination of the basic energies. It is through this gradual development of senses and organs that the plant eventually develops into an animal.

The Animal Kingdom (Orange Section)
THE DEVELOPMENT OF PHYSICAL SENSES

In the animal kingdom the predominant energy is the energy of gravity. The energy of instinct has lost ground and so has the energy of memory or bliss. The energies of feeling and intelligence have gained ground and the energy of intuition is latent. This combination of energies is what constitutes the animal. We have now moved into the orange section of the symbol. The energies of gravity and feeling, whose interplay constitutes the life force of all physical beings, have grown and we see that the animal has a stronger life force than the plant. In this way the animal has a stronger and more vigorous body than most plants and it has become mobile. Through the growing capacity of the energies of gravity and feeling and through the effects on its body of the outer forces such as light, darkness, heat, cold, wind, and rain, the animal has developed the physical senses: eyesight, hearing, smell, taste, and feeling. It is through the effects of the forces of the outer physical world on the being that the physical senses evolve. Because there is light and darkness the being gradually develops senses with which it can distinguish light from darkness. In other words, the beings develop eyes. Because there is silence and noise in the outer world, the being evolves its ability to hear. All the senses are evolved because of the influences of the outer world on the being. If there were no light and no darkness, there would be no reason to develop eyes. If there were no sounds there would be no reason to develop hearing, etc.

DAY-CONSCIOUSNESS ENTERS THE PHYSICAL PLANE

With developing senses the being is able to perceive many more details of the physical world, and with its growing intelligence it is gradually able to know what is going on in its surroundings. As the energy of intelligence grows, the being becomes able to analyze what goes on in its surroundings. At the same time its day-consciousness enters the physical plane. The plant was not very conscious of what was going on in its surroundings as it still had its day consciousness on the spiritual plane. In the animal kingdom it is no longer through a vague sensation that the being experiences its physical surroundings, but through a full perception of the physical, material facts. In this way the animal has its day-consciousness on the physical plane just as we, the humans have it. The animal can only experience what goes on on the physical plane. It is no longer conscious that the spiritual plane exists. Its only reality now is the physical plane.

THE INTRODUCTION OF PAIN

Through the development of the senses the animal also reaches a point where it can begin to feel pain. The concept of pain is only introduced when the being reaches the animal kingdom and its body has developed to the point where it has a nervous system. The plant can feel no pain and can only vaguely sense what happens in the outer world. With the development of the physical senses the concept of pain is introduced, so to speak. If there were no pain the animal would not be able to effectively reap experiences from its actions. The accumulation of experiences about what hurts and what does not hurt will teach the animal certain appropriate patterns of behavior. This accumulation of experience will eventually develop the animal into a human being. If there were no pain there could be no effective reaping of experience. Without experiencing what is painful and what is not, the animal would not develop into a human being.

Pain is present only in the animal kingdom or orange section of the cycle. We saw that the plant could feel no pain. Once we enter the yellow section, the real human kingdom, again there will be no pain. The spiritual realms are completely devoid of pain. So pain, suffering, and misery are present only in one-sixth of the cycle. Most of the cyclic passage is painless.

THE GROWTH OF INTELLIGENCE

The animal can gradually begin to actively participate in the sustenance and creation of its life. The primary forces that drive the animal are its nourishment and its procreation through which it secures the survival of its species. The wild animal has a strong sense of self-preservation, which extends to its mate and offspring. Outside its sphere of mate, offspring, and flock there exists only a war zone. The animal has to have all its senses on high alert in order to protect itself from its enemies. If it wants to maintain its physical life, it has to fight for it and at the same time it has to kill other beings to live. If the animal were not driven by a strong sense of self-preservation based in selfishness, it would soon perish.

As its intelligence grows, the animal can gradually begin to understand what goes on in its surroundings and it can begin to adjust its activities to this understanding. As the animal gains experience and with the growing influence of the energy of intelligence it will gradually learn which is the best way to secure its nourishment and its survival. No longer will it depend solely on the energy of instinct for its survival as it did as a plant. Dawning intelligence begins to play a role in the behavior of the animal.

SELFISHNESS

With the predominance of the energy of gravity, which conveys all mental explosions such as rage and violence, the animal is driven by a strong sense of self-preservation or selfishness to maintain its physical existence. Either it kills and sustains its own body by devouring the bodies of other beings, or it falls prey to the appetite of other animals and is itself eaten. In the animal kingdom there is no room for mercy or pity. It is either eat or be eaten. It is either get a meal or be a meal. A polar bear that finds two unprotected seal pups does not first stop to think how sweet and endearing they look, nor does it feel any kind of compassion for them. It simply kills them without any more ado and devours their bodies. The animal in its pure manifestation has no mercy whatsoever. In the animal kingdom it is kill or be killed; only selfishness will determine survival.

The animal kingdom is the killing zone of the cycle, and as you reap as you sow, the animal reaps nothing but killings. As it kills, it must itself be killed. This killing zone is the realm of darkness. In this darkness there is no mercy, no pity, no lenience, no compassion, no love. In this zone there is only selfishness, greed, and a fight for power.

In spite of being driven by selfishness, the animal still has no self-perception or "I" consciousness. It has not discovered its own identity and being. The tiger that hunts its prey and the prey that is being hunted have no idea about an "I" behind their bodies. Their whole consciousness is concentrated on the outside world. The outer world is full of dangers and all their senses are directed toward this outer world. They still have not turned their vision inward toward their own self. It is only when the animal develops into a human being that it begins to perceive its own self as something apart from the outside world. This means that the difference between a "pure" animal and an earthly human being is that the latter has an "I" consciousness and the first has none.

THE UNFINISHED HUMAN BEING

If we take a closer look at the orange portion of the circle we can see ten and a half pointed sections. The first six pointed sections counted counterclockwise from the red part represent the real animals, the beings that have animal bodies such as lions, tigers, hyenas, dogs, cats, apes, etc. The two short but equally long pointed sections, numbers seven and eight, symbolize the very primitive human stages. These are stages that are more apelike than human and represent the so-called "missing link." These stages are no longer to be found on this planet, but exist on other planets that are further behind in development than Earth. The next pointed section, number nine, represents the stage of our present "primitive" or aboriginal people representing the ancient world impulse as explained in chapter 4. This stage will also soon be over on the planet. The next pointed section, number ten, the one just before the section that is part orange and part yellow, represents the stage of the present cultural human beings or mainstream of our cultural societies. It is in these societies that the materialistic sciences have reached their present fairly high level of unfolding and consequently it is in these societies that we find the materialistic and godless beings, the beings that have no idea of a spiritual reality.

In the last pointed section of the animal kingdom, the one that is half orange, half yellow, we find the people who have outgrown the ability to believe in the religions. These people have passed the culmination of darkness. They are very humane and are against war and bloodshed. They are advocates for peace and internationalism, they cannot find it in their heart to hurt other beings, they live only on a vegetarian diet, they don't wear animal skin, they avoid all confrontations, and they forgive their enemies easily. They begin to understand that the solution to the mystery of life is not to be found on the physical plane. These are the people who through their sufferings have outgrown all their animal tendencies, and their cosmic organic connection with God begins to stir. In these people the new world impulse will find foothold, and they are the candidates for cosmic glimpses.

In the range between sections number nine and up to the vicinity of the yellow section we find ourselves, the humans such as we are today. Martinus says that we are unfinished human beings. We are still partly animal and partly human. We have a humanlike body, but this body is still not a real human body. The real human body is finer, frailer, more beautiful, and with no hairs. We have a humanlike mentality, but our mentality is still not completely free from the animal thought climates that are vestiges from our many lives as animals. In order to survive, the animal has to have a mentality characterized by selfishness, greed, jealousy, possessiveness, anger, intolerance, etc. These thought climates have been with us for millions of years and they were necessary for our survival as animals. As we develop a humanlike body these thought climates are still with us as they have developed into an automatic function, and it takes a long time to "unlearn" these. When we are faced with some kind of confrontation, we automatically react through our million-year-old patterns of behavior from the animal kingdom. That is why we react with anger or rage or even killing. If at the same time our human thought climates such as compassion, understanding, mercy, forgiveness, and love are still fairly weak in our mentality, it is no wonder that our animal patterns of reaction often take control. We belong to the animal kingdom to the degree that our mentality is still characterized by the animal thought climates.

DEVIL MENTALITY

We know that there are animals that are dangerous, but the most dangerous beings alive on Earth are not to be found in the jungle but in the middle of our so-called cultural societies, as we shall soon see.

In sections nine and ten of the animal kingdom we find the "humans" that still have a strong animal mentality. As already explained, the animal has to maintain its physical existence through the exercise of pure egoism. Egoism is a purely animal though climate. As we approach the real human kingdom the energy of intelligence grows. This means that at a certain point in evolution there are beings that have an animal mentality characterized by egoism linked together with a fairly high intelligence.

These are beings whose mentality is purely selfish but at the same time they are equipped with a fairly developed intelligence. This is a very, very dangerous cocktail. With the growing intelligence the "human" being is able to develop weapons that are thousands of times stronger and more dangerous than the mere claws and teeth of the animal. Take the completely selfish mentality of a polar bear and provide this polar bear with intelligence enough to build a machine gun. Now let the polar bear be free to use the machine gun and see what happens. The man or woman with a mentality of a polar bear will kill everybody and keep killing even after they have eaten their full. Just to demonstrate how important they are, they will go on killing. They have no mercy and no thought for anybody but themselves. They only want power and riches for themselves. A man with animal mentality provided with nuclear weapons or bacteriological weapons is the most dangerous being alive in the universe. It is so bad that we can no longer talk about animal mentality, but we have to call it devil mentality. The people with devil mentality are the real "devils." They are the only existing "devils." There are no other "devils" and there is no other "underworld" than the orange section of the physical plane.

In the past century we have seen many examples of persons with devil mentality. These persons are led entirely by their selfishness and, with the lethal weapons that they have at their disposal as a result of their merciless climb to power, they have been able to create Armageddon on Earth. Examples of beings with devil mentality could be any dictator or despot. They are egoistic and merciless but fairly intelligent beings. They have thoughts for nobody but themselves.

But the law of karma sees to it that we reap as we sow, and the people that have so mercilessly destroyed the lives of millions of their fellow beings through torture and mass executions will inevitably fall victims to their own devilry. The fate that you have imposed on others will inevitably be your own. More about this in chapter 13.

It is through the manifestation of the devil mentality that God creates darkness. Darkness is necessary as a contrast to the light of the spiritual worlds. Because there is light and love in the spiritual worlds, there has to be a place in the cycle where there is darkness and lovelessness. If there was not such a place, there could be no contrast and without contrast there can be no experience of life. The physical plane is the realm of darkness and the animal kingdom constitutes the culmination of darkness.

To bring about the culmination of darkness, the energy combinations have been so brilliantly thought out that the fact that the energy of intelligence is allowed to grow before the selfishness conveyed by the energy of gravity has been allowed to wane gives way to the creation of the being with a devil mentality. If there were no dictators there could be no darkness. But if there were no darkness we could not experience a contrast to the light. The darkness may be unpleasant, it may be painful, but it is there for a reason. So the beings with the devil mentality are there for a reason, they function as catalysts for our descent into darkness.

THE MEANING OF SUFFERING

When we sow misery, we reap misery. Through misery and suffering we develop the ability that we call compassion. So it is through suffering that we develop our humane abilities. Suffering is absolutely necessary and the only way in which we can "unlearn" our animal mentality. Suffering exists for the sole reason of being instrumental in eradicating our animal tendencies. Suffering does not just exist for its own sake and it is not a punishment. It is a means through which we can learn compassion. We feel compassion in the areas where we have once suffered ourselves. The suffering that we have once experienced leaves a mental image in our consciousness. Although we cannot actively remember the situation in which we suffered, an echo of this suffering is still present in our consciousness and when we see a person who is suffering, as we once suffered ourselves, we are able to feel compassion for this person. We want to help this person and somehow alleviate his suffering. Through sufferings our humanity is born.

Through this we see that God is not letting us suffer because of our sins or because he takes pleasure in seeing people endure pain. Our suffering is the necessary experience of darkness. But our suffering is also the necessary means through which we can develop humanity. We have to suffer our way out of the animal kingdom. Through suffering we are able to shed our animal frame and become loving and forgiving real human beings.

The Real Human Kingdom (Yellow Section)

In this kingdom we see that the energy of feeling is predominant. Because of the predominance of the energy of feeling, the beings in this kingdom are kinder, milder, and more loving than people are today. They no longer nurture thought climates belonging to the animal kingdom such as jealousy, envy, greed, intolerance, revenge, hatred, bitterness, pride, and contempt for others. As the energy of gravity is on the decrease, the beings no longer have such a strong and powerful body as they had in the animal kingdom. The bodies will be finer, leaner, and more beautiful than they are today. The energy of intelligence is increasing so intelligence and logic will rule society in the real human kingdom. The energy of instinct no longer plays an important role, whereas the energy of intuition is growing and through the influence of this energy almost everybody will have reached the point at which they have cosmic glimpses or cosmic consciousness. The energy of memory is at its latent stage with only enough strength to get people through the day.

The human being that has reached the real human kingdom

is a being that has passed the zone of darkness in the cycle of the spiral. All darkness is now behind it, but the experience of darkness is "fresh" in its subconscious. It has renewed its knowledge of darkness and is now ready to start its climb toward the light of the spiritual realms. The real human being has totally outlived all animal mentality and is now a being of light. It emanates love toward its neighbor no matter if this neighbor is a plant, an insect, an animal, or another human being. The being is now in contact with the basic tone of the universe, which is love. It is now a being in the image and likeness of God and is one with God. It is now an organ in God's primary consciousness.

In the physical part of the real human kingdom (most of the real human kingdom is on the spiritual level, above the black line to the left in the symbol), the beings will eat only vegetables and fruit. This food will be the only natural food for people that have reached this stage. The human being in the image and likeness of God cannot be a person who kills and devours the bodies of dead animals like a wild beast in the jungle. The finished human being cannot participate in killing, cutting up, frying, or boiling the physical bodies of other living beings just in order to swallow their bodily parts as elaborate dishes, as steaks, sausages, ragouts, patés, or similar. No, finished human beings live only on a vegetarian diet. Neither can a finished human being wear clothes or shoes made of animal skin. In the real human kingdom all clothes will be made from man-made, synthetic fibers.

Vegetarian food will make all nutritional diseases disappear. Everybody will be very healthy and fit and will carry only their natural weight. Hospitals will have disappeared because illnesses will no longer exist. The killing principle will have been completely abandoned. The beings will sow no killing and consequently they will reap no killing in the shape of illnesses. This aspect will be explained in the chapter about the law of karma.

The bodily structure of the beings will be slight, and toward the end of the physical part of the real human kingdom almost ethereal. There will be no need to have a very strong body, as there is no need to defend oneself. There is no brutality, no assaults, no killings, and no wars. An atmosphere of absolute humanity reigns as everybody serves everybody. "It is better to give than to take" has long been the rule of conduct. As everybody lives to serve his fellow man, an atmosphere of all-pervading love reigns. As the energy of intelligence is increasing, this kingdom is one of wisdom, science, and knowledge, and everybody will have cosmic insight. This is again the same as having a day-conscious experience of the spiritual facts that exist behind the physical world. In this kingdom the human being is conscious of his own immortality, of his oneness with God and of the solution to the mystery of life.

In the real human kingdom, all human beings on Earth and all states will have been united in one people and one state. There will no longer be various states that can oppose each other. There will be no national states and consequently no special national interests. The national languages will be only spoken locally, if they will be spoken at all. One supranational language will be the official language and will be spoken by everybody. According to Martinus this language will be Esperanto, as Esperanto is a perfect language free from all grammatical irregularities that all national languages have. There will be only one language and one kingdom on Earth, the world-kingdom. This is what Jesus refers to when he says, "*So there shall be one flock, one shepherd*" (John 10:16).

Money will no longer exist and all the riches of the Earth will be evenly distributed to everybody. There will be no private property, as all living beings on Earth are heirs to its riches. All materials are free and everybody is rich. Poverty has long been eradicated. Huge computers calculate how much work has to be done each day of the year to keep the desired standard of living. On the basis of this calculation, each grown-up person is told how many hours he has to work per week. This is likely to be only a few hours per week.

Only our ability to work has value and we will work only in the fields where our interests and abilities lie. When we have worked the hours designated, we will get a receipt that allows us to make use of the many facilities that are on offer. Everybody will be employed only in what they are good at and all hard physical labor will have been taken over by machines. Children will be educated in what they are best at and in what they most want and all old people will be cared for. Nobody will be able to exploit any other person. Everybody is equal. Peace, prosperity, and happiness reign.

According to Martinus it will take us approximately another three thousand years to reach this kingdom of love. Over the next millennia we will outgrow all types of warfare and we will gradually be able to allow internationalism and common interests to define our societies. But if we look around us today we can already see many signs that point in that direction.

The growing internationalization such as the European Union is a step toward this. The many different European countries that have been at war with each other for close to two thousand years have now been united. The United Nations has a growing influence and it is the embryo of the supranational government that will one day rule the world. Credit cards are a step toward the abolition of money. The Internet is a huge step toward global cross-frontier communication. Technological development is a step toward the abolition of hard labor.

In the real human kingdom the being will develop away from the need to reincarnate in physical matter. But in its last period on the physical plane the being no longer has to be born by a woman. It can materialize on the physical plane when it wants to and dematerialize when it has no more need to manifest itself in physical matter. This ability to materialize and dematerialize is an ability that we acquire when we reach a very high moral standard. All beings that have cosmic consciousness have this ability. In the New Testament we read how Jesus dematerialized his dead body from the cave and how he materialized in front of the disciples when he visited them after he was crucified. Martinus also had this ability and did materialize and dematerialize himself at some occasions,[1] but he used this ability only very rarely, as it was not in his mission to do this. The process of materialization and dematerialization will be enlarged upon in chapter 14.

Once the being has reached the point where it can materialize and dematerialize at its own free will, it has reached so high a level of moral perfection that it no longer needs to reincarnate in physical matter. It simply has no more to learn on the physical plane. It has remembered that it is part of God. It has no more animal mentality, it lives only to serve its fellow beings, and helps, supports, and loves everybody. It has "passed its exams" and has graduated itself out of the need to incarnate in the heavy physical matter. "School" is over and the "holiday" in the spiritual realms is ready to begin. The being will now continue its experience of life as a spiritual being. The being has now reached the black line at the right in the symbol.

We have now passed through the physical planes of existence and we have seen how *everything was very good*" (Genesis 3), although the passing of darkness was full of tears, pain, and suffering. We have seen that this darkness was a necessity for the renewal of our experience of life and we have seen that there was a reason for our sufferings. The darkness was there to constitute a contrast to the light of the spiritual realms.

The being now continues its existence in the spiritual realms where it is one with God's primary consciousness. We now pass the black line at the right of symbol number 22 and enter the spiritual realms.

The Kingdom of Wisdom (Green Section)

In this kingdom the energy of intelligence is predominant and the energy of intuition is at its stage just before its culmination. The energy of instinct is latent as the beings on this plane are so knowledgeable that they do not need to be led by instinct. The energies of gravity and feeling are decreasing, and as we know that these two energies are responsible for the physical bodies it means that the being is no longer a physical being—his body consists of spiritual matter only.

The beings in this kingdom are the highest capacities of perfect creation of the universe. They are the sublime masters of wisdom.

It is these beings that design and shape the organisms of future plants, animals, and humans on future planets, just as it was beings from this kingdom who designed and shaped the plants, animals, and humans that we see on Earth today. Our own bodies are no exception. All bodily manifestations that we see in nature have been designed and made functional by beings on this plane of existence. No process of creation exists that does not originate from this realm of wisdom. Everything that is created in physical matter is first created in thought matter on this plane.

The physical bodies of all living creatures have been designed and made functional by beings in the kingdom of wisdom. The plants and animals that we see on Earth today have been designed and created first in spiritual and later made to function in physical matter by beings from this kingdom.

The thought creations from the kingdom of wisdom may sometimes "spill over" onto the physical plane and be accessed by scientists, engineers, technicians, and artists. These "spillovers" are experienced by the physical beings as flashes of inspiration and thus they can be transferred to the heavy physical matter. Most of our best works of art, our most brilliant symphonies and operas, our greatest literature, great ideas, and answers to difficult questions have been transferred from the kingdom of wisdom to physical beings through flashes of inspiration.

The kingdom of wisdom is God's drafting room, God's design study.

The Divine World (Blue Section)

In the divine world the energy of intuition is predominant. In this kingdom we are at the center of God's primary consciousness or the holy spirit, this is as close to the light and as "high" as we can get. On this plane of existence all answers to all questions are found, but here the beings have no questions, as everything is revealed. This plane is the home of all of God's consciousness. God's consciousness is all knowledge that exists about the universe or cosmos. It is a sea of knowledge and wisdom and we are one with this universal bank of data in the divine world. Here the beings can experience the totality of answers from the whole universe, from remote inhabited planets, solar systems, and galaxies. The whole of God's countenance shines unhindered upon the eternal sons of God in this the highest of all cosmic life spheres. This is the closest we can get to God.

It is from this kingdom that all ideas for macro and micro life forms and structures originate. These ideas are then made functional in the kingdom of wisdom from where they are transferred to the physical worlds. It is also from this world that cosmic glimpses and cosmic consciousness can be transferred to highly developed beings on the physical plane.

The divine world is the culmination of light and it is as far away from darkness as we can come. This kingdom forms a contrast so great to the animal kingdom that it is difficult to grasp its all-encompassing light for beings living in the animal kingdom. In this divine kingdom we are outside time and space, only the eternal "now" exists, there is no yesterday and no tomorrow. All the details of the past and future can be experienced in this "now." All matter shapes itself according to the desires of the being, as spiritual matter is so light that it obeys the mental energies of the being. We have only to think of something and it will unfold before our very eyes. We do not have to move or travel, all matter shapes itself at our beck and call, and all communication takes place as a direct transfer of thoughts.

In this kingdom the being has reached a level of development so high that it has become one with God. This is the highest, most harmonious, and beautiful constellation of the basic energies: a perfect intelligence, a culminating intuition, an increasing energy of memory, and a low level of unfolding of the "physical" energies of instinct and feeling and a total absence of the energy of gravity, the purveyor of the killing principle. The presence in the divine world is the culmination of the experience of light.

The Kingdom of Memory or Bliss (Indigo Section)

The last kingdom in the cyclic spiral is the kingdom of bliss or memory. In the divine world the energy of memory is already increasing and it is this energy that is predominant in the kingdom of bliss. This means that it is the energy of memory that carries the consciousness of the being in this realm. We also see that the energy of feeling is latent and that the energy of gravity is weak. This means that the capacity of the being to sense in the outer world is minimal, indeed so minimal that the being has no perception of the outer world. In the kingdom of bliss the being lives only in its inner world, in its memories.

But the memories that it can access at this point, where the energy of memory culminates, are innumerable. It can remember every detail from every life it lived during the whole cycle through which it has just passed. This means that the being can remember every detail from millions of lives. It can remember how it was a plant in the jungle and how as a flower it was picked by a young lover, it can remember how it was a wild animal and devoured the bodies of other animals, it can remember how, as an unfinished human being, it killed its brother in a civil war and how it later had to pay with its own life for this deed. It can remember how it lived in peace and happiness in the real human kingdom and how it designed interesting new fish in the kingdom of wisdom.

The passing through the kingdom of bliss is like sitting in a time machine in which you can go forward and backward just as you please. You can reexperience every detail of all your lives in the cycle. You remember your friends and lovers and because the energy of memory is culminating, the memories are of a much stronger nature than the memories that we experience now on the physical plane, where the energy of memory is almost latent. As the memories ripen with time to become "gold copies" as mentioned earlier, the experience that the being has in this kingdom is one of pure bliss. As all the memories present themselves at the beck and call of the being, the being gets to experience itself as a God in its own little kingdom. This is the perfect conclusion to the passing through the cycle.

Once the being has reached the kingdom of memory it has lived for millions of years in the light. The light is beginning to need a contrast. As the being also reexperiences its lives in the darkness as gold copies, it begins to desire a return to the darkness and its growing body of instinct begins to prepare the being's return to the physical plane. And thus the being starts to leave the kingdom of bliss and prepares to enter a new cycle, but on another level than the previous one.

We are now back at the black line at the left of the symbol. The two indigo shapes below the black line at the physical plane represent the first manifestations of the being in the kingdom of bliss on the physical plane. These manifestations are crystals in ice and mineral matter or stone and they are the forerunners of the being's manifestations as a plant. When we observe ice crystals being formed on our windowpane, these are the first physical manifestations of a spiritual being who now desires to reenter the physical plane.

All mineral matter such as stone, rock, and crystal are manifestations on the physical plane of beings whose day-consciousness is still in the kingdom of bliss and who are in the process of reentering physical matter.

This, then, is our present spiral cycle. We saw how every kingdom offered new possibilities for the eternal "I" to experience life through a series of different physical and spiritual bodies. We saw that we have physical bodies in the plant and animal kingdoms and in a fairly small part of the real human kingdom. But in these kingdoms we do *not only* have physical bodies.

Our Various Bodies

While we are on the physical plane we have six spiritual bodies apart from our physical body (our body of gravity). We have a body corresponding to each of the basic energies, all of them embedded in the mother energy, so we have a body of feeling, a body of intelligence, a body of intuition, at body of memory, and a body of instinct. These spiritual bodies can be seen in our aura, and their strength depends on the level of unfolding of the corresponding energy as depicted on symbol number 12. When we die or shed our physical body the next energy in strength (in our case the energy of feeling) takes over our day-consciousness. Those who have had a near-death experience say that they left their physical body, but that they still had their consciousness. They could still experience things. This is because the consciousness is now carried by the body of feeling. I will elaborate this further in the chapter about death and the afterlife.

In the major part of the real human kingdom, in the kingdom of wisdom, in the divine world, and in the kingdom of bliss we have only spiritual bodies, and the combination of these bodies changes according to the unfolding of the energies as seen on symbol number 12. There will, however, always be small individual differences.

Our spiritual bodies form a field of energy. This field of energy vibrates on a particular wavelength defined by the type of energy of which it consists. This means that our energy field or spiritual body has a particular wavelength on which it operates. This is an important feature because it means that we will automatically be attracted to beings whose spiritual bodies operate on the same wavelength. The law of attraction and repulsion determines that like wavelengths attract each other and dissimilar wavelengths repel each other. We sometimes feel that there are people with whom we are on the same wavelength and we generally get on very well with them. But when we are discarnate our wavelength becomes even more significant because we will automatically be attracted to wavelengths in the spiritual worlds that are similar to our own. As the spiritual world is an electric world operating on a large range of different wavelengths we will, once we have been severed from our physical body, be drawn to a wavelength similar to our own. We shall see what this means in later chapters.

We have come to understand that there is a spiritual reality behind the physical reality and that the criterion that "it is not visible" does not mean that it does not exist. Today we know that there are many things that exist even though they are not visible. Sound waves, microwaves, and television waves exist, but we cannot see them. Our thoughts exist, but we cannot see them. Today we can measure thought waves, so gradually we accept that non-visible "things" exist. There is a whole world "out there" that is not visible, and accepting that invisible matter exists is the first step up the mountain of understanding that we have to climb to reach insight. As we move ahead in our development toward the spiritual realms, we shall see how more and more details of the spiritual world will be revealed to us. This will happen once the energy of intuition begins to stir.

The Spiritual World Is the Primary World

The spiritual world is the primary world and the physical world is the secondary world. The spiritual world is "*the Spirit of God over the face of the waters*," it is the home of God's consciousness, and it existed before the physical world. It is from this world that the physical world has been created. The physical world has been created through a process of condensation of spiritual matter. The physical world exists only as a place where there can be a contrast to the light. It exists as a place where "it hurts to think wrongly."

We think that the physical plane is the only existing world, but we are as ignorant as the manacled prisoners in Plato's "Republic" who lived in a subterranean world and could see only the shadows of the people in the light and thought that the shadows were "the real thing."

As the spiritual plane exists on very fine wavelengths it offers no resistance. On the spiritual plane all matter is very light, so light that all matter automatically shapes itself after our thoughts. Spiritual matter is thought matter and when we are on the spiritual plane what we think about will materialize before us through the working of the law of attraction and repulsion. Spiritual matter is so light that it automatically obeys our thoughts. Because the spiritual world offers no resistance, it is not a good place to learn to distinguish between good and evil. There is simply too little resistance. As soon as we have made a mental picture in our mind, this picture materializes before us because spiritual matter is very moldable.

And because the spiritual world is a world of light, it cannot produce any darkness. The darkness has to exist in a place that is not spiritual. For that reason the physical world was created.

In order to learn to think and act in the correct way we have to come into the heavy physical world where every creative process takes a lot of effort and where it hurts if we act wrongly. To act wrongly means to act selfishly, because acting selfishly is to act against common interests and against the basic tone of the universe, which is love. In the physical world we furthermore have to express our thoughts through a physical voice and all our creations have to be shaped in heavy physical materials.

We can logically deduce that the spiritual world is the primary world because every man-made thing that exists on Earth started as an idea, as a construction in thought or spiritual matter. Not a single man-made thing exists on Earth that was not first a thought. A thought is a construction in spiritual matter. As with all other spiritual matter, thoughts are invisible but they exist all the same. The fact that everything man-made was a thought before it became a physical thing shows that the spiritual world is the primary world as it was there before the physical world. Consequently the physical world is the secondary world, the world of hardships and darkness.

The Expulsion from Paradise

Before we leave our present cycle I would like to share with you how the act of leaving the spiritual realms (i.e., the act of crossing the black line at the left in the symbol) and restarting reincarnation in the physical realms has been symbolically expressed in the Old Testament.

We know from the above that the experience of contrasts is fundamental for our perception of life. We can only perceive life if we experience contrasts. Through our eternal wanderings we pass through both spiritual and physical planes of existence, as we have just seen. When we are in the spiritual realms we are completely enveloped in the wisdom and light of God's primary consciousness. Everything is light. After having spent eons in these kingdoms of light, our eternal being or "I" becomes satiated by light and starts longing toward a contrasting experience. Without contrast the light becomes meaningless. The being starts longing for darkness.

It therefore has to leave the kingdoms of light in order to experience darkness. This leaving the kingdom of light is what has been so brilliantly expressed in a symbolic way in the Bible's narrative of the expulsion from Paradise (Genesis 3).

Adam and Eve living in Paradise represent the eternal beings living in the spiritual realms. These are kingdoms of light where you are one with God's primary consciousness. The light and love of these spiritual kingdoms are all-encompassing, there is nothing but light and love. In the Bible these kingdoms are referred to as Paradise.

So what the Bible explains in Genesis is that we have the eternal beings, represented by Adam and Eve, living in the light, living in Paradise. The beings that live in the realms of light know no evil, they know only good. This again means that they know no contrast to good. But sooner or later they have to experience the contrast to good in order to renew their experience of life. If they do not renew their experience of life, life becomes dull. If the beings do not renew their experience of life, God does not renew his, as I have explained in chapter 7. The renewal of the experience of life is absolutely fundamental. In this sense life becomes dull in Paradise because there is no contrast to the light and love. So Adam and Eve cannot forever live in Paradise because they need to have new experiences that Paradise cannot offer.

In Paradise, Adam and Eve are allowed to eat from all the trees of the garden, but not from the Tree of Knowledge. Now why are they not allowed to eat from the Tree of Knowledge? Because the Tree of knowledge represents both light and darkness. There can be no "knowledge" with only light. In order for there to be real knowledge, there has to be darkness also. In order to obtain knowledge you have to see both sides of the coin. He who eats from the tree of knowledge will be like God, "knowing good and evil."

So in Paradise the serpent comes along and tempts Eve to try the fruit from the tree of Knowledge, but Eve refuses, saying that God said, "*You shall not eat of the fruit of the tree which is in the midst of the garden, neither shall you touch it, lest you die.*" However the serpent says "*You will not die. For God knows that when you eat of it your eyes will be opened, and you will be like God, knowing good and evil.*" (Genesis 3:5).

So, tempted by the serpent, Eve ate of the fruit of the Tree of Knowledge, and she convinced Adam to have a bite, too. The consequence was that God threw them both out of Paradise saying to Adam, "*Because you have listened to the voice of your wife, and have eaten of the tree of which I commanded you 'You shall not eat of it' cursed is the ground because of you; in toil you shall eat of it all the days of your life; thorns and thistles it shall bring forth to you; and you shall eat the plants of the field. In the sweat of your face you shall eat bread till you return to the ground, for out of it you were taken; you are dust, and to dust you shall return.*"

To Eve God said, "*I will greatly multiply your pain in childbearing; in pain you shall bring forth children, yet your desire shall be for your husband and he shall rule over you.*"

With this tirade from God, Adam and Eve were thrown out of Paradise. But this was necessary in order for them to learn to distinguish between good and evil. In this sense we see that the serpent was not evil, he was just instrumental in the development of Adam and Eve. They could not stay forever in Paradise and something had to prompt them to leave. They had to come onto the physical plane and experience darkness. They had to forget that they were part of God so that, once forgotten, they could again start the process of remembering their eternal link to God.

On the physical plane the beings have to operate in the heavy physical matter, and here it hurts to think wrongly. To think wrongly means to act in selfish and nonloving ways. When you think wrongly and act in selfish ways you also reap the fruit of your selfish actions. Through the reaping of the selfish seeds you have sown, you yourself get to suffer and through suffering you experience darkness. Through the experience of darkness you obtain the much-needed contrast to the light and at that point you have obtained knowledge of what is good and what is evil. It is through the passage of darkness that the being eats from the Tree of Knowledge. When he has eaten from the Tree of Knowledge, he knows "good and evil" in the same way that God knows this difference, just as the serpent promised. This again shows that the serpent was not an evil and malevolent being, but a divine tool that prompted Adam and Eve to get on with their development.

We see that the expulsion from Paradise was not something that could have been avoided if Eve had been more obedient and had not listened to the serpent. The expulsion from Paradise was absolutely necessary for the sake of the renovation of Adam and Eve's experience of life. The expulsion from Paradise was unavoidable, as it was part of God's plan. The expulsion from Paradise symbolically represents the point in time when the being starts reincarnating again in physical matter after having spent eons of time in the spiritual realms.

The many grim prospects that God promised Adam and Eve when they were outside Paradise are indeed what we are experiencing today. The predictions, "*In the sweat of your face you shall eat bread,*" "*I will greatly multiply your pain in childbearing,*" and "*He shall rule over you*" speak for themselves, but the prediction "*You shall not eat of the fruit of the tree which is in the midst of the garden, neither shall you touch it, lest you die*" (my emphasis) needs an explanation.

God said to Adam and Eve that they would die if they ate from the Tree. But just as the serpent said, they did in fact not die in a traditional sense. They were still alive after they were thrown out of Paradise. They became farmers and they had two sons, Cain and Abel, so they were anything but dead. But what did God mean when he said that they would die, when in fact they did not die?

The death that God mentioned is not the "ordinary death" where our eternal being or "I" sheds its physical vehicle (or as God puts it, *"till you return to the ground, for out of it you were taken; you are dust and to dust you shall return"*). No, the death that God promised Adam and Eve is the so-called cosmic death. The cosmic death means that the being has come so far away from the light or the divine life force or Paradise that *it believes in death instead of in life.* It believes that it is one with its physical body and that when the physical body perishes, the "I" perishes as well. It believes that an absolute and total death exists. It has lost the knowledge that it once had that it is an eternal being and part of God.

This cosmic death is what we are experiencing at this point in time where the majority of the people on Earth believe in death. We think that we are identical with our physical body, that the death of the body means that we cease to exist and that we have only one life. This is to live in a death cult. It is as far away from the truth as we can come; it is the experience of the cosmic death, the peak of the experience of darkness. This is the point at which we find ourselves today. The belief in death instead of in life, the belief that we only have one life is the predicted *"lest you die,"* the immersion in cosmic darkness. This belief in death is a necessary step in our development and it defines the culmination of the experience of cosmic darkness and the point where we are apparently very far away from God. We have reached the pit bottom of darkness when we believe in a total and all-destructive death that rules in a godless universe.

So, in our eternal wanderings through the kingdoms of God we are now passing or have just passed the deepest point of darkness in which we believe in death instead of in life and in which there are wars, killings, and misery. We *had to pass* this deepest point of darkness in order to renew our experience of life. There can be no complete darkness without a belief in total death. Our present belief in death is absolutely fundamental to our descent into darkness.

Now that we have passed the deepest point of darkness, we will again be able to experience light as we are becoming so satiated with darkness that we are hungry for the light. We long for the contrast to war, terror, killings, strife, unrest, famines, assaults, fear, torture, pain, poverty, illness, sorrow, unforgiveness, etc. We long for peace and love. We have had enough darkness and we are so full of it that it makes us loathe it. This darkness is what Jesus predicted when he said, "*And when you hear of wars and tumults, do not be terrified; for this must first take place, but the end will not be at once. Nation will rise against nation, and kingdom against kingdom; there will be great earthquakes, and in various places famines and pestilence, and there will be terrors and great signs from heaven*" (Luke 21:9–10).

The century that we have just left has probably been the culmination of darkness, with two world wars and several other wars; wars so horrible that mankind has never before experienced anything like them. Especially the Second World War with its large-scale slaughter on the battlefields, its concentration camps with torture and gas chambers, its airborne bomb attacks, its Holocaust, and its nuclear bombs was so horrible a contrast to love and light that it is difficult to imagine that we can come further away from the light or steep ourselves more in darkness. We have now become experts in darkness and we know every nook and cranny, every aspect and every inch of it.

We have reached the rock bottom of darkness and are now ready to start our climb toward the light. Our yearning is now toward the light as a contrast to the darkness that we know so well. In our wandering through our eternal existence we are now about to enter the better part of the physical world where we move away from darkness prompted by the new world impulse which will lead us into the real human kingdom and into the spiritual worlds beyond, so that we can complete our present cycle.

Because Adam and Eve needed to experience darkness as a contrast to the divine light, they were thrown out of Paradise. But this was not a punishment, it was a divine measure. The darkness is there for the sole purpose of constituting the contrast to the light of the spiritual realms.

The Unfinished Human Beings of Today

The average man and woman on Earth today are creatures with both animal and human mentalities. As we have seen previously, the feelings of greed, revenge, intolerance, envy, possessiveness, harshness, selfishness, jealousy, anger, irritation, hatred, etc. are thought climates that belong to the animal kingdom. However, through their sufferings many people today have developed thought climates that belong to the real human kingdom such as compassion, mercy, pity, tolerance, forgiveness, understanding, affection, devotion, and love. The more we are influenced by the animal thought climates, the more animal are we and the more we are influenced by the human thought climates the more human are we.

Sooner or later every person will reach the point at which all the animal thought climates have been cleansed from his mentality. At this point we are no longer part animal, part human but we are real human beings. When enough of us have become real human beings all war, strife, and unrest will have been eliminated from the planet and peace will reign. This is the Promised Land that Jesus talks about and it is "*not of this world*," because when Jesus lived this land of peace was only to be found on more advanced planets.

It has already been mentioned that every person on Earth stands at a different level in development. The level that each person stands on depends on when he or she entered the present cycle. So the level of development has nothing to do with being better, the level is defined solely by the time factor. But at the same time every person also stands at the highest point of his development. We are all a result of the trials and tribulations that we have been through during our passage of the cycle. No person can be any different than he is today. Every single one of us is as good as he can be, based on the experiences he has had through his previous lives. Every one of us stands at the peak of his evolution. Through millions of years as animals we have learned to survive through selfish actions, as these are the only actions that will have carried us through the animal kingdom. The animal mentality has been very strongly embedded in our mentality and it takes many, many lives to "unlearn" the animal behavior. We are now in the process of unlearning our animal mentality and this can only be done through suffering, as it is only through suffering that we can develop compassion and love for our neighbor.

No person can help it if he is still very much dominated by animal mentality. That person will one day become a perfect human being, and reproaching that person for his position on the ladder of evolution is as unreasonable as reproaching the apple that is not ripe. As mentioned, we all stand at the highest point of our development and we are as good as we can be. It is only a question of how far we have come in our progress through the cycle. Nobody can be any better than he is today.

The culmination of darkness or Armageddon on Earth is the consequence of the animal mentality linked with a growing intelligence. The "devil" mentality that was the result of this dangerous cocktail is what has led to the depths of darkness that we saw in the previous century with its two world wars and many other smaller wars. The deepest darkness is when everybody is at war with everybody, where men, women, and children are killed, where women are raped, and where whole cities with their cultural treasures are destroyed together with the lives of many, many people. When women are widowed and children are orphaned, when men lose their limbs and have to hump around on wooden legs or sit in wheelchairs, when there is no compassion and no mercy—that is the culmination of darkness.

But that is exactly what the living beings or Adam and Eve set out to experience when they were expelled from Paradise. We saw that in order to renew their experience of life, the living beings that were full of the light, *had to* experience darkness. They needed a contrast to the light. Seen in this perspective the darkness becomes a necessary thing, and although it is unpleasant to experience, it is a divine measure, a blessing. Seen from the point of view of God, there is no evil, there is only the pleasurable good (light) and the unpleasurable good (darkness). The unpleasurable good is a necessary arrangement as it permits the living being to experience the contrast to the light and thus to renew the experience of life. Without contrast life cannot be experienced. The world can only be perfect when the two extremes of darkness and light exist.

The situation that I have just described is the one in which we find ourselves today. We are passing through or may have just passed the deepest point of darkness. We have read how suffering is necessary for us to develop compassion. It has been explained that there is a meaning to wars and suffering and that these unpleasant experiences are not a punishment for our sins. In a cosmic sense there are no sins. There are only actions whose consequences we shall reap, as we reap as we sow. God is not a revengeful, bloodthirsty being that sits up in heaven and takes pleasure in seeing people suffer. God is pure love, and love is the basic tone of the whole universe. There is no hell apart from the hell that we experience in our passing through the darkness of the animal kingdom on the physical plane. There is no other hell. And the darkness of the animal kingdom is as necessary as the light of the divine world. We need both darkness and light in order to experience life. This is the only reason why darkness exists. And here we have the answer to the question that theologians have asked for centuries: How can God be good when at the same time there is so much suffering in the world?

Now we have answered this age-old question.

Martinus sweetly points out that darkness only reigns in one sixth of the cycle, in the animal kingdom. The other five sixths are dominated by light. So darkness is a relatively short experience in our passing through the cycle. The majority of the passage is dominated by light. This fact should give us comfort.

As has been explained, we are approaching the real human kingdom in accordance with the growth of our humanity. Through our own sufferings we develop compassion and love for our neighbor. The more developed our humanity or moral is, the closer are we to the real human kingdom. As we approach the real human kingdom, we start having cosmic glimpses. Getting a cosmic glimpse is really a question of morals. Only when our morals have reached a high enough standard will we get our first cosmic glimpse. As long as our mentality is still dominated by animal thought climates such as greed, revenge, hatred, anger, etc., there are no cosmic glimpses likely to come our way. Martinus calls these vestiges of animal mentality "the guardians of the threshold." We can only pass the threshold to a day-conscious realization of the existence of the spiritual realms when "the guardians" have been eradicated.

The Godless Human Being

As long as we are still under the influence of the energy of instinct we will be satisfied with the explanations offered by the religions. Then we do not necessarily demand a logical explanation to the mystery of life, but we are happy with what the minister preaches. We go to church and get comfort from the words of the minister; we are impressed and full of awe when we see and listen to the ceremonies, the beautifully decorated churches, the candles in the expensive chandeliers, the minister in his fine robe, the playing of the organ, and the chanting of the hymns. All these things convey an elated feeling, a feeling of belonging, and this feeling offers us comfort. We leave the church comforted and assured that there is a meaning somewhere. We do not know what this meaning is, nor do we ask this question. This attitude is still predominant in millions of people today and it is conveyed by the energy of instinct.

As we experience sufferings, our humanity grows. At the same time and in tune with the growing influence of the energy of intelligence our religious instinct degenerates. We see that many people today have lost the ability to believe in the religions. The churches are drawing smaller and smaller congregations. People generally no longer really care about the directions dictated by their religion. Religion is losing its grip. This is due to the decreasing influence of the energy of instinct in people's mentality and the increase of the energy of intelligence.

As the intelligence grows, more and more people become godless because the dogmas of the various religions cannot stand the clear light of logic. Christianity teaches us that God is omniscient, almighty, and all-loving. We are told to believe in this at the same time as we witness an infinite number of unequal fates. Now, the intellectual person who no longer can be seduced by the magic of religion starts to analyze the concept of an omniscient, almighty and all-loving God and he thinks, "If this God is omniscient, then he already knows that the fate of the child in the womb will be unhappy and end in an early death from starvation. But if God know this, then why does he not stop his creation of this child? It would be more loving if that child were not born. If God does not know what fate awaits the child, he is not omniscient. And if he knows what fate awaits the child and does not want to prevent it from having an unhappy fate, he is not all-loving. And if he cannot prevent the child from having such an unhappy fate, he is not almighty." In this way we see how logic can undermine a religious dogma. It can undermine a particular concept of God. Through this and similar analysis, people gradually outgrow the ability to believe and their intellect tells them that there can be no God.

Those who can still believe have a foundation on which their soul, spirit, and morals can rest, they have somewhere to go when they need reassurance and comfort in a time of need. But those people whose intelligence has undermined this foundation have only the materialistic sciences to turn to. They can look for a solution to the mystery of life only on the physical plane. As the materialistic sciences are based only on physical facts, such as a knowledge about all physical matter, weight, length, height, volume, substance, etc., these sciences can in no way constitute even the smallest foundation for the soul, spirit, and morals. So the people who, after their exodus from the religions, have turned to science have nowhere to turn in their time of need. A book about physics or chemistry offers no comfort whatsoever when you have lost a loved one. These people have lost all foundations for their spiritual life; they have nowhere to turn in their time of need; they have become godless materialists. They have come as far away from God as it is mentally possible. They think that the universe is a conglomeration of the chance play of dead forces and that all living beings have come into existence by pure chance. As they only see what can be weighed and measured, they think we are one with our physical body and they believe in an all-destructive death. It is in this death cult that a very large part of Earth's population lives today.

Criminals

The different manifestations of people that reveal the stage of the development they have reached are many and it could be relevant to say a few words about where the skinheads, certain members of motorcycle gangs, members of the Mafia, drug dealers, criminals, murderers, and terrorists stand. Most of these people have most likely only recently reincarnated on Earth from other planets that are further behind in development than the Earth or they have reincarnated into the so-called civilized societies from more "backward" societies on Earth. In the society that these beings came from, it was still the strongest and most powerful man who was admired by everybody. If you killed and raped and dominated your enemies and stole from them, you were a hero. Killing and raping brought you acceptance and admiration. With this mentality, these beings are reincarnated into the civilized societies of Earth. But why do they reincarnate here? They do so because their "natural" planet or society has no more possibilities for growth to offer. In order to learn new lessons, the beings have to step up one grade, so to speak. On their "former" planet they can take the "sixth" grade only one more time, because the societies there have not yet evolved beyond admiring the killing principle. In order to go into the "seventh" grade the war-loving beings have to change schools, so to speak. As the Earth has reached a level of development at which the natural behavior of these beings is no longer accepted, the Earth is a good school for them. They then reincarnate here in order to start "unlearning" killing, revenge, rape, stealing, etc. As these activities are not accepted social behavior in civilized societies, they have to reincarnate in such a society in order to start learning a new rule of conduct.

But the lesson that these beings have come to learn here is an expensive lesson for the "natural" inhabitants of the Earth to teach them. The "natural" inhabitants of the Earth are those who have lived for several incarnations here and who represent the general level of civilization. On the Earth special arrangements have to be made for the "newcomers," such as extra help in schools, special schools, extra social services, or special institutions. If all these fail there are the prisons. If the "newcomers" are incarcerated for their crimes, they do not understand this, because what they did was considered heroic where they came from. In the societies they came from it was the powerful person who could dominate and subjugate others who was admired and respected. They still feel that killing and raping is the "right" thing to do and the natural way to behave. But now they are looked down upon and despised. But this is the only way in which these people can start learning that their "old" social pattern was no good and that it has to be "unlearned," so that they can begin to learn humanity and learn to love their neighbor instead of persecuting him. These people will begin to suffer from their old mentality and thus gradually their humanity is born.

How to Accelerate Our Own Development

Now, we have seen that nobody can be any better than they are today and that nobody can help it if they are not advanced. This is true. But it is also true that at our present stage we can do a lot when we become aware of traces of animal mentality that we still have left because we can begin to avoid the animal thought climates. We can start to channel our mentality toward expressions of compassion and tolerance and love. The only way to be good at something is to practice. The more we practice humanity, the better we get at manifesting it. If our animal thought climates never get used they will perish and die. What we do not use will die from lack of attention. So if we concentrate on doing good and helping others we will shorten our way toward the light.

As individuals we cannot save the world, we can only save ourselves. Providence will take care of the world; that is not our job. But we can help Providence by cleansing our own mentality and by promoting peace, equality, and love.

Once we become aware of our manifestations of animal mentality we can actively do something to avoid these. We can start thinking nice, loving, positive, and forgiving thoughts instead of greedy, hateful, and negative thoughts. Every time a hateful or negative thought crops up we can mentally smack ourselves over the fingers. We can start sending loving thoughts to people that we may not like so much. When we have thought lovingly about people that we did not like we gradually stop not liking them. The more we concentrate on thinking positive thoughts, the more we concentrate on weeding out our animal mentality, the better we will get at this. We have to practice. The more we practice, the better we get.

It is the animal mentality that sabotages all friendship, all positive cooperation, all peace and harmony. In order to start weeding out our animal mentality we have to be aware that we have it. We can start this process by taking stock of the strength of the animal mentality still reigning in our mental setup. This is the first step. We can think about the situations in which we display animal thought climates and be honest with ourselves. Now we can think what we want to do the next time we find ourselves in a situation in which we would normally display for instance anger, irritability, or jealousy. We can prepare an alternative reaction in our mind. We can mentally practice manifesting this alternative reaction. We may not be able to manifest this alternative reaction the first time we find ourselves in a critical situation, but then maybe we can the next time or the next. We have to make a start and we must not be hard on ourselves if we do not succeed the first time, but it is taking the first step and practicing that will make us succeed. If we do nothing, the process will take much longer.

We can promote our own exit of the animal kingdom by show-ing tolerance toward other people. We should look upon other liv-ing beings as "works of art in progress." We are all in the process of being transformed from animals into real human beings. If we meet a being that still exhibits animal tendencies, we should re-member that we have an unfinished being before us and should treat this being with tolerance and understanding just as we would show tolerance and understanding toward a child. To the degree that a being exhibits animal mentality, to the same degree is it unfinished. When we are faced with people who show animal ten-dencies, we should treat them with tolerance and forgiveness and thus demonstrate a different pattern of reaction than their own. If we can do that, we have not only demonstrated that we are able to curb our own animal tendencies, but we have also demonstrated that an alternative pattern of reaction is possible. And hopefully this alternative pattern of reaction will be noticed and give food for thought and thus it may help change others. We can all start practicing tolerance.

Martinus points out that "unlearning" our animal mentality and practicing humanity and love is our meaning of life right now.

There is a very important side effect to practicing humanity and positive thinking. We improve our health. Martinus says, "*Our thoughts are the highest outer force of nature for the micro beings of our organism.*" (*Kosmos* no. 2, 1993). Our thoughts are the outer force of nature for our cells and with the quality of our thought matter we attract our micro life. Our thoughts constitute the "spir-it moving over the face of the waters" of the universe of our body.

When we think thoughts of a killing nature we attract micro organisms of a corresponding killing nature, and when we think kind and loving thoughts we attract microorganisms of a loving nature through the working of the universal law of attraction and repulsion. When we think loving thoughts, we attract health-creat-ing microorganisms to our body.

Furthermore, Martinus says that our thoughts are the same as our life force. This means that the electrical impulse of a thought is life force. Thoughts are life force. In this way the thoughts become the main decisive factor of both physical and mental health of the individual. The negative and hateful thought climates of the animal kingdom are very harmful for our cells or microcosmos at our present stage. A display of anger sends impulses through our organism of the same dark energy as the one that kills—the energy of gravity. When we display a fit of anger we poison the environment in which our cells live. The more anger and negative thoughts we experience, the more we pollute our inner environment. We know that a very negative person is much more susceptible to developing an ulcer, a nervous breakdown, or even cancer than a very positive person.

Loving and positive thoughts send waves of sunshine through our whole body. If a person experiences something very uplifting and joyful, this energy also sends impulses through the body, but these impulses convey only health and joy. Martinus says, "*Each thought or impulse that goes through the mentality of the being sends constructive or destructive impulses through the body of the being depending on the quality of the thought impulse*" (*Kosmos* no. 2, 1993). In this way Martinus tells us that our thoughts are much more important to our health than we may think. In a sense we _are_ what we think. If our thoughts are positive, we are healthier than if they are negative. Our thoughts can make us ill or well because they constitute the outer environment of our cells. When the environment is positive the cells are happy and pay us back with good health, and when the environment is negative the cells live in darkness and pay us back with illness. Our thoughts bring either sunshine or thunder to our cells, and the cells react to these changes in environment in exactly the same way as we react to changes in our environment. In this way Martinus also tells us that our cells do have an experience of life. Our cells have an X 1 or "I," an X 2 or creative ability, and an X 3 or body just as all living beings have. Our cells have a consciousness at some level of development. It may not be a consciousness as advanced as ours, but it is a consciousness nonetheless. Our cells have a life experience and this experience is influenced by our thoughts.

Avoiding dark thoughts such as hatred, bitterness, anger, or irritability is much more important for our health than we may think. Dark and negative thoughts can make us ill. Laughter and positive thoughts can make us well. Our thoughts are a very decisive factor in our health.

A healthy body will not only be beneficial to us in this life, but it will lay the foundation for our health in future lives, as we shall see in the next chapter about the principle of reincarnation.

12

The Principle of Reincarnation

A Logical Development

Reincarnation is a universal principle. Every living being reincarnates, be it particles, atoms, molecules, cells, organs, plants, animals, humans, planets, suns, etc. As the being reincarnates, it also slowly develops from life to life. This development follows a logical progression in tune with our advance through the spiral cycle. This means that when we are, for instance, humans, we will reincarnate as humans in the next, and in the next, and in the next life, etc. For each life our bodily looks may evolve slightly, we may outgrow illnesses, we may develop talents from one life to another, gradually our bodily structure will be finer, but our bodies will have to follow a logical line of development. We cannot be a human being in this life and a rat or a whale in our next. That is impossible, because in order to create a specific body, we have to have talents for the creation of that specific body. We develop and refine our talents for bodily creation as we progress through the cycle. We cannot just create a body out of the blue. We have to have some "tools" in order to create a body and our talents are those "tools." The body that we have today has mainly been created by ourselves through the accumulation of talents for body creation that we have been developing through practice during many, many lives. The genes of our parents play only a minor role, as we shall see later. Because our talents know "only" how to make a body like the one we have today, the body that we will have in our next life will resemble the one we have now, with the exception of a few traits we will take from our parents.

Let us take a closer look at reincarnation.

The "I" Is a Field of Energy

According to Martinus the living being has a double analysis. It is partly a being of physical matter and partly a being of spirit. The being of spirit is its true identity. The being of physical matter is only a temporary state. Martinus points out that we have various bodies apart from our physical body, because we have a body for each basic energy. Our physical body is our body of gravity, but as we have six other bodies consisting of ray-formed matter, we do not cease to exist when the physical body dies. When the physical body dies, our day-consciousness is transferred to our spiritual bodies and we live on in these bodies of ray-formed matter.

These spiritual bodies are primarily defined by the level of unfolding of the basic energies at the point in development each individual has reached. The energies unfold according to their eternal fluctuations depicted on symbol number 12. Out of these energies the "I" creates its bodies with all the individual characteristics that the "I" has cultivated and accumulated during its many lives. We have to understand that the creation of bodies takes place as an automatic function, as something we can do without consciously knowing how in the same way as all our other bodily organic functions are also automatic.

The energies that define the individual form a field of energy, and this field "sits" inside and around the physical body. It is this field that can be observed in our aura. This field of energy is indestructible.

The Creation of Consciousness

Our consciousness has been created through an accumulation of experiences during our passage of the cycle. In the plant we witness the creation of the first feeble forms of consciousness—the plant could vaguely sense what was going on. Through the influence of the outer forces such as rain and drought, cold and heat, the plant gradually becomes more and more conscious on the physical plane. Once it has developed into an animal it has a whole range of physical senses at its disposal with which it can experience life on the physical plane. For each physical life the animal adds experience to experience and thus it builds its consciousness. In this way we can say that our consciousness is a result of a huge accumulation of experiences and learning. All these experiences are embedded in our eternal structure (X 2) in the shape of ray-formed matter and they accompany us from life to life. At our present stage we may not be able to access all the information embedded in our consciousness directly, but still it is there. We generally cannot remember former lives (although many young children can), but still our former lives are with us in the shape of our talents, our moral capacity, our tastes and dispositions, our patterns of reaction, our anxieties and phobias, our likes and dislikes, and our sense of self. Our consciousness is a field of information, and as this field of information consists of ray-formed matter or energy matter it is indestructible and it accompanies us from life to life. The field of information, which constitutes our consciousness, is the core of our "I," it is our eternal and primary being, it is who we really are. The physical body is just an instrument for the eternal "I." We create our physical bodies according to the information we have stored in our field. Our physical bodies are a reflection of the information that lies stored in the field. It is on the basis of the accumulation of information we have stored in our energy field that we create our physical bodies.

All Talents Are a Result of Practice

In order to account for the accumulation of information that lies in the human energy field or consciousness we could look at something that forms an essential part of who we are: talents. Talents are abilities we have, things that we are good at, special gifts. The general notion is that all talents are embedded in our genes, so consequently we inherit our talents from our parents. However, we very often see that children exhibit talents that none of their parents have. A child may, for instance, show great talents for learning foreign languages even though none of the parents have this ability. The parents can only speak the vernacular, but their child is fluent in, say, English, Spanish, and German apart from the vernacular and has learned these languages with great ease. The parents really cannot explain where this talent comes from, and they look to their ancestors to find somebody who could have supplied the gene that gave rise to the talent in their child. But among the ancestors there was nobody who spoke a foreign language and the question remains a mystery.

Even more mystifying are so-called "wonder children," or child prodigies. These children exhibit extraordinary talents and a very high IQ. In most cases the IQ of such a child prodigy is much higher than that of their parents and nobody can explain how a child can have a number of talents that none of the parents, have and an IQ that is considerably higher than that of their parents.

Until now it has been largely accepted that all our talents are based in the genes and that consequently we are a result of a combination of the genes of our parents. But this is not so, says Martinus. The genes only form the basic physical material for the creation of a new body. This basic material is practically identical for all mammals. The Human Genome Project[1] has stated that there are only three hundred genes that distinguish a human from a mouse. This makes it quite obvious that the genes alone cannot account for who we are.

From where then do we get the talents that we have, when these talents do not coincide with those of our parents? How can a specific talent suddenly crop up? Well, it cannot. The talents that we have, we get from ourselves, so to speak, and we only have the talents because we have worked hard to get them. Every talent that we have is a result of practice, a practice that we have carried out and perfected during former lives.

We are not just a result of a mere combination of parental genes. A gene is nothing but a recipe for a protein. How can a number of recipes for proteins create a complicated body and create consciousness and talents? Our sciences are at a loss to explain how this can happen. The genes may give rise to certain illnesses and to blue or brown eyes and black or fair hair, but how about all the other abilities we have that are not based in the genes? Where is the gene for playing the piano, where is the gene for cooking, where is the gene for humor, for fixing cars, for playing football, for doing business, for caring for children, for writing novels, for drawing pictures? These abilities are not in the genes, but still we have them. How can we account for these abilities when they are not in the genes and when we clearly exhibit them as an intricate part of who we are even though we have never been taught how to perform them?

The question of where talents come from and how the process of embryo genesis is controlled and why some cells suddenly "decide" to become brain cells while others "decide" to become lung cells is something that our materialistic sciences cannot explain. How consciousness is created from a number of recipes for protein is another thing that our sciences cannot explain. They cannot explain this because they do not take the existence of the spiritual plane into account. But once we accept that the spiritual plane exists and that we have a body of spiritual matter, we have a basis for explaining how a body can be created and how reincarnation exists and why there is no death. We can then also explain how consciousness can exist as nonphysical matter and thus we can account for the existence of our own consciousness, not as something created from two sets of genes, but as something that is ours and ours alone and that accompanies us from life to life.

The "I" of the individual, the "I" that makes *you* the person you are, is not a mere result of the genes of your parents. The "I" is what gives you a strong feeling of individuality, and it is this "I" together with its combination of talents that are embedded in the supraconsciousness (X 2) that reincarnates into a new body at the time of fertilization. The "I" is eternal, and with the talents that the "I" has accumulated through practice during life after life, the "I" creates a new body in its mother's womb after fertilization. We shall look at this process later.

Martinus accounts for the existence of talents in the following way: We all know that there is only one way to be good at something and that is to practice. We can only become good at playing the piano if we practice. The more we practice, the better we get. Martinus explains that there are three stages of learning.

The first stage is the beginner's stage, the theoretical stage, when the being is not very good at something. This stage Martinus calls the A stage. At the A stage we have to receive instruction and concentrate hard to do what we are trying to learn. Let us say that we are trying to learn to play the piano. At the A stage we are clumsy and disorientated and every tune takes a lot of concentration. We are very uncertain about how to play and each step of progress requires a lot of hard work.

At the next stage, the intermediate or B stage, we have reached a point where the process is better controlled and we no longer have to concentrate all that hard. We can play the piano with a fair amount of ease. We feel more comfortable about playing and we slowly start to enjoy it.

The C stage is reached only after a lot of practice. At the C or final stage we master the playing of the piano to a degree of perfection. We have become virtuosos and we really enjoy playing. We do not even have to think about what we are doing, the playing just flows automatically through our fingers. Playing the piano has become an automatic function. We do not consciously know what we are doing; the playing just flows through us on its own accord. When we have reached the C stage the things we do are felt to be *so* easy that we cannot understand how they could ever have felt difficult.

How does this process work? Martinus explains that when we practice something, a small talent kernel is formed in our supraconsciousness. This talent kernel is very much like a seed; it is a small individual body of spiritual matter, a spiritual seed. The talent kernel is formed as soon as we start practicing a certain skill, and the more we practice, the bigger the talent kernel gets. In the end, when our perfection has reached the C stage, the talent kernel takes over the whole process of performing the act at hand. We can say that with practice the talent kernel has developed to become a beautiful flowering plant. All our automatic bodily functions such as our bowel movements, our breathing, heartbeat, menstruation cycle, etc., have become automatic functions in exactly the same way.

An example could be our ability to walk. When we walk, we do not have to think: now I put my right leg forward and now I put my left leg forward. In fact we do not even consciously know which muscles to activate in order to walk. When we walk we do not have to think at all. We just walk and the actual coordination of the muscles is completely controlled by the talent kernel.

All abilities that we have are preserved in a talent kernel, and as these are embedded in the supraconsciousness, which forms part of our eternal structure as shown on page 74, these talents accompany the individual from life to life.

There are innumerable examples of this. The example of Mozart is probably the best known. Ever since Mozart as a four-year-old sat down at the piano and played a tune, the world has wondered how this was possible, as he had not yet learned to play in his life as Mozart. But the explanation is simply that he had learned in a former life and that playing the piano had already reached the C stage in his supraconsciousness.

Some children are able to read a book already at the age of four, even before anybody has taught them how to read. The parents then think that the child is a "wonder child" with an extraordinary intelligence, but the explanation is simply that the child already knows how to read from his or her last life. The ability to read is embedded in the talent kernels and it is the accumulation of talents that is responsible for the early reading.

As talents are a result of practice, we have to have been in a position to practice them somehow. What can this position be other than a former life?

Several Bodies Are Used in a Single Physical Life

But there are even more obvious exemplifications of reincarnation. In front of our very eyes we see the principle of reincarnation manifested in the transformation of the butterfly.

The butterfly starts as a larva. After some time the larva transforms into a cocoon. And then after some more time the butterfly crawls out of the cocoon.

The butterfly makes use of three different bodies in one and the same life: the body of a larva, the body of a cocoon, and the body of a butterfly. It reincarnates from the larva into the cocoon and then into the butterfly. It is still the same individual, but it uses three different bodies in one lifetime. This is the principle of reincarnation exemplified for all to see.

In an almost identical way we also reincarnate from one body to the next in one physical lifetime. This reincarnation is, however, partial and not complete as in the case of the butterfly or when we "die." Try to look at the three photos of Martinus in this book.

In the first photo on page 21 he is eleven years old, in the next on page 25 he is thirty years old, and in the last on page 31 he is sixty-eight years old. When we look at the three photos there is no doubt that we are looking at three different bodies: the body of a child, the body of a young man, and the body of a middle-aged man. We know that most of our cells live approximately three months. Then they die and are replaced by new cells. In this way our body is in a constant process of renewal. All the cells in the body that we have today are different from the ones we had a year ago. This means that all our physical material has been changed. Still we are the same individual. This means that our "I" has currently reincarnated into various different bodies throughout one and the same life. This reincarnation is partial as we do not, as in the case of the butterfly or when we "die," exchange all the material of the body at one and the same time. But the principle of reincarnation still applies here. As the physical matter of our body is under a constant process of renewal, our "I" reincarnates into a new physical body on a regular basis.

The Process of Reincarnation

When we are "between lives" or discarnate in the spiritual realms, we do at a certain point in time wish to reincarnate so that we can continue our development on the physical plane. There are still things we have to learn, there is still animal mentality to unlearn, so we have to go "back to school," so to speak. We have to go back to the heavy physical plane where it hurts to think wrongly. There are certain things that we have to learn, and these things can only be learned on the physical plane. So even if the fate that awaits us is an unhappy and miserable fate, we have agreed to it ourselves, because this fate was the only way in which we could evolve. So both the famous millionaire and the starving child in Africa have chosen their fates themselves. They have chosen to come "down" to learn exactly the lesson that they most needed in order to get on with their development.

As the development will lead the beings out of the animal kingdom and into the real human kingdom of light and love, it is in everybody's best interest to get this unpleasant but necessary part over with. Therefore the discarnate beings agree to come into the physical world to experience both happy and unhappy fates. The unhappy fates will teach the being compassion and love for his neighbor, so although the unhappy fates may not be pleasant to experience, they are more enhancing for growth than happy ones. It is through suffering that our humanity is born.

The discarnate being on the spiritual plane will, when the time comes for it to reincarnate, automatically be drawn to the two people who will become its future parents. The universal law of attraction and repulsion is at work here. This law determines that energies on similar wavelengths are attracted to each other. This again means that the discarnate being is attracted to precisely the lovemaking couple that fits its own mental and bodily setup.

All incarnation into physical matter takes place from the kingdom of memory or bliss such as it was explained in chapter 11. This applies whether we reincarnate after only a "short" visit to the spiritual realms "between lives" or whether we restart reincarnation in physical matter after having lived for millions of years as a spiritual being. In the kingdom of memory the discarnate being recalls its former incarnations. Because the discarnate being experiences its former incarnations as "gold copies," it starts to long toward the physical plane once again. The memories of the previous incarnations as gold copies are experienced as bliss, and this is an ecstatic energy. As this energy is on the same wavelength as the energy of ecstasy emanating from a lovemaking couple on the physical plane, contact is established, as similar wavelengths attract each other.

During the act of lovemaking the two people involved in this act produce a very high amount of emanation of a highly spiritual energy. This highly spiritual energy is felt as the culmination of sensual pleasure or bliss and its cosmic interpretation is that it is the very spirit of God or the "highest fire." It is this "highest fire" that is experienced during orgasm.

This high charge of energy of bliss attracts the energy field of the discarnate being who is ripe for reincarnation. The remembrance of former incarnations recalled as "gold copies" sends a high charge of ecstatic energy out from the discarnate being. This ecstatic energy from the discarnate being and the ecstatic energy from the lovemaking couple are on the same wavelength and the two energies are attracted to each other and merge. Through the gateway that the energy of ecstasy opens for the discarnate being, the "I" of this being then incarnates in the fertilized egg in the womb of the woman and thus begins the creation of an embryo, which with time will grow into a fully finished physical organism.

Martinus explains that once fertilization has taken place the creation of the new physical body in the womb of the mother is completely controlled by the discarnate being who supplies not only the life force or the electromagnetic field of the new body but also the "know-how" for bodily creation, its talents, and consciousness. As soon as fertilization has taken place, the talent kernels of the discarnate being take over control of the process of bodily creation. The discarnate being "knows how" to create a body, as it has done so millions of times before. This knowledge lies embedded in the talent kernels of the discarnate being and it has become an automatic function. The looks, the talents, the abilities of the new being soon to be born are all mainly defined by the discarnate being. Martinus points out that at our present stage about 40 percent of our physical and mental characteristics are defined by our own talents and we take 30 percent from each of the parents. As we develop toward the perfect stage of the real human being, the percentage defined by the parental genes diminishes, so the closer we get to the real human kingdom, the smaller a role will the parental genes play and the more will our own talents define our physical bodies. This also means that we have many traits that are the same from one life to the next. So in our next life we will have a body that looks much like the body that we had in our last incarnation. The discarnate being can "only" create a body according to the level of perfection that its talents have reached. Slowly it develops its talents from life to life through practice and new talents are added, but generally speaking the discarnate being can "only" create a body quite similar to the one it had in its latest incarnation, perhaps with a few embellishments added and taking the necessary percentage from the parental genes into account.

Martinus emphasizes that we have to understand that when children have the same or similar characteristics and talents as their parents, these have not been inherited from the parents, but these had already been more or less developed by the being itself in previous lives. It is the universal law of attraction and repulsion that determines that we are born to parents that resemble us in certain aspects. But most of the qualities and abilities that a person has are the results of his practice and level of perfection developed through former lives and not something that he simply gets for

THE PRINCIPLE OF REINCARNATION

free from his parents.

It is the being's own inheritance from former lives that causes it to be attracted to parents who have qualities similar to its own, and through this it generally comes to resemble its parents in respect to talents, looks, and gifts. We have to understand that this process takes place in an automatic way through the attraction that similar wavelengths have on each other. The parents have a specific combination of energies in their mental and physical setup and these energies operate on a specific wavelength. The discarnate being is automatically attracted to parents who have an energy combination operating on a wavelength similar to its own.

The genes supplied by the mother and the father form the physical basic material for the discarnate being to use in the process of reincarnation. From the pool of genes the discarnate being selects which genes come into play in the new child. This selection is done on the basis of the accumulated talents of the "I" who is about to reincarnate. It is the "I" with its accumulated talents for bodily creation that activates and deactivates certain genes, thus creating its specific DNA code. It is the "I" which controls and initiates the cells differentiation of the fertilized egg, thus telling which cells become brain cells, lung cells, heart cells, spine cells, muscle cells, etc. And finally it is the discarnate being, which supplies consciousness to the new child. From where would the egg and sperm cell get hold of a consciousness to put into the new child if the discarnate being did not participate in the process of embryo genesis? No new child could come into existence without the participation of the discarnate being. The egg and the sperm cell cannot do the job alone. And because the discarnate being orchestrates the process of embryogenesis and selects which genes come into play, the new body will resemble the body the being had in its last incarnation. It will fundamentally and essentially be the same being, now in a new body with a few new traits it has taken from its new parents.

Identical Twins

I have just explained that each individual looks very much like "himself" as a result of the talents he has for bodily creation, developed through many lives.

You may now logically ask how identical twins can look alike. Identical twins are two beings that, through their mutual attraction developed during various lives, have decided to incarnate together. They may have karmic ties that bind them together or they may have lessons to learn that they can best learn together. Nothing happens by chance, and when two beings decide to reincarnate together it is for a reason.

Although identical twins look alike, they are not exact "copies" of each other and they don't have identical fingerprints. One twin may have diseases that the other does not have, so there may be different genetic setups even though identical twins mostly are genetic doubles. But they are certainly not doubles on a personality level. They may look alike, but as persons they are not the same. They have two different personalities. This fact demonstrates that they are not "just" copies of each other. They are two different individuals with similar looks. At birth and during the early years the twins look very much the same, but once they have passed the age of thirty, when they start on their present incarnation as will be explained later in this chapter, they begin to look more and more different.

Martinus explains that the genetic material predominates mostly in the early years of a physical life. A person may resemble his or her parents considerably while young, but after the age of thirty the genetic material has more or less outlived its mission and the person looks more and more "like himself." It is fairly easy to tell the difference between identical twins over the age of thirty. This point is also confirmed by Ian Stevenson in his book *Where Reincarnation and Biology Intersect* where he not only confirms that identical twins show many different character traits but also that their "identical looks" wear off as they grow and they become much more easily distinguishable in later life.

Artificial Insemination

We saw that the energy of ecstasy that emanated from the lovemaking couple during intercourse "opened the door" for the discarnate being to incarnate. However, we know that fertilization can also take place even though there is very little energy of ecstasy present in the act of lovemaking as in the case of rape, or even when there is no act of lovemaking at all as in the case of artificial insemination. In these cases, however, there is enough energy of ecstasy present in the sperm cells to allow fertilization. At the moment of ejaculation the male of the species discharges a considerable amount of ecstatic energy. This energy is transferred to the sperm cells that conserve enough of this to allow fertilization to take place even after some time, indeed even after deep freezing. So fertilization can take place when only one of the parties experiences the "highest fire."

Incarnation of Beings from Higher Realms

Let me just mention that when beings from higher realms reincarnate on Earth such as the case has been with Jesus and Martinus, the process of reincarnation is exactly the same as described above. No "Holy Spirit" was needed to fertilize the women who were to become their mothers.[2] The sperm cells of ordinary males would do. The process is anyway controlled by the discarnate being about to reincarnate. So Joseph was the father of Jesus just as Lars Larsen was the father of Martinus. The reason why the "Holy Spirit" has been proclaimed to have fathered the child Jesus is that at the time when Jesus was born, nobody would have been able to understand why Jesus was so special if his father had "only" been Joseph. So Providence issued the rumor that the Holy Spirit had something to do with it. In that way it was easier to understand why Jesus could be called the Son of God and why he could perform miracles. It was anyway the "I" of the advanced being Jesus that determined who he was, and consequently he stood at a level high above the people among whom he had incarnated.

But Jesus also had to take some traits from his physical parents Mary and Joseph, and these traits were responsible for his less advanced manifestations. For instance, in the garden of Gethsemane, the night before he was arrested, Jesus showed signs of fear for the fate that awaited him. Jesus knew that he was going to be crucified, he had agreed to this fate before he reincarnated, but he now had second thoughts. He thought about the suffering that his microcosmos would have to go through and to some extent he feared his crucifixion. He said to his disciples, *"My soul is very sorrowful, even to death; remain here, and watch with me." And going a little farther he fell on his face and prayed, 'My Father, if it be possible, let this cup pass from me; nevertheless, not as I will, but as thou wilt.' And he came to the disciples and found them sleeping; and he said to Peter, 'So could you not watch with me one hour? Watch and pray that you may not enter into temptation; the spirit indeed is willing, but the flesh is weak.' Again, for the second time, he went away and prayed, 'My Father, if this cannot pass unless I drink it, thy will be done.'* (Matthew 26:38–42).

In this we see how the unfinished sides of his mentality, inherited from his parents, take hold of him and make him experience fear. Had Jesus not been under the influence of the less advanced traits from his parents, he would have felt no fear. In his own right he stood high above any feelings of fear *("The spirit is willing")*. But because he was also a being of flesh and blood and because *"the flesh is weak,"* it made him ask God to *"let this cup pass from me."* But we see how Jesus conquered this crisis by putting his fate in the hands of God with the words, *"Thy will be done."*

How Long Are We Discarnate?

How long we stay on the spiritual plane between physical lives depends on how and when we died the last time. If we have died as children, we reincarnate quite quickly again, maybe after only a few years or less. A soldier who has died in war will typically reincarnate after seven years. If we have died young, say we were newly married or had just given birth to young children, we may long very much to go back to the physical plane to finish our unfinished business. We then reincarnate again fairly quickly.

If we have lived a whole life and have died of old age "full of days," normally around seventy years will pass between each reincarnation, but this varies a lot and is quite individual and in accordance with our desires.

When we have fulfilled the physical part of the spiral circle and have become perfect human beings in the image and likeness of God, we no longer need to reincarnate and millions of years will pass before we feel a longing for the physical plane again. We will then live as a spiritual being for millions of years. But at a certain point we will again need to reenter physical matter in order to renew our experience of life. This point is when we are "expulsed from Paradise," as we have seen in chapter 11. We will then enter the physical plane in a new cycle one level up from our previous cycle, as already explained in chapter 8.

Where we stay and what happens when we are discarnate will be explained in chapter 15.

Guardian Angels on the Physical Plane

The parents have, through their act of lovemaking, not only created the physical setup of the conditions for a discarnate being to reincarnate in physical matter, but they will normally also accept the role of "guardian angels" for the being, as it is completely helpless on the physical plane as long as its physical body is still young and unfinished. Through this we see how everything has been divinely organized, so that the discarnate being can pass happily through the gateway from the spiritual to the physical plane. Normally the being is received on the physical plane by a couple of loving "guardian angels" in the shape of its parents, who will watch over it until it has reached the time when it can fend for itself.

It is a well-known fact that babies, puppies, kittens, and all other newborn mammals look incredibly cute and endearing. This,

Martinus says, is because they still retain a sheen from the spiritual kingdom of bliss, which they have just left. This spiritual kingdom of bliss "shines through" and still has an effect on the looks of the young during the first years of their lives and this divine sheen makes them so endearing to their surroundings that they cannot help being loved and looked after.

Abortion

We saw that the process of creating a physical body is taken over at the time of fertilization by the discarnate being. We also saw how it was the "I" of the discarnate being that gave the embryo its life force and consciousness. This means that the discarnate being already incarnates in the womb at the moment of fertilization. If the embryo is aborted, the discarnate being is forced back to the spiritual plane. Through this process the discarnate being loses life force. It now furthermore has to wait on the spiritual plane for new parents that fit its mental setup to appear. In this way its development is halted and it cannot get on with its progress. A possibility for growth has been "missed," not only for the child but also for the parents. After a while it again has to put its talent kernels to work to create a new body.

Martinus points out that aborting an embryo is an unnatural thing to do. The persons who were to be the guardian angels of the new being on the physical plane, the persons who were designated to love and protect the new being, become its murderers. Martinus says that abortion can only be justified if the life of the mother is at stake. Then and only then can abortion be justified, as the life of the mother should be spared in preference to that of the child. The mother's development is already ongoing whereas the development of the child can be recommenced. In all other cases abortion should be avoided because its karmic consequences are serious for everybody involved.

Deep Freezing

The principle of reincarnation is also at play when we deep-freeze our food. When we bring the temperature down to minus 38 degrees Celsius we create an artificial mineral matter in, say, a steak. The steak becomes hard as rock. At that temperature we force the "I"s that incarnated the cells of the steak out of the physical matter. The "I"s of the cells that incarnated the steak now have to seek incarnation in other (unfrozen) matter where they can continue their physical lives. When all the "I"s have left, there is only the dead bodies or corpses of the cells left in the steak. As these have been forced into mineral matter where there is only a minimum of vibration or movement, they will keep for a considerable time. But as long as the steak is frozen, its cells are dead and lifeless.

But then when the steak is defrozen, the cells become alive again. This has led our scientists to believe that the cells were not dead, but only dormant. However, the original cells in the steak do die when exposed to subzero temperatures. What happens is that new discarnate cell "I"s reincarnate in the steak as soon as there are living conditions there, that is as soon as a normal temperature has been reached. But the cells that reincarnate in the steak are cells of a slightly inferior quality than the original cells. That is the reason why food that has been frozen tastes slightly different from fresh food. It tastes different because it is different "I"s with different vibrations that now inhabit the cells.

This process works only on the cell level. You cannot deep-freeze a person and then expect a discarnate being to reincarnate into the body once it is defrosted. The human body is much too complicated a structure to allow this to be possible.

Repetition of Former Lives

A child that is born repeats its former lives until it is thirty years old. This explains why boys play soldiers and Indians and like to shoot with guns while girls play with dolls and play "house." They repeat their former lives in which they were soldiers or warriors or housewives with young children. Children at play are totally absorbed and mostly totally happy in their replay of former lives and tend to forget their present surroundings completely.

When you watch children play, it is possible to get a very accurate clue to who they were in former lives. Their choice of play, their dispositions and inclinations tell you very clearly who they were before.

The fact that children repeat former lives during childhood also explains why some children display a very primitive behavior. If they do they may be repeating a life in which they lived as, say, primitive hunters. This does certainly not mean that they will be "primitive" when they grow up, it only tells something about the life they repeat at the time. Childhood play shows what the children did in former lives.

In this connection it is completely futile to try to persuade boys to play with dolls or girls to play with guns as has been tried in Denmark in the holy name of sexual equality. At some point in the 1970s it was supposed that sexual injustice could be eliminated and sexual equality be obtained if boys and girls from a young age were told to play with the same kind of toys. So the boys were forced to spend endlessly boring afternoons dressing and undressing dolls so that they could learn to become politically correct adult males. I think this practice has now been abandoned, mostly because it didn't seem to work, which is not surprising.

It is best if the child is left alone when he or she plays, so that the former lives can be duly repeated without interference, as the repetition of former lives is the necessary preparation to the present incarnation in physical matter, which only starts at the age of thirty.

In our twenties we start repeating our former marriages. We date a lot of different boys or girls and normally we change partners quite often. This is perfectly logical as the twenties is a period when we are still repeating former lives. We repeat our last life at the end of our twenties. The repetition of the last life takes a fairly long time, maybe a few years. The further away from our present life we come, the shorter the repetition of a life is. In the womb as an embryo we repeat our whole bodily evolution through time. As a child we repeat the lives quickly, but the older we get the repetition of each life takes longer and longer.

It is only when we are thirty that we start on our present incarnation. When we are thirty, we start doing what we came here to do in this lifetime. We saw that Martinus had his initiation when he was thirty. We also know that Jesus was thirty when his mission started (when full cosmic consciousness was opened in his mentality during the transformation on the mount). As we know Jesus' mission was short, as he was only thirty-three years old when he was crucified.

Let me just mention in this connection that Martinus says that the most productive years in the life of a human being are from fifty to seventy. At the age of fifty the person has accumulated a lot of experience and it is in the years from fifty to seventy that the person can best put this experience to work, can be productive and useful. If the person has children, these have then in general grown up, and the person has time to concentrate on what he came to do on the physical plane. In this connection it seems completely illogical that many people are considered "finished" and have problems finding new employment if they are over fifty. It is in the years from fifty to seventy that a person can best contribute to society and bring his life to fruition.

Addiction

Reincarnation is a fundamental principle. All life reincarnates. Also our cells.

When we live a healthy life, we attract discarnate cells that correspond to our specific combination of energies. Again it is the law of attraction and repulsion that is at play. These cells Martinus calls our normal cells. These cells convey our normal health. But if we, through the constant intake of drugs or alcohol, alter the conditions of life in our organism, the "I"s of our normal cells can no longer reincarnate there, because there are no longer the right life conditions for them. They then reincarnate in beings where life conditions are suitable for their level of development.

But what happens then in our organism? When living conditions in our body are no longer suitable for our normal cells because of, say, a daily intake of alcohol, then "I"s of cells of a lower and coarser quality will reincarnate in our body. These cell "I"s have a more robust disposition than our normal cells and they can stand the daily influx of alcohol. The more we drink, the coarser the cells become. After some time of alcoholic addiction the cells that incarnate in our body are really sturdy ones, so sturdy that the alcohol is their life sustenance. They can only exist if there is alcohol. The robust alcohol-loving cells gradually take over the control of the body and the first thing they do when the body wakes up in the morning is to express a collective cry of *"Whiskey!!!!"* The person who through his abuse has reached this stage has no choice but to go to the whiskey bottle and pour himself a fresh drink.

This is the principle behind all addiction. We get addicted to coffee, tea, and tobacco in exactly the same way. The daily influx of poison into our body makes this body unsuitable as a home for the "I"s of our normal cells and these "I"s have to find somewhere else to live. "I"s of cells of a coarser nature, which can stand the poisonous daily influx, then reincarnate in our body. They then gradually take over the control of the body and make a constant demand on the body to have their desires fulfilled.

We see this very clearly with people who have withdrawal symptoms. The coarse poison-loving cells make a collective demand on the being to have their thirst for the poison quenched. The "I" of the being then starts a fight with the coarse cells. No, he says, you are not going to have it; I want to get out of this abuse. But this is easier said than done, as the demand of the cells is very strong. The person has to muster an extreme amount of self-control in order to ignore the cry from the cells. If the cells win, he walks to the bottle and pours himself a new whiskey. Then the cells are satisfied, he feels relief, and peace reigns in his body for a short time. But not for long. After a short time the demand is there again, and he goes to the bottle again. These unnatural needs have no satiation. A natural hunger and thirst can be satiated, but these unnatural hungers have no satiation, they only have a momentary relief. After a short time the need arises again and the being has become dependent.

If the person through the mustering of great self control wins the battle and stops serving whiskey for the whiskey-loving cells, these will gradually stop reincarnating in his body as the right conditions for them are no longer there. With time the normal cells will return. Once the normal cells have returned, the person will find that he can no longer drink even a single glass of whiskey without having a colossal hangover. This is because the normal cells cannot live in whiskey-infected surroundings and they react strongly to the presence of the whiskey in their habitat.

Possession

There is an even grimmer aspect to the intake of alcohol. When a person drinks a lot of alcohol, which is really a material of a certain spiritual quality and therefore also called "spirits," the aura or energy field of the person is gradually debilitated. Once the aura has debilitated, the body is left without proper protection from outside spiritual beings. Martinus explains that there are spiritual beings everywhere around us and that our aura, which consists of our spiritual bodies, protects us from being possessed by those spiritual beings. There are spiritual beings around us of very different dispositions. Our spiritual guides or guardian angels are around us and they are there to help and protect us. But there are also beings of a coarser nature "floating around." These coarse spiritual beings are beings that, because of their attraction to earthly vices such as alcohol and tobacco, have not passed on to the spiritual realms after their own physical body was made useless and "died." They therefore linger on wavelengths close to the physical plane where they, so to speak, are lying in wait for a body to pour enough alcohol into himself so that the aura will debilitate, thus allowing the discarnate being to enter and take control of that body. These "addicted" bodiless beings generally "hang around" in cheap pubs or bars where they have the best chance of finding a drinker. Through the possession of the physical body of the drinker, the normally discarnate and now incarnate being experiences a certain pleasure from the alcohol to which it now has access. The "I" to whom the body normally belongs has been "dethroned" and is no longer in control. We then experience how the person changes personality. The person we normally know is no longer there, but a completely different person with different tendencies and different behavior and speech pattern has taken over the body of the person we know. The body has become possessed.

When the drinker eventually falls asleep, the usurper leaves the body, as there is no more fun to be had. The following morning the person to whom the body normally belongs remembers nothing and is not aware of any embarrassing behavior the night before. This is logical, as the original "I" simply wasn't in control.

Reincarnation is a Fundamental Principle

Reincarnation explains not only how we can have talents that are different from those of our parents and how we can exhibit talents for things that we have not yet learned in a particular life, but it also explains how a body can be created in the womb of the mother. The genes alone cannot do the job, and it is the accumulated talents of the discarnate being that control cell differentiation of the embryo. If we did not reincarnate, we would not be able to create a body. We have to have the ability to create a body from somewhere. An ability does not just crop up on its own. As the ability to create a body has been practiced throughout our whole sojourn on the physical plane while we lived as plants and animals and humans, we can understand that the ability for body creation is something that evolves. Our first manifestations on the physical plane were in mineral matter. Later we developed plant bodies and through the influences of the outer forces such as rain, wind, cold, and heat we developed our physical senses and our bodies became more and more physical.

Gradually, and in tune with the changing combinations of the basic energies, we developed stronger and stronger bodies, we became mobile, we became conscious on the physical plane, we developed animal bodies, and later we developed human bodies. This is a long, gradual process, and for each body we create, we perfect our talents for bodily creation. It is through this process that we can be who we are today. We would not be here if it were not for the process of reincarnation.

The egg and the sperm cell cannot create a new body on their own. How would those two cells know how to select a specific combination of genes (the DNA code) and initiate cell differentiation? From where would they get that information? And what about the consciousness that inhabits the body? Is the consciousness also just created by the egg and the sperm cell?

Also what would the purpose of a human life be if reincarnation did not exist? For what reason would we accumulate experiences, accumulate knowledge and learning if we lived only one life? If we lived only one life all the effort of learning would have been in vain. A long life spent accumulating knowledge would have been a gigantic waste of time if the knowledge accumulated could not be benefited from later. The things that we have laboriously learned, the experiences that we have reaped, the whole process of trial and error that a human life consists of would all have been in vain if there were no reincarnation. We would have spent a lot of time and effort for nothing if our experiences could not be used to our benefit later. Life would be pointless if we lived only one life. Living only one life would be a complete waste of time. There would be no perspective and no reason for reaping experience. Would an omniscient and all-loving God create a world with such a human waste?

In nature we see how everything has a purpose and nothing is wasted. Even the smallest breadcrumb is consumed by some living creature, if not by an ant then by bacteria. In nature nothing goes to waste. If all our experiences gathered in one life were wasted, life would be pointless. But life is not pointless and all our experiences are not wasted but accumulated for our own benefit later, if not in the same life then in the next.

What justice could there be in the world if there were no reincarnation? If we really had only one life, why are we then not all born under exactly the same conditions so that our one life can be the same for all humans? What kind of God would allow one person to live a long and happy life and die of old age and another person to die of starvation at the age of one and let that life be the only one? Only a very imperfect and unjust God would create such discrimination. And how can some beings represent advanced stages of development and others less advanced stages when they have never existed before? How can children exhibit talents that none of the parents have if they have not lived before? Those who believe that we live only one life have a lot of explaining to do.

There would be no logic in having only one life. All the evidence points toward reincarnation as fact. It is much easier to "prove" reincarnation than it is to disprove it. It is only a question of looking at the evidence. Reincarnation is absolutely fundamental. If it weren't for this process, no living creature would exist in the physical world. The concept of reincarnation is fundamental for our understanding of the world.

But if reincarnation is such a fundamental principle, then why haven't we been told about it before? Why is it only the Hindus and the Buddhists who have been taught this? Why didn't Jesus tell us about this? Why does the Bible not say anything about reincarnation?

Martinus answers this question in a very interesting way. Obviously Jesus knew about reincarnation. He also mentions it in the New Testament when he speaks to Nicodemus and says: "*Truly, truly, I say to you, unless one is born anew, he cannot see the kingdom of God*" (John 3:3). "*Truly, truly, I say to you, unless one is born of water and the Spirit, he cannot enter the kingdom of God*" (John 3: 5). Martinus explains that by the kingdom of God, Jesus refers to the real human kingdom, which we will eventually reach through reincarnation or being "born anew." Being born of water means being born in a new physical body, as this body consists of 70 percent water. These words of Jesus have not been interpreted by "the church" to be a reference to reincarnation, but they were.

Indeed, the belief in reincarnation was present in early Christianity, but in the year AD 533 the Roman emperor Justinian issued an official edict condemning the doctrine of reincarnation. As a consequence, all followers of the belief in reincarnation were persecuted, tortured, and killed. This happened for instance to the Cathars, who lived in the south of France in the early Middle Ages.

Abandoning the belief in reincarnation, Martinus explains, was not just something that was decided by the Emperor Justinian, this was prompted by Providence. But why? This was done in order to speed up development on Earth.

When you are completely convinced about reincarnation, you tend to become a little bit lazy. You'll say, "Well, what I don't achieve in this life, I'll achieve in the next. I'm in no hurry. I have all the time in the world. Eternity is before me."

This general attitude is not productive for scientific and technological growth. There is much more dedication to achievement in one life if you believe that you only have this one life. You want to make a mark; you want to make a difference. You become single-minded and diligent and much more ambitious. So the nonbelief in reincarnation enhances and speeds up scientific and technological advances.

It seems obvious that this is what has happened. At the risk of not being considered politically correct, I think that it is clear that most scientific and technological advances have taken place in the Western world, where belief in reincarnation had been abandoned. Very few new inventions and technological advances have come from countries where belief in reincarnation is predominant.

So in this way we have to understand that nonbelief in reincarnation in the Western world was not something that could have been avoided if the Emperor Justinian had not banned this belief. The nonbelief in reincarnation in the Western world was a necessary step in the development of mankind. Without this our technological level would not be what it is today. As our technological development is fundamental for our progress toward the real human kingdom, it is only logical that it should be enhanced.

However, through the influence of the new world impulse we are now ready to be made aware of the fundamental principle of reincarnation also in the Western world, not as belief but as logic. Our technological and scientific level has reached a point where it has to progress beyond the physical plane in order for us to know more. So knowledge about the principle of reincarnation is now in the process of being revealed to the Western world. We have progressed enough both scientifically and technologically. We are now ready to be told about the fundamental principle of reincarnation and the existence of the spiritual world.

There is no getting away from the fact that we reincarnate, and the sooner we learn to accept this fact, the better, as we shall see in the following chapter about the law of karma.

13

The Law of Karma

The Science of Fate

The Laws that Govern the Reactions of Physical Matter

It has been explained that beyond, behind, and before the physical world there is a spiritual world. The spiritual world is the primary world, as thoughts or constructions in spiritual matter come before constructions in physical matter. Consequently the physical world is the secondary world, the heavy and burdensome world—the world in which we have to incarnate in order to learn to think correctly, in order to learn the difference between good and evil.

We all know that there are laws that govern the reactions of physical matter. These laws are defined by our materialistic sciences such as physics and chemistry, and these sciences have reached a high degree of sophistication today. The laws of physics and chemistry describe the properties and reactions of the various physical materials or elements, and once these properties have been defined, this knowledge can be made use of in our manipulation of physical matter. We know that iron has one set of properties and that silver has another set of properties. Furthermore, we know that these properties never vary. Silver is not silver today and gold tomorrow. Silver is silver and silver has the properties that silver has. All specific types of matter have completely constant characteristics.

When an engineer wants to build a bridge, he knows how to combine the various physical materials such as concrete and steel in order to make the bridge. He knows that the characteristics of a specific alloy of steel are always constant. He can count on that. He knows that steel is always steel. It is not steel one day and wine gum the next.

When he builds the bridge he takes it for granted that the characteristics of steel are always constant. He accepts that there are rules that govern the reactions of all physical matter. If he does not abide by the rules, he may make the bridge too weak and it may collapse. The engineer knows exactly how to combine the various physical materials, so that the end product will suit his needs. He knows that when he does not respect the specific properties of each material, he simply cannot build a bridge that will meet all the requirements.

When we bake a cake in our kitchen, we also assume that sugar will always sweeten and flour will always give substance. We do not expect that sugar will sweeten one day and salt the next. We know that sugar is sugar and its property is to sweeten and that it will always do that.

Everybody accepts that all physical matter has properties that are constant and that there are laws that govern the reactions of physical matter. Furthermore these laws are international and universal. The law of gravity does not have one manifestation in France, another one in China, and yet another one in Sweden. There is only one set of laws that governs the reactions of physical matter, and all over the globe we agree about what the properties of physical matter are.

The Laws that Govern the Reactions of Spiritual Matter

However, when it comes to the spiritual world our confusion is enormous. The Catholics have one way of looking at it, the Jews another, the Protestants yet another, the Buddhists, the Hindus, the Mormons, the Baptists, the Muslims, the Jehovah's Witnesses each have their version of how the spiritual world works. It is logical that all these different interpretations should arise as long as ignorance about the spiritual world is still widespread. But isn't it logical to assume that there is also only one set of laws that governs the spiritual world, just as there is only one set of laws that governs the physical world? Isn't it logical to assume that when one level of existence, the physical, is ruled by the strictest laws then the other level of existence, the spiritual, is also ruled by the strictest laws? Is it logical to assume that one level should be ruled by laws and another level be ruled by chaos? Did God have a bad day when he created the spiritual world so that he forgot to apply laws? Or is it just that we are still completely ignorant about the laws that govern the spiritual level of existence just as we were once ignorant about the properties of physical matter? Isn't the answer that our sciences have not yet reached a level of cognition at which they can account for what goes on in the spiritual world, let alone recognize its existence?

What logic would there be in a world where one level of existence is ruled by the strictest laws and another level is ruled by complete chaos? Isn't it more logical to assume that it is our own ignorance or lack of insight that is responsible for this misinterpretation and that both the physical and the spiritual worlds are governed by laws?

However, now Providence has found the time to be ripe for us to step out of this darkness of ignorance and let the laws that govern the spiritual world be revealed to Mankind. With this revelation we can gradually learn how the spiritual world works and what it "looks" like. We can learn how to be spiritual or cosmic chemists and mix the spiritual energies correctly and thus create a happy fate instead of an unhappy one. How can we ever be able to create a higher and more humane culture on Earth without knowing the laws that govern the spiritual world and the way to create happiness? How can we make the planet a peaceful place if we do not know the recipe for peace?

How can we create happiness without knowing its recipe? Many of us have the impression that happiness has something to do with money and we struggle and fight to achieve riches, but sooner or later also the rich and mighty realize that they are as little immune to unhappiness as the pauper. Also the multimillionaire can risk losing his loved ones, and all the money in the world cannot assure him good health and a sane mind.

How can we make the planet a place where happiness reigns as long as we believe that everything happens by chance? We think that the existence of each one of us is a result of a chance meeting of two people who happened to run into each other and whose lovemaking resulted in two chance cells getting together and creating a chance person. When it comes to our fate, we think that this is also a result of chance. We think that happiness is dished out randomly like the food in a cheap canteen. If we are lucky we get a decent helping and if we are unlucky a single overcooked carrot lands on our plate. We think that we have been lucky if we live in good circumstances and are healthy. And we think that people who are ill, poor, or who have met with accidents are very unlucky. When we hear about a neighbor that has been crippled in a car accident we think how unlucky he was. We are glad that we are not in his shoes. We think that being happy is a result of pure chance and that we have nothing to do with it ourselves.

On television we watch the news and see children starving or suffering from AIDS in Africa. We are grateful that it isn't us and we think how unlucky these children are. We see young children that have died and think what a waste of life. We think that life is very unjust because we live a happy and healthy life and a child in Africa starves and dies before the age of two. We see how some children are born to loving and wealthy parents, they get a good education, and live in harmony and prosperity. But we also see other children who are born to poor and negligent parents, who live in suffering and misery—the father drinks and beats both the children and the mother, who has to beg in order to feed her children. Life is so unjust, we think, and if we believe in God we say that the ways of the Lord are past understanding. We believe that life is governed by pure chance.

We do not realize that the spiritual world is governed by laws in exactly the same way as the physical world, nor do we realize that nothing happens by chance and that everything that occurs is a result of the highest form of justice. There is no good or bad luck, no injustice, and no accidental occurrences. Everything in the spiritual world is governed by the strictest laws in exactly the same way as in the physical world. But until we know these laws, we cannot make use of them and we cannot mix our energies in a way that will give us a happy fate. Getting to know the laws that govern the spiritual world is, according to Martinus, the greatest challenge facing Mankind today because getting to know these laws is a prerequisite to getting the world out of the mess it is in today.

Jesus tells us about these laws when he says, "*Are not two sparrows sold for a penny? And not one of them will fall to the ground without your Father's will*" and "*But even the hairs of your head are all numbered*" (Matthew 10:29 and 30). Jesus is talking about the laws that govern all matter and when he says that a sparrow does not fall to the ground without it being the will of God, he is referring to the law of gravity. The sparrow falls to the ground because the law of gravity pulls it and makes it land exactly according to this law. Jesus called this law the will of God, because at the time he pronounced these words nobody had ever heard about the law of gravity. As there was no point in referring to a law that nobody had ever heard of, he called it the will of God. But then in a cosmic sense all natural laws are the will of God. Jesus knew exactly what he was saying.

The hairs of your head that are numbered is a reference to the law of karma. The law of karma is a strict law and everything you do has to be accounted for. Everything you do comes back to you. The accounts have to be balanced. The hairs that are numbered symbolize this.

Throughout the New Testament there are many references to the law of karma. Jesus refers to the law of karma at various occasions, such as, "*Judge not, that you be not judged. For with the judgment you pronounce you will be judged, and the measure you* give will be the measure you get" (Matthew 7:1–3), "So whatever you wish that men would do to you, do so to them; for this is the law and the prophets" (Matthew 7:12) "Put your sword back into its place; for all who take the sword, will perish by the sword" (Matthew 26: 52), "For if you forgive men their trespasses, your heavenly Father will also forgive you; but if you do not forgive men their trespasses, neither will your Father forgive your trespasses" (Matthew 6:14). All these quotations from The New Testament can be summed up in the words, "What you do to others you eventually do to yourself." As you yourself judge, so will you be judged; the measure you give will be the measure you get; do to other what you want them to do to you; if you kill by the sword, you will be killed by the sword and if you forgive, you will be forgiven.

Everything in the universe goes in cycles and spiritual energies are no exception. Karma is a cycle. Every energy you send out comes back to you in the same shape as it was sent out. A hateful energy comes back as a hateful energy and a loving energy comes back as a loving energy.

The works of Martinus are also called the science of fate, and Martinus clearly points out that learning the laws that govern our fate is the biggest challenge facing Mankind today. If we want to create happiness for ourselves and for our fellow beings and create peace on the planet, we simply have to learn about the laws that govern our fate. How can we mix spiritual matter in the correct way so that the mixture brings us happiness if we do not know the workings of the laws that govern all spiritual matter?

Martinus calls this cosmic chemistry, which is about mixing the energies that all matter consists of in such a way that we can create a happy fate instead of an unhappy one. We can only become successful cosmic chemists when we know the properties of spiritual matter in exactly the same way as we can only become successful physical chemists when we know the properties of physical matter. A knowledgeable physical chemist knows that there are certain chemical mixtures that are dangerous, but very few people realize that there are spiritual mixtures that are equally dangerous.

Stealing, beating, deceiving, and killing are examples of spiritual mixtures that are dangerous because they will bring unhappiness to their originator.

The Law of Karma

This may sound complicated, but it is really quite simple. The law of karma governs our fate and the law of karma is very easy to express: *"We reap as we sow."*

Every child knows that when we sow seeds of carrots in our garden, it is carrots that we are going to reap. We do not expect to reap turnips when we sow carrots. Very few people, however, realize that this universal principle of sowing and reaping also applies to our nonphysical manifestations. If we are angry and bad-tempered toward our surroundings, it is anger and bad temper that we are going to reap. If we are kind and loving toward our surroundings, it is kindness and love that we will reap.

Many people complain that they do not get enough love. They lean back in their pillows and moan and wait for love to come their way. Passively they wait and wait. When no love comes they get disappointed and bitter. Then they feel unjustly treated by fate. They do not realize that there is only one way to make love come your way and it is a way that will work with absolute certainty: give more love, sow love profusely, and it is love that you will reap.

The law of karma can also be expressed like this: what you want other people to do to you, you must do to others first. First you give it out, and then you get it back. You have to sow before you can reap. If you want good things to happen to you, you must first let good things happen to others. You cannot expect to reap where you have not sown. But if you sow good seeds, you will reap good seeds. If you sow love, you will reap love. It is as simple as that.

The law of karma is unrelenting. Let us look at how this law works.

We know from our school days that there is no such thing as a straight line in the universe. What looks like a straight line is really just a segment of a circle. However, the circle can be so big that even a large segment looks like a straight line. But physics has taught us that a straight line does not exist in the universe. Everything moves in circles and sooner or later all matter, be it physical or spiritual, will return to where it came from.

Furthermore, the law of thermodynamics has taught us that the sum of energy is constant. Energy does not just disappear. Energy cannot disappear nor can it be destroyed. It may be transported to some other place and it may enter into a new combination of energies, but it does not disappear or dissolve.

All our actions are energies that we send out into the world. As there is no straight line in the universe, these energies will sooner or later return to us. That is the law of karma. As we reap as we sow, all the energies that we send out will return to us at a later stage in the same shape as we sent them out. A loving energy will return as a loving energy and a hateful energy will return as a hateful energy. This again means that *we are the only ones responsible for our fate.*

Many people tend to blame others for their unhappy fate. Many people think that someone else was responsible if they had an accident, that the accident was somebody else's fault. They do not think that they were responsible themselves. They think that fate is blind. But we are all responsible for our fate. Fate is not blind and happiness is not dished out randomly. Everything that happens to us, good or bad, is our own karma. Our karma is presented to us by our fellow beings, as these beings are the only instruments available for Providence to show us the effects of our deeds. But the first and only reason for our fate is the seeds that we have sown ourselves.

Let us look at a few examples.

One day in the Danish news there was a story about a man who had lost his purse containing a large amount of cash in a street in Copenhagen. Naturally the man was very upset, because the money represented a considerable part of everything he had. But one hour later the purse with all the money was returned to the local police station and after that to the man. He was happy and then he told the astounded policemen that he had twice found a purse with money in it and each time had returned the purse to its rightful owner. This man had first done to others what he wanted others to do to him and consequently his purse was returned to him. "What a coincidence," people said, but it was no coincidence, it was the law of karma. The man had sown what he wanted to reap, so his purse was returned to him.

The Peace Pilgrim, who walks the roads of the USA for peace with no luggage and only a thin windbreaker to protect her, tells a story of how she was once very close to being beaten up. Needless to say, the Peace Pilgrim could not hurt a fly and had always treated people kindly. At a certain place she gets involved in a situation in which she wants to protect a child from a violent and angry step-father. The stepfather is about to start beating the child up when she steps between them to protect the child. Now logically you would think that she would get the beating. The stepfather lifts his fist ready to hit the Peace Pilgrim when something stops him. In the middle of the movement of hitting, something holds his arm back; he stops in his action and retreats. The child and the Peace Pilgrim are allowed to go. In this case we see that being hit was not the Peace Pilgrim's karma, as she had never hit anybody. Hitting people was not part of her psychological setup and consequently it was not her karma and she was protected from being hit.

Protection

We saw that the peace pilgrim's karma protected her from harm. Because she could do no harm, she was herself protected from harm. Martinus says that this is our *only* protection. We are protected from harm to the same degree that we protect others from harm. There is no other real protection.

People think that they can protect themselves from harm by owning a gun. They think that if they own a gun, then they can protect themselves and their family from being attacked by gunmen. If the need arose, they would be willing to use the gun against an intruder. They do not realize that this is no protection at all.

As long as they own a gun and are willing to use it against their fellow man, they are not protected themselves. The only protection against being attacked by a gunman is not to be willing to use a gun and not to own a gun. When we could never dream of hurting a fellow human being and consequently do not own weapons, then we have real protection.

But, you may say, what if I were attacked by gunmen and I had no gun to protect myself with, then I would be killed! But the point is that if you are a 100 percent peace-loving person, who could never dream of attacking another being, animal or human, you would never be attacked by gunmen. You would be protected by Providence from gunmen, your karma would protect you. Nothing happens by chance and our fate is ruled by the strictest laws. We are protected to the degree that we protect others.

This does not, however, mean that we can behave in any silly way we want and expect the law of karma to protect us in all situations. If we step out in front of a passing truck or if we walk into the line of fire we cannot expect the truck not to hit us or the bullets just to pass us by. We have to take proper care of ourselves and not challenge fate. If we behave sensibly and do not challenge fate we will be protected while in our own natural surroundings.

Martinus mentions the example of the Christian missionary who goes into the jungle to preach to the cannibals and ends up in the soup pot. This missionary left his own natural and cultural surroundings and entered the natural surroundings of people who were not at a cultural level equal to his own. He knew they ate other people. If against his better judgment he enters the natural habitat of cannibals, he can expect to be eaten. He had not made use of his better judgment, and in a case like this his karma cannot help him. He had acted like the fool who walks safely where angels fear to tread.

But if we do not challenge fate and do not act against our better judgment, we are protected by our karma. Let us look at some more examples.

If we are completely honest in everything we do, we are protected against burglary and theft. If we cannot ever dream of stealing and if we always pay our debts, there is no way that we will be the victim of burglary or theft. But, you may say, what if I were a burglar in a former life, could that karma not hit me in this? The answer to this is yes, but the karma can only hit you if you are still able to steal. If your "old" desire to steal has not yet been outlived, then you are still liable to be the victim of a thief.

But if our mentality has been cleansed of all tendencies to steal and we are completely honest in everything we do, then we do not attract theft. Now why is this? It is because karma is not a punishment and karma does not work like "an eye for an eye and a tooth for a tooth." Karma is a loving instruction and once we show that we have learned the lesson, no more instruction is necessary. We do not go on teaching a child the alphabet once it has clearly demonstrated that it can read. That would be completely unnecessary. Once we, through our behavior and actions, have shown that we are completely honest and truthful, the old "stealing" karma will be dissolved. There is no need for further instruction when our behavior clearly shows that we have learned the lesson. This is really the principle of the forgiveness of sins. Through our honest and truthful behavior our old sins are forgiven.

It is the vibration in our aura, the electromagnetic field that surrounds our body, which attracts or repels our karmic energies when they return. As soon as we outlive a certain mentality, the vibration of our aura changes, it vibrates on different wavelengths. Once our aura is "free" from, say, energies of anger, we will no longer attract these energies and consequently, when old karmic arches of anger return to us, they are repelled by the aura and will not affect us. Again it is the law of attraction and repulsion at work.

Through the Darkness of Initiation

Let us look at two very central symbols in Martinus' teachings, symbol number 19 called "*Through the Darkness of Initiation*"

(Hell or Armageddon), and symbol number 23 called "*The Finished Human Being in the Image and Likeness of God.*"

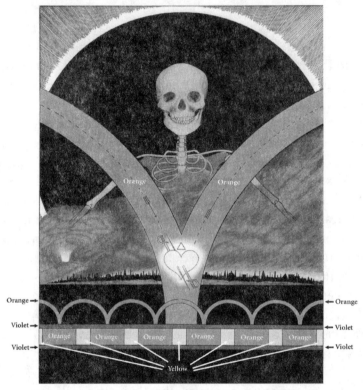

Symbol 19. Through the Darkness of Initiation.[1]
© Martinus Institute

The symbol shows the culmination of darkness and the conduct of the unfinished human being. This conduct is founded in the predominance of the energy of gravity in the mentality of the being and it means that the killing principle predominates. All dark fate is received with anger and desires for revenge, and this leads to more dark fate and its effect is the general image of Armageddon that the symbol expresses.

1. The yellow fields between the two horizontal violet lines at the bottom symbolize the spiritual existence of the being, while the orange fields are its physical lives.

2. The little triangle above the heart-shaped figure shows the living being. The heart-shaped figure symbolizes the organism of the

living being and the two sabers the killing principle, which means that the being is still lacking the ability to love and forgive.

3. The big orange arch at the left is a dark arch of fate occasioned by the being itself, which now returns.

4. The big orange arch at the right shows that the being receives the dark fate with revenge and killing and thus the being sends out another dark arch of fate that will return to the being in a future life.

5. The row of physical lives at the bottom of the symbol stays orange, which means that through this way of receiving his dark fate the being remains in the animal kingdom.

6. The representative of death symbolized by the skeleton expresses the panorama of death, which is occasioned through this unfinished conduct.

7. The burning city from which a huge dark cloud of smoke is pouring out and the erupting volcano also symbolize Armageddon in the shape of natural disasters, wars, revolutions, unrest, poverty, need, and misery that are the result of the lacking ability to love and forgive.

8. The radiance of light behind the black sky of death expresses the light from the highest spiritual worlds.

The first impression we get when we look at symbol number 19 is that all hell is loose. We see an enormous skeleton on a pit black background above a burning city. A volcano is erupting and clouds of smoke are reaching into the sky. This situation symbolizes the culmination of darkness, which has been explained in chapter 11 about our present spiral cycle.

It has been explained that darkness is at its maximum in the animal kingdom and especially in the part of the animal kingdom where the unfinished human beings live, i.e., the human beings who have a humanlike body with a mentality of an animal. We remember that the mentality of an animal is defined by thoughts of revenge, envy, jealousy, possessiveness, greed, power, selfishness, hatred, war, murder, intolerance, anger, irritability, etc. We called this the culmination of the killing principle and we called the mentality responsible for this the "devil mentality."

At the center of the symbol is a white heart-shaped figure with a white triangle above it. The white triangle symbolizes, as we have seen before, the eternal "I" of the living being, and the heart symbolizes the body of the "I." The heart and the triangle together symbolize a living being. The two sabers that penetrate the heart symbolize the killing principle.

At the bottom of the symbol are a series of orange-colored fields separated by yellow squares. Each orange-colored field symbolizes a reincarnation or a physical life. The color orange indicates the animal kingdom, the zone of the killing principle dominated by the energy of gravity. The yellow squares symbolize the spiritual life of the being between physical lives. The yellow color indicates that in the spiritual life the energy of feeling is predominant, thus making spiritual life a rest away from the predominance of the energy of gravity, the purveyor of the killing principle. The two purple lines that frame the orange squares symbolize the mother energy, which is responsible for the release of the arches of karma. The orange arches that jump from one physical life to the next represent actions carried out in one life whose effects are to be felt in the next life. The fact that there is only one arch does not mean that there is only one effect per life. This is only to illustrate the principle that karma from one life can affect us in later lives. Of course karma can also come back to us in the same life. The orange arches only illustrate the principle.

In the center of the symbol we see a grinning skull. This symbolizes the cold materialistic concept that death is a total annihilation of the living being. The skull is surrounded by a pit black sky with no stars or moon. This symbolizes the spiritual darkness of the godless materialist who believes that death and total annihilation is the final outcome of life.

The burning city symbolizes the cultural creations of mankind that perish in wars, revolutions, insurrections, strikes, lockouts, political struggles, religious wars, poverty, illness, distress, and misery. The volcano symbolizes natural catastrophes that befall mankind such as earthquakes, typhoons, floods, and volcanic eruptions.

Just underneath the skull is a very heavy arch of karma that is going to affect the living being in a particular life. Let us say that this is a murder that the being once committed. For the sake of simplicity we will call this being Arthur. The effect of the murder which Arthur once committed is now due to him. The murder which Arthur has owing to him is being carried out by another being, let us call him Sven, but the only and real cause of the murder is the act of murder that Arthur once committed himself. The person Sven, who by Providence has been appointed to execute the resulting murder, is only an instrument and is therefore not the being responsible for the act that is now going to be carried out. However, Sven has been selected by Providence to carry out the act of murder because Sven's mental setup is fit for this. Sven is still very much under the influence of animal mentality and thus he is a perfect instrument. Had Sven been a saint who could not dream of killing, he would not have been made instrumental in a murder. But Sven is the perfect instrument and he goes to kill Arthur. However, the real cause of the killing is an act of killing committed by Arthur himself.

But Arthur, who suddenly stands face to face with Sven, who wants to kill him, sees Sven as the person responsible for the lethal attack. So what does Arthur do? He kills Sven. This is symbolized by the two sabers in the heart. Through the killing of Sven, Arthur has sown more new dark karma for himself. This is represented by the orange color of the big arch of karma that goes out to the right. The orange color of the small arches of karma on the line at the bottom also indicates that each return of karma has been met with anger, revenge, and more killing. Thus the line of lives will be characterized by the killing principle symbolized by the orange color and the being will remain in the animal kingdom.

If Arthur had forgiven Sven and met his murderous attack with kindness, and offered Sven friendship and invited him to stay the night and have dinner and a chat, then he would have averted the karma of his previous murder. But as Arthur's mind was not set for forgiveness and he was damned, he fought Sven and in the end he killed him. In this way he has sent out a new arch of killing karma for himself, which will come back with more killing and strife in a later life. Dark arches of killing karma could never arise if the being itself did not create hateful, egoistic acts of killing.

Arthur looked upon Sven as his enemy, but in a cosmic, absolute sense Sven is not the enemy. Those that we think are our enemies are God's instruments through whom he reveals to us the effects of our own murderous or unloving acts. Our enemies are God's instruments in teaching us the effects of our own deeds and without "enemies" we could not reap as we have sown.

But just as Arthur was the first and only reason for the suffering he received from Sven, so Sven was also the first and only reason for the suffering that he received from Arthur. Both Arthur and Sven are instruments for each other's previous acts of darkness. Sven is Arthur's instrument and Arthur is Sven's instrument. They are each other's instruments because their mentalities are the same.

Through this we see that everything that happens is an expression of the highest form of justice. No living human being can be the victim of injustice, nor can he do injustice. To think that it is our enemy who is to blame for our unhappy fate is incorrect. Only we are to blame. As long as we hate and persecute other living beings, thinking that they are the reason for our dark destiny, will we live in the shadow of hate and persecution. Revenge, hatred, and killing are the shortcuts to Armageddon, the panorama of death that the symbol shows.

As we are all responsible for our fate, it is up to each one of us, whether we live in unhappiness and suffering or in happiness, joy, and bliss.

The root to all existing evil or darkness in the world, the root to all unhappy fates, is a lack of knowledge of the workings of the law of karma. If we knew that everything we do to others we eventually do to ourselves, if we knew that every act we do comes back to us, chances are that we would stop performing unloving deeds. Darkness and unhappy fate is a result of a lack of love for our neighbor. To avoid darkness and unhappiness we have to learn to love our neighbor as we love ourselves. If we meet every situation that we are faced with, kind or unkind, with love, then we have effectively stopped all unhappiness in our own life. If we send out nothing but love, we will get nothing but love back. It is as simple as that.

Our Inner Fight Between Good and Evil

However, this is easier said than done. We know that the apostle Paul said, "*For I do not do the good I want, but the evil I do not want is what I do*" (Romans 7:19). Now why is it that we cannot always be as good as we want to even when we know the consequence of unloving acts? Why is it that we are sometimes carried along on a surge of anger, envy, jealousy or selfishness even though we know that we should not? It is because we are not yet "finished," we are still not "real human beings." The animal mentality, that these reactions express, is so deeply rooted in our mentality that we cannot control it even though we want to. We should remember that we have lived as animals through millions of years. In the animal kingdom the only mentality that will carry us through is selfishness. If we are not selfish, we will either starve to death or be killed. In the animal kingdom it is kill or be killed. Selfishness has become "C" knowledge in our mentality as a result of our passing through the animal kingdom. Without even thinking, our animal mentality just simply takes over automatically in certain situations and we are carried along on an incontrollable surge of anger.

This is really a natural reaction given the many, many lives we have lived as animals. The animal mentality still reigns in our mind. In order to respond with kindness in a critical situation we have to count to ten, pour cold water on the wrists (the energy of feeling contained in the coldness of the water counterbalances the energy of gravity that is responsible for the anger) and muster the human mentality that we have, which has probably only reached the "A" stage in development. Making a strong mental effort, we manage to smile at our adversary and stretch out our hand in friendship. Thus we have disarmed the situation and have sown good karma for ourselves. But this is not always easy at our present stage in development because the animal mentality may still have a firm hold. That is why we actively have to practice kindness, forgiveness, and love so that these thought climates can reach the "C" stage in our mentality, thus letting the animal thought climates die from lack of attention. The only way to be good at something is to practice, so the more we practice kindness and love, the better we get at mastering it.

Because the animal thought climates reached the "C" stage in our mentality many, many lives ago, we cannot "*do the good that we want to do.*" When we are in a critical situation, we are on "automatic pilot" and before we can even think we have manifested a reaction, which we did, in fact, not want to manifest. We have shown that our animal mentality still has a firm hold on us.

The Finished Human Being in the Image and Likeness of God

Let us look at the next symbol, number 23, called "*The Finished Human Being in the Image and Likeness of God*" to see what happens when we meet our dark karma with love and forgiveness.

Again we see the line of lives at the bottom of the symbol with the periods of "rest" on the spiritual plane in between. In the center we see the heart-shaped figure with the triangle above, which represents the living being. The heart and the two hands symbolize that the being has a perfect ability to love and forgive. Again we see the big orange arch of fate that returns to the being to inflict him with the effects of a dark deed that he once committed to a fellow being.

The fact that the arch of fate is orange, the color of the energy of gravity, means that the deed was one of darkness such as killing. But in this symbol we see that the being Arthur meets his dark arch of fate with great kindness, symbolized by the handshake

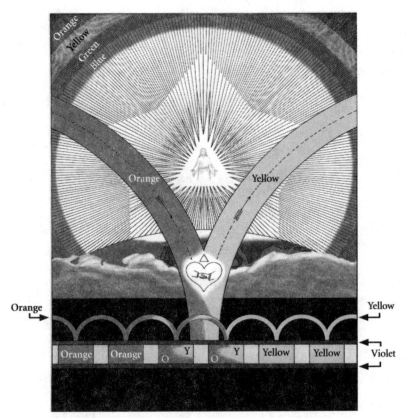

Symbol number 23. The Finished Human Being *
© Martinus Institute

The symbol shows the attitude of the finished human being. This attitude is based on a harmony between intelligence, feeling, and intuition and expresses itself through sympathy for all living beings. When this being is faced with dark fate, it knows through experience that the reason for this is its own dark deeds.

1. The whitish yellow square fields between the two horizontal violet lines at the bottom symbolize the spiritual existences of the being, while the orange fields are its physical lives.

2. The little triangle above the heart-shaped figure shows the living being. The heart-shaped figure symbolizes its perfect ability for love and the hands its perfect ability for forgiveness.

3. The big orange arch is a dark arch of fate occasioned by the being itself, which is now returning.

* Original title: The Finished Human Being in the Image and Likeness of God.

4. The big yellow arch shows that the being receives the dark fate in a positive way and in this way it sends out a light arch of fate. This perfect way of receiving its dark fate leads the being out of the animal kingdom and into the real human kingdom where it will experience cosmic consciousness.

5. The change in colors from orange to yellow on the figure at the bottom shows the change in fate of the being toward the free state of love.

6. The big triangle with its sea of rays symbolizes God. The halo of rays is the all-encompassing primary consciousness of God. The colored fields in the halo of rays show the planes of existence.

7. The Christlike being shows the finished human being.

8. The mass of clouds, which symbolizes dark fate, is dissolved through the humane development of Mankind.

inside the heart figure. In this case Arthur understands that it is the effect of one of his own dark deeds that he once committed against his neighbor that he now has to face up to. He now shows understanding, love, and forgiveness toward Sven, who has come to pay back the dark deed, and thus all enmity is dissolved and a great friendship arises between the two. With his forgiving and loving attitude Arthur has not only averted the effects of his dark karma, but he has also sent out a new arch of karma. As Arthur in this case has shown love and forgiveness, the karma that he has sent out will also be loving and forgiving. So he has sown karma of light and happiness for himself to reap later. The yellow color, the color of the energy of feeling, of the big karmic arch that goes out to the right symbolizes that the karmic effect will be one of love and forgiveness.

This way of receiving one's karmic arches has the effect that it leads the being out of the animal kingdom and into the kingdom of the real human being. This is shown on the line of lives at the bottom. The lives change from being dominated by the orange color to being more and more dominated by the yellow color. With his change in attitude Arthur has lifted his lives up from belonging to the animal and killing zones to belonging to the happy zones of the real human kingdom.

In the center of the symbol we see a large triangle from which rays of light emanate. This symbolizes God. The halo of rays symbolizes God's all-encompassing primary consciousness. Inside the triangle there is a being that is intended to resemble Christ. This being is the finished human being in the image and likeness of God. In the white halo of light is a five-pointed star. This star symbolizes the principle of world redemption, which was mentioned in the chapter of the Parent Principle. The principle of world redemption sees to it that world redeemers are sent "down" to teach the inhabitants of the various planets new morals at times when it is considered that these are needed. The colored fields in the outer part of the halo represent the planes of existence.

Underneath the symbol of God we see a part of our planet. We see a dark and heavy band of clouds. These clouds symbolize the dark and killing thought climates and manifestations of war. But just as the sun dissolves the rain clouds, the manifestations of love and forgiveness dissolve the dark thought climates and the manifestations of war.

In this way we see how the acceptance of one's fate, through the manifestation of love and kindness toward the instrument that God uses to show us the effects of our own dark deeds, can not only dissolve the effects of dark karma but can also sow good karma and start a domino effect on others. Through our demonstration of love and kindness in all situations of life, we will set an example for others and thus start a chain reaction of love and kindness whose effects can only be positive. Just as the sun shines on both the righteous and the wicked, so our loving mentality must shine on everybody. This may be easier said than done, but if we do not start practicing, we will never become experts and so find it easy said and done.

Familiarizing ourselves with the law of karma and learning how it works is the greatest challenge facing us today. Once we have learned to treat others as we ourselves would like to be treated and once all our manifestations demonstrate that we sow only what we would like to reap, we have effectively eradicated unhappiness from our own lives. If we sow nothing but happiness, we shall reap nothing but happiness. The sooner we internalize the workings of the law of karma the better, because the sooner we can stop fighting war with war, the sooner peace will reign on Earth. We have to learn that the *only* protection against war is disarmament and that as long as we keep designing and producing new lethal weapons, we are still in the war zone. Jesus advocates the desired attitude when he says, "*But if any one strikes you on the right cheek, turn to him the other also*" (Matthew 5:39). Martinus explains that this means that when anyone strikes you on your animal side, turn to him your human side. Forgiveness and more forgiveness, love and more love are the only way forward, the only way out of the darkness of the animal kingdom. The recipe for world peace is to sow peace. We cannot sow war and expect to reap peace.

Karma from the Killing of Animals

Martinus says that of the ten Commandments the most important one is the fifth: "*Thou shall not kill.* "This commandment does not specify the "not killing" to apply only to other human beings. It simply says, "You shall not kill." This means that you shall not take any life, including the lives of animals. Let us have a look at this aspect.

It is a supposition among many human beings today that it is necessary to eat meat for the sustenance of our body. This is, however, not true. The amount of protein that our body needs can easily be covered through a vegetarian diet. Recent research at both the Karolinska Institute in Sweden and the Max Planck Institute in Germany confirms that most vegetables, fruits, seeds, nuts, and grains are excellent sources of complete protein and that indeed the needed daily intake of protein is only 35 to 45 grams per day, which can easily be attained by using a vegetarian diet. Twenty years ago it was believed that our necessary daily intake of protein was 150 grams, but this has been disproved by recent research. Today it is becoming accepted that a vegetarian diet is much healthier than a diet that includes meat. A recent investigation into vegetarianism showed that vegetarians are by far healthier than meat eaters, have fewer days off from work because of illness, are less prone to get a whole number of diseases, including heart diseases and cancer, and they live longer.

The Bible also clearly states what our food should be. When God had created man he said, "*Behold, I have given you every plant yielding seed which is upon the face of all the earth, and every tree with seed in its fruit; you shall have them for food*" (Genesis 1:29). God says nothing about eating the flesh of other living creatures for food.

Let us look at how meat eating affects us in two ways. The eating of the bodies of other living beings gives two different arches of karma, short ones and long ones.

Long Arches of Karma from the Eating of Meat

When we participate in the killing of animals, we become liable to dark killing karma in exactly the same way as when we participate in the killing of another human being. The law of karma makes no distinction between the killing of another human being and the killing of an animal. A living being is a living being and a murder is a murder. Whether it is a man or a beast that we kill is of no consequence. All life must be respected.

We can participate in the killing of animals in two ways: Actively or passively.

Some people have made the killing of animals into a kind of sport or pastime. Hunting and angling are "sports" in which the killing of other beings has been made into a pastime, even a pleasure. Foxhunting is considered the thing to do for the so-called upper class. Nobility and royalty gather and dress up in a certain "fashionable" gear in order to hunt the poor foxes to exhaustion and to show how "superior" they are. They have probably no idea that in a cosmic sense this activity reveals that the participants are no better than the predator in the jungle, indeed they are worse, because the predator kills only to satiate its hunger, whereas the "upper" class kills for pleasure.

Bullfighting is another example of killing as a pastime. Bullfighting is even considered a kind of "art" by some people. The bullfighter dresses up in a certain fashion with a special black hat and a special dress with small mirrors to give off a certain impression. A lot of paraphernalia are used in the bullfight such as "picadores," "banderillas," "muletas," short and long swords, etc. The bullfighter that can kill the bull in a certain fashion is considered a hero and consequently he can make a lot of money, be admired by a lot of people and have easy access to members of the opposite sex, who admire his courage. But seen from a cosmic point of view a bullfight is nothing but a brutal killing staged in a certain "fancy" way. The "artful" dressing up of the killing does not change the fact that the bullfighter is a murderer.

The less "artful" killers are those who kill for a living such as butchers and fishermen. These people have made killing their profession.

Butchers, fishermen, hunters, anglers, and bullfighters are active participators in killing.

But to participate in killing we do not have to kill the animal ourselves. If we eat meat we also participate in killing. We are accomplices in the killing through our intake of meat. Why should the butcher kill the animal if there were no customers for it? Our demand for meat causes the butchers to kill the animals, so if we are meat eaters we are the real source of the killing, even though we do not execute the actual murder.

Meat eaters are passive participators in killing.

The animals that we eat such as pigs, cows, and lambs are highly developed beings that are not very much below ourselves on the ladder of development. Just as we were animals once, the animals that we eat are beings at a certain point in evolution toward becoming "man in the image and likeness of God." They have not progressed quite as far as we have, but they are not very much below us. They have their day-consciousness on the physical plane just as we have, and their intelligence has reached a fairly high level of development, as explained in chapter 11. And they are, just as we, capable of feeling physical pain and fear. When we kill an animal for its meat, we cause the animal a sudden, surprising death. If the animal that we kill is a domestic animal, we may be under the false impression that it is all right to kill animals and that the animals are only put on this Earth in order to serve as food for us humans. But the animals are born on this earth with their own agendas; they are here, just as we are, in order to get on with their own development. They are definitely not here to end up on the dinner table, served up as some elaborate dish on silver plates.

When we confine the animals to small sties and let them live there in miserable conditions, where they can hardly move, in order to kill them when they have become sufficiently fat, we sow dark karma for ourselves. When we seek out animals in their own natural surroundings in order to scare, hunt, injure, and kill them, we sow dark karma for ourselves.

Meat eaters and hunters have to pay for this killing of animals with their own lives. The law of karma does not make a distinction between killing an animal and killing a human being. The law of karma is unrelenting: what we do to other living beings, we do to ourselves.

However, the karmic effects of something we do on purpose and something that we do accidentally are different. If we unknowingly step on an ant or if an insect is killed against the windscreen of our car, these killings will not affect our karma in the same way as a purposeful participation in murder. This aspect is mentioned by Jesus on the cross when he says, "*Father, forgive them, for they know not what they do*" (Luke 23:34). Because they "know not what they do," forgiveness will be granted. But if we purposefully and in cold blood kill another being, then the law of karma is unrelenting.

The killing of animals to satisfy our bloodthirsty palates has taken gigantic proportions and it shows that we have no real human feelings toward the animals. For this callousness we have to pay later and in this case the situation is the same as we saw before.

Because we have caused the animal a sudden, surprising death, we ourselves will have a sudden, surprising death. Many, many accidents in cars, trains, planes, etc. are the return of arches of karma for the killing and eating of animals. The only protection against being killed in an accident is not to participate in killing, that is not to eat meat. If you never participate in any kind of killing, your karma will protect you from being killed. Nothing happens by chance. Everything is governed by laws. So it is very unlikely that a person who never participates in killing can be killed in an accident. It is as simple as that.

An interesting examination has been made in which scientists investigated the number of people present on board trains and planes that crashed. It turned out that on the day of the accident, there were fewer people on board than on an average day. This was strange and the fact was there, but it could not really be explained. But the explanation is quite simple. Only those people whose karma it was to be killed were on board. Those who had no killing arch of karma coming to them had either been late for the train that day, or had decided at the last minute to take the car instead or another form of transportation. The fact is that if it was not their karma to die in an accident, they were not on board.

The large number of deaths that occurs every weekend on the highways all over the world is karma for either the eating of meat or other killings that the victims have done to their fellow humans, animals or birds, and fish. Wars, concentration camps, and sufferings can also be karma for the killing of animals. As long as we humans kill animals, we cannot go free from sufferings or from Armageddon on Earth.

The dark arches of karma caused by all kinds of killings are normally compressed to be released at intervals. This means that a being can live several relatively happy lives without being hit by dark arches of karma. When then the dark arches of karma come, they are generally very concentrated and will affect many people at the same time, such as we see in wars or natural disasters or accidents involving hundreds of people.

These are the long arches of karma caused by killing and meat eating.

Short Arches of Karma from the Eating of Meats

But there are also short arches of karma caused by the eating of meat. Illness is a short arch of karma from meat eating.

Our organisms have reached a fairly high degree of refinement if we compare them to the organisms of animals such as lions or crocodiles. The more refined an organism is, the more refined must its nourishment be.

If we eat nourishment that is too coarse, the digestion of this makes a very high demand on our body and causes it to muster a very high degree of effort to digest the food. In order to extract the nourishment in the coarse foodstuffs, our body experiences a loss of power. We have probably all tried to eat a heavy meal and then felt exceedingly tired afterward, so tired that we had to go and lie down. This is the loss of power that the body experiences after eating a meal of foodstuffs that are coarse.

The power or level of vibration in meat is so strong that it is practically at the same level as the vibration in our body. This is logical, as meat is muscle fibers similar to those in our own body. All muscle fibers vibrate at more or less the same frequencies. As our body has to overpower the power in the food in order to digest it, it has very little margin to do this with. The body has to muster all its power to digest the meat, and that is why we feel tired after a heavy meal including meat. There is practically no surplus power left to deal with bodily functions other than digestion. We therefore have to go and lie down. In such a case our body goes into a kind of shock and this is extremely unhealthy. The coarse food that we eat becomes a kind of poison for our body, as it is an irrelevant and powerful foreign energy that we incorporate in our body.

If we, on a daily basis, fill our body with foodstuffs that take too much energy to digest, we slowly but surely undermine our own health.

Foodstuffs such as meat, flesh, fish, fat, lobster, crabs, shrimps, snails, mussels, etc., are so coarse that they are only suitable as food for animals such as lions, tigers, panthers, hyenas, dogs, cats, snakes, sharks, etc. These animals have a digestive system suited to digest meat.

To the same degree that we as humans stand above these animals in development, to the same degree are these foodstuffs unsuitable for us.

In the question of our nourishment we are still very much behind our own level of development. Our nourishment is in reality very outdated. In fact it is our palates or taste buds that still demand blood. Our taste buds have not yet developed away from wanting the taste of blood. Our taste buds determine to a very high degree what we eat. We strive to experience new tastes to a degree that has become an obsession. We are extremely focused on having new taste experiences. How the food tastes is more important than its nutritional values. We stuff ourselves with unhealthy "tasteful" food and we are so much slaves of our taste buds that we have ruined our natural regulation of hunger. We eat although we are not hungry, just to experience yet another taste. As a result many of us have become grotesquely overweight. But the idea is to eat to live and not to live to eat. We should eat what is good for the health of our body and not what our palates dictate. We should eat only when we are hungry and stop eating when we are full.

The foodstuffs that are suitable for us at our present level are all kinds of vegetables from the relatively coarse roots such as potatoes, carrots, and beetroot to the fruits of plants such as tomatoes, beans, peas, and cucumbers. All food derived from cereals such as bread and pasta is suitable. Nuts, stalks, leaves, and bulbs (e.g., asparagus, lettuce, and onions) and all kinds of fruit such as bananas, apples, pears, plums, grapes, apricots, mangos, and oranges are appropriate as food at our present stage. The vibrational level in these foodstuffs is relatively low in comparison to the vibrational level in our body and consequently the energy in the food is easily overshadowed by the energy of our body. This again means that this food is easy to digest and our body does not experience a loss of power after eating. Fresh milk is also easy to digest and can be added to this diet for its nutritional value.

Martinus says that the intake of meat is the real cause of many different kinds of illnesses such as cancer, boils, rheumatism, tuberculosis, arthritis, gallstones, renal calculus, overweight, heart problems, anemia, digestive, and bowel movement problems.

If we look at the general state of health of the population of the Earth today, it is not exactly uplifting. Hospitals all over the world are full to the brim with people suffering from various diseases. Doctors, nurses, scientists, surgeons, and other medical personnel are overworked trying to cope with all the diseases that people have. But the human body is created to be a healthy and perfect tool for its "I" to experience life on the physical plane. It is only when this fantastic tool is left in the care of man that it loses its health. If man were so developed that he could tend to his body in the best possible way, the amount of illnesses would be drastically reduced. We humans still lack the knowledge of how to treat our divine tool in a way that prevents diseases. In this field we still do not know what is good and what is bad, we are still ignorant.

Meat intake cannot take place without promoting all sorts of illnesses and our own premature death. The person who has not yet realized what is the correct nourishment for his level of development is, through his intake of meat and blood, not only guilty of killing other beings but also of killing himself. He is a murderer and a suicide at the same time. Most suicides are committed with a knife and fork. It is true that this kind of suicide is committed through ignorance, but it is a suicide nevertheless. Through excessive eating and drinking, lack of exercise, and smoking we slowly but surely kill ourselves.

Martinus ironically says that a well-laid table with flowers and candles at which we serve the quartered limbs of our fellow beings accompanied by wine is a festive shortcut to death.

Alcohol

We have just seen that the intake of meat is very harmful to the cells in our body or our microcosm. When we put meat into our body, we put our cells on overwork. But even worse effects come from taking drugs and alcohol.

In the chapter about reincarnation we saw that alcohol could cause our aura to debilitate, thus weakening our body's defenses against the usurpation by foreign spirits that are trapped in the spiritual zones adjacent to the physical plane. Another effect is seen at the cell level.

How does the intake of alcohol affect our cells? Let us start by stating that alcohol is a neurotoxin. Imagine that neurotoxins were poured out all over the Earth, so that every breath we take was infected by poison and everything we ate was equally infected by poison. The whole atmosphere would be covered by a heavy neurotoxin. This is the effect that alcohol has on our cells. Once we pour alcohol into our body, the alcohol is immediately absorbed into the bloodstream and through the blood it is led to all parts of the body. The cells are affected by the alcohol and they no longer work as well as they could. The cells become poisoned, they cannot avoid absorbing the alcohol, as it is everywhere. There is no unaffected or "clean" blood, and if the drinker also smokes, there is no "clean" oxygen. The whole atmosphere in which the cells live is polluted.

Furthermore, alcohol causes the liver to work overtime in order to get rid of the toxin. With continued consumption of alcohol the liver gets debilitated, develops a fatty slate, and later cirrhosis of the liver sets in. Through this process, which takes many years, the talent kernels that are embedded in our supraconsciousness for making a healthy liver gradually degenerate. This is very serious because in the end (after many years' abuse) our talent kernels become so damaged that we are no longer able to make and keep a healthy liver. As a consequence it is likely that in our next life we will be born with a deformed liver or some kind of liver disease or weakness.

Alcohol has other harmful effects on our body. The bloodstream is polluted by poison, and the poison is taken into each and every organ and cell and into the brain. Our memory suffers, our skin suffers, our digestion suffers, and our health in general deteriorates drastically. In the end and after heavy drinking for a number of years, our talent kernels for creating a healthy body will be destroyed and in the incarnations to come we might be born insane or mentally retarded.

Martinus very clearly points out that all kinds of intake of unnatural or unnecessary elements into our body, be it alcohol, drugs, tobacco, coffee, or meat, undermine the health of the body. Our body is a divine instrument for our experience of life on the physical plane and it is our job to take good care of it. The body will only yield a perfect experience of life to our "I" when it is kept in optimum condition. The right kind of nourishment and sufficient exercise and sleep are essential for the optimum functioning of the body. It is only when the body is kept completely free from unnatural and harmful elements that it will yield a perfect experience of life to its originator. When we fill our body with alcohol and tobacco, all our senses are blurred and our experience of life is blurred as well. We simply do not experience life at its maximum potential. We might as well walk around with a sack over our heads.

Alcohol is a substance of a certain spiritual quality. This means that it affects our spiritual bodies, thus causing the aura to debilitate. Alcohol is particularly harmful to the energy of intuition. Alcohol and the energy of intuition are incompatible. It is through the growing influence of the energy of intuition that we will begin to experience cosmic glimpses. But the intake of alcohol will completely prevent us from getting anywhere near the energy of intuition. Martinus was once invited to a reception and through the strength of social pressure he accepted and drank one glass of sherry, the only glass of alcohol he ever drank. The effect of this was that he was cut off from his cosmic source of knowledge for two whole days. For two days he was not able to write a single word, because the energy of intuition could not coexist with the alcohol in his body. This example illustrates that alcohol should be avoided if we want to be able to access the higher spiritual energies.

All Diseases Are Karma

All diseases that we are born with are karma. A disease in a child is not something that the child inherits from its parents, nor is it due to unfortunate circumstances or chance. If a child is not born healthy, the reason for this has to be found in its former lives. Through autodestructive abuse or accidents in former lives, the talent kernels of the "I" may have been damaged and consequently the "I" is no longer able to create a completely healthy body. The effect of continued abuse of alcohol is mental deficiency in the following life. The person who has abused alcohol throughout a whole life has effectively destroyed his talent kernels for the creation of a healthy body. The talent kernels are so degenerate and debilitated that they can only do the job of creating a body in an imperfect way. The body that is created by degenerate talent kernels is anything but perfect. It is crippled, debilitated, and possibly insane.

In this connection I think it is worth mentioning that beings that have destroyed their talent kernels for creation of a healthy body and consequently become mentally deficient still have to be born. If they are not born onto the physical plane they will not be able to get on with their development. They can only develop away from abuse and gradually regenerate their talent kernels for bodily creation through incarnations on the physical plane. If they are forever stuck on the spiritual plane, their development is halted. They simply *have to* be born.

In Denmark it has for some years now been the practice to offer all pregnant women over the age of thirty-five a so called amniotic fluid test. Through an analysis of the amniotic fluid it can be determined if the embryo is normal or if it suffers from, for instance, Down's syndrome or mongolism. If the fetus suffers from Down's syndrome, abortion is recommended and in most cases accepted and carried out. It is very understandable that most parents will opt for abortion, as caring for such a child is very demanding and burdensome. Still these children have to be born. And when they *are* born they are born to parents whose development in some way will benefit from the experience of caring for a sick child. This experience, burdensome and unpleasant as it may be, will surely develop tolerance and a greater ability to love in the parents. Having this experience may well be a very decisive step in the development of the parents. When such a child is aborted, the development of both the parents and the child is postponed.

But as I said, the mentally deficient children, the new bodies of the beings that destroyed their talent kernels in a former life, have to be born. So what happens? It has been seen in recent years that children with Down's syndrome are born to younger and younger women, women that are under the age of thirty-five and who consequently are not offered the amniotic fluid test. As these children have to be born, they will get born. We cannot "outsmart" the law of karma, nor halt development. The talent kernels that have been destroyed through autodestructive behavior in former lives have to be regenerated, so the children with Down's syndrome have to be born.

If talent kernels have been destroyed, be it through autodestructive behavior or injuries, this will affect the body in the next incarnation. This is pointed out by Martinus, and it is confirmed by regression therapists who have demonstrated how our present physical body can be affected by incidents or accidents in former lives. It is not only the psyche that may have suffered from injuries or sufferings in a past life. Severe physical pain in determined areas of the body may have its origin in a past life.

Also, scars that we are born with and birthmarks are vestiges of injuries to the body inflicted in past lives. Ian Stevenson's books *Twenty Cases Suggestive of Reincarnation* and *Where Reincarnation and Biology Intersect* have many examples of how scars originating in one life are still visible on the body in the next life. One of the best examples of this is probably the case of Ashok Kumar/Ravi Shankar. Ashok Kumar was the son of Sri Jageshwar Prasad and at the age of six he was brutally murdered by two men who slit his throat with a knife or a razor. Not long after the murder, a boy was born to parents not far away from the town where Ashok Kumar lived. The boy was named Ravi Shankar and when he learned to speak he claimed to be the son of Sri Jageshwar Prasad although he did not know this man. He could give details of the murder of Ashok Kumar and could even identify the murderers. I quote: *"Ravi Shankar's mother testified that the boy had a linear mark resembling closely the scar of a long knife wound across the neck. She said she first noticed this mark when he was three to four months old. The mark was apparently congenital."*[2] Again, this is an example of how talent kernels are affected by injuries in a past life so that the next physical body of the being will show these injuries as scars or birthmarks.

Martinus clearly points out that both our bodily health and our fate are results of our own former behavior. Everything that happens to us has been caused by ourselves in a former life. The reactions of our fellow human beings toward us are life's mirror. Our bodily state and our fate are harvests of seeds that we once sowed ourselves. Nobody is responsible for our fate but ourselves. There is no one else to blame. If we are crippled, unhappy, or miserable we did this to ourselves. There are no martyrs. The strictest justice rules the universe.

Most people do not like to hear that they themselves are responsible for their own fate. People can get really upset when they hear this. It is much nicer to have somebody to blame, because then it is not our own fault if we are miserable and unhappy. We all seem to have a tendency to prefer having somebody to blame and not to want to take responsibility ourselves. But isn't it much more just that things do not happen by chance and that nobody has to suffer for wrongs other than those of their own doing? Would you rather that the universe were organized so that it was your neighbor who caught a cold when your feet got wet? Would that be sensible and logical? Isn't it more logical that you get the cold when it is your feet that get wet?

Would you rather pay other people's bills than your own? Would you prefer having to pay the bills of your neighbor, whose extravagant spending is completely outside your range of influence? When it comes to paying the bills, don't we normally insist on paying only our own share? We normally do not accept to pay other people's debts, but when it comes to our fate we automatically assume that it is other people's offenses that we have to pay for. Somehow it makes us feel better to think that we are the victims of injustice, because then we are free from responsibility ourselves. But would it be a better world if our neighbor caught the cold when our feet got wet and if we had to pay our neighbor's debts instead of our own? Isn't it better that it is only our own acts that we have to pay for? Isn't it preferable that we only get to reap the effects of our own seeds?

How could we learn anything if we were not taught how our actions affect others? And how could we become real human beings if the effects of our actions were not shown to us? It is through our own sowing and reaping that we accumulate wisdom and are transformed from animals into real human beings. This can only be done when we are shown the effects of our own actions. Karma is life's pedagogic.

How can we outgrow our animal mentality and become real human beings if we are not shown the effects of our acts? Karma is a loving instruction that reflects our own actions. If we were not shown the effects of our actions, no learning could take place. We would never learn to distinguish between good and evil if we were not shown the effects of our own actions. It is only when we reap the effects of our own former deeds that we eat from the tree of knowledge, that we learn and accumulate experience.

Let me just stress that nobody gets to suffer more than anybody else when you look at things in a perspective that encompasses several lives. We all get a similar amount of suffering and we only get the suffering that is necessary for us to learn. As the basic tone of the universe is love, no being can forever remain in darkness or in suffering. We only suffer to learn compassion, and when we have become sufficiently loving, no more suffering is necessary.

Karmic Effects

As long as we can find it in our heart to do wrong to our neighbor, we will be used as instruments in the dark fate of others. The fate that we thus inflict upon our neighbor is his own doing, not ours, but because we had it in our heart to carry out an unloving act, we sowed dark karma for ourselves to reap later. When we can do no evil and can manifest only love, we are no longer suitable instruments in the unpleasant karma of others and we will be instruments for good karma only, thus sowing only good karma for ourselves.

But until we reach the point when we sow only good karma we will reap the unpleasant karma that we once sowed ourselves.

In his book *Other Lives, Other Selves*, Roger Woolger has this example from regression therapy: *"A man remembers a late medieval life where he took great sadistic pleasure in the torture and execution of witches. After this he finds himself in another life where he is the political victim of the Nazis and is tortured to death for information he does not possess. As he dies he recognizes a version of his previous cruel self in the figure of his torturer and realizes the potential for an endless, hellish, sadomasochistic spiral of vengeful lives. Instead, he is able to forgive his adversary and seems to be released from further karmic violence either to himself or to others."*[3]

In this case we see not only how the man reaped what he had sowed, but we also see how his ability to forgive broke the otherwise evil circle and released him from karmic violence. As he was no longer a suitable instrument in the evil fate of others, his fate changed for the better.

Let me again underline that karma is not a punishment. Karma is simply the return of energies that we once sent out ourselves. The energy will return in the same shape as it was sent out. A loving energy will return as a loving energy and a hateful energy will return as a hateful energy. This is simply how things work, so it cannot be a punishment. Karma is a loving instruction of how to mix our energies, so that we do not create unhappiness for ourselves. Karma is life's own speech, pointing us in the right direction. We could never accumulate wisdom if we were not taught by life itself, and karma is the greatest teacher.

Obviously, also all good things that we do give us karma. From good deeds we reap a good karma. If we have helped others, shown compassion, shown understanding, been a good and supportive friend, been generous, loving, and positive, it is help, compassion, understanding, friendship, generosity, and love that we will reap.

But as we are now passing the last part of the animal kingdom and as we through our animal mentality have sown a lot of dark karma, it is logical that we are now reaping a lot of misery and unhappiness. The unpleasant karma that we have sown in former lives through the predominance of the animal mentality in our consciousness is the reason that there is so much unhappiness and misery in the world today. We are in the process of reaping the "wild oats" that we sowed as animals or unfinished human beings. But the reaping of these "wild oats" and the consequential sufferings are our "passport" out of the animal kingdom, the passport that will eventually give us access to the real human kingdom.

When we think about the difficulty of the process that we are undergoing it is no wonder that there is so much upheaval, misery, suffering, and pain. We are in the process of being transformed by God from an animal to a human being in the image and likeness of God. Think of a crocodile trying to swallow a hindquarter of a gnu in one go. And then think of Jesus. In these two mental pictures we have the two extremes of where we come from and to where we are going. Changing a being from a crocodile to a Christlike person is not easy. The crocodile and the Christ are as different as night and day. One is pure selfishness; the other is all unselfish love. One is brutal and bloodthirsty; the other is altruistic and forgiving. It is no wonder that this process of transformation is long, difficult, and painful. It is no wonder that it takes a lot of practice and suffering to "unlearn" the animal mentality and to learn humanity. It is no wonder that a world in which such a difficult process is happening is a world with all sorts of sad fates and misery. It takes a harsh medicine to cure a vicious disease. Our sufferings are the harsh medicine we have to take to become man in the image and likeness of God.

Free Will

If everything that happens to us is karma, then it may seem that our fate has already been shaped and that we have no free will. But this is not so. We do have free will. We can exercise our free will at exactly the moment when we are confronted with our own karma. We can choose how we respond to our karma, how we receive it. We saw that Arthur manifested two different reactions to the dark arch of karma that had caught up with him. In the first example he responded with hatred and in the second example he responded with love. He had free will to choose how to react. It is in the confrontation with our karma that we have the freedom to exercise free will.

We also have free will in many other instances, e.g., in our choice of nourishment. We can choose to eat the flesh of other beings or to eat only a vegetarian diet. Through this choice we affect our karma.

We can choose to be friendly and kind or to be angry and unkind. Again we have free will and again our choice affects our karma.

Martinus also points out another important aspect of free will. He says, "*The law of fate determines that we only have free will to the extent that we, with our own free will, do not block other beings' normal use of their free will*" (*Livets Bog* VI, paragraph 2275). This means that if we prevent others from exercising their free will, our own free will will be blocked. If we confine people to small rooms or restrict their abilities to move and thus prevent them from exercising their free will, our own free will will be affected. This again is karma. What we do to others, we do to ourselves.

In fact, we can say that we have free will to promote our exit of the animal kingdom or to stay there. We have free will to practice humanity. If we choose not to start practicing humanity, we delay our exit of the animal kingdom. We have free will to make this decisive choice.

Compassion and the Meaning of Suffering

There are people who interpret the law of karma to mean that we should not help people in need because it is their karma to be where they are. But this is not so and this attitude shows that the people who have it have no compassion. We should always endeavor to help. By helping we not only alleviate the suffering of our fellow beings, but we sow good karma for ourselves. There is no excuse for not helping people in need. This help may be only a few dollars, a hot meal, or a kind word of comfort, but whatever it is, it demonstrates that we feel compassion for our suffering neighbor and that we are not completely callous. Whatever shape the help takes it will be received by the sufferer as a beam of light, as a comfort, and it will, if only just for a short time, alleviate his suffering. If we see a miserable beggar on the street, we could try to imagine what we would want somebody to do for us, if we were in the same situation. Would we rather that everybody just walk by, or that somebody show us kindness and compassion in order to alleviate our suffering?

In the fields where we have experienced sufferings ourselves, we will have compassion for others. As adults we cannot actively remember our former lives, but still our former experiences are with us in the way we react in different situations. When we are faced with a situation that resembles one we have been in ourselves, we recognize this situation at a subconscious level. It is our feelings in a particular situation that reveal our own former experiences. If we feel compassion, we recognize the situation from our own experience. If we feel nothing, we have no experience. Let us again consider the really miserable beggar on the street. Some people just pass him by thinking that he ought to get up and get a job. They feel no compassion whatsoever and may even spit in his begging bowl. These people have no mental recognition of what it is like to be a miserable beggar, because this is not within their experience. Other people, on the other hand, may feel compassion for the beggar and give him money or offer him a meal or just simply show him kindness. These people have a mental recognition of what it is like to be miserable and want to help the man.

Martinus says: "*Even though people cannot remember their sufferings from former lives, these sufferings still exist in their consciousness as a limit to what they can find it in their heart to do to others*" (*Kosmos*, Nov./1992, page 206).

Whenever we feel compassion, whenever we are touched by other peoples' sad fate, we experience a situation similar to one we once have been in ourselves. The callous person is consequently a person who has not suffered a lot yet. The compassionate person has suffered a lot through many lives and has developed a great empathy and a great sensitivity for the sufferings of others. It is through our sufferings that we learn to think correctly, that we eat from the fruit of the Tree of Knowledge. In this way we see that the sufferings are a divine measure that is able to transform the being from an animal to man in "the image and likeness of God."

In a time of suffering it may be a comfort to think that our sufferings have a purpose and that we are in the process of being transformed into real human beings, full of compassion and love. In our darkest hour, when perhaps we are suffering the loss of a loved one or the loss of health, it will be a comfort to know that our suffering is not in vain, that there is a meaning with the hardship. This thought may make the suffering more bearable. It is easier to accept the things that happen, when we know why they happen. When we accept that our suffering has a higher purpose and that it is the will of God that we be transformed into real human beings, comfort will come to us.

The Concept of Sin and the Forgiveness of Sin

In the New Testament there is a lot of mentioning of sin, and the Christian churches have emphasized the concept of sin to a very high degree. We have learned that there are seven "deadly" sins and that we have to pay for our sins. The concept of sin has been used by the Christian churches to control the congregations and make people behave. We have even been told that we shall pine eternally in hell for our sins.

Now Martinus tells us that in a cosmic sense there is no sin. This may be quite surprising to hear and somehow it may seem difficult to accept, as there are certainly acts that one should not do, such as killing. Killing may seem like a sin.

However, Martinus says that God does not judge and there is no experience that God does not grant his son, the human being, in order for this son to reap experience and learn. The human being is allowed to try everything in his accumulation of experience. If he were not allowed to try all possible scenarios, how could he reap experience? He can only reap experience when his range of experiments is unlimited. God does not judge and say that this act is better than another act. God has laid the whole field open at our feet and there is nothing that we are not allowed to try. In this way everything is allowed and any experience is granted. In this way the planet is like one big experimental laboratory where a large number of different experiments takes place. There is no experiment, however fantastic, that the son is not allowed to carry out. If the son wants to carry out torture on his fellow man, then he can go right ahead and do it. If the son wants to kill his brother, he can go right ahead and do it. God will not interfere in these acts and prevent his son from carrying them out.

But, the son will have to reap the consequences of all his acts, just as we have seen through the look at the law of karma. The son is allowed to sow whatever seeds he wants to, but he will have to reap the subsequent harvest. There is no escaping the harvest. There is no degree of judgment in the harvest and so it cannot be called a sin. It is simply the way things work. The harvest is simply an effect of the seed. And God is telling his son, "If you sow thistles, you will reap thistles and if you sow wheat, you will reap wheat." It is no sin to sow thistles; the seeds are there and you can try them if you want to. You just have to learn what the consequence is. Once you have learned that, you have become wiser. How could we ever learn anything if things did not work this way? How could we learn if our range of experiments was restricted?

When the son has harvested a number of bitter harvests, he has become wiser. He has learned that there are certain acts that will cause his own suffering and he learns to avoid those acts. When he has learned his lesson, he no longer acts as he did before. When he has learned his lesson, no more instruction is necessary.

Let us say that the son has taken 149 lives through his passage of the animal kingdom. For these killings he has himself been killed 89 times. But after the 89th time of being killed, the son has learned that killing is no good; that it will only make him reap unhappiness, and he is no longer able to kill. He simply cannot kill anymore and he stops carrying arms and becomes a vegetarian. He shuns away from all brutality and becomes an advocate for peace. But in his "account books" he still has a "deficit" of 60 lives. There are still 60 lives that he has taken and that he has not paid for. But because he has now become a completely peace loving individual who cannot even kill a fly, the "deficit" of the 60 lives is canceled in his "account book." He never gets to pay those back. He has shown that he has learned his lesson and consequently the old debts are forgotten about. This is, explains Martinus, "the forgiveness of sin" in the shape of the dissolution of all the old arches of dark karma whose mentality we have outgrown. We get only the necessary amount of suffering to learn the lesson. Once the lesson has been learned, no more instruction is needed. When we outlive a certain mentality the vibration of our aura changes, and when the old arches of karma return they will be repelled because their wavelength is no longer compatible with our own. This means that the old karma is dissolved, or the "sins" are forgiven.

Collective Karma

A nation creates karma just like a person. A nation is an entity in its own right.

A nation consists of many individuals, and these individuals have come together to act with a common desire and with a common voice in the nation. The nation as such therefore sows seeds whose consequences it will reap later, just as an individual being does.

Germany before the Second World War is a good example of this. Through the sowing of attacks on neighboring states, the occupation of neighboring states, through armament, bombings, shootings, and aggression, Germany sowed a karma of war. This led to the subsequent harvest it so bitterly reaped in the last years of the war. The once so high and mighty nation whose aim it was to conquer the world was a miserable country in ruins with a wounded and starving population when the war ended in 1945. Germany sowed war and it reaped war. Germany's pride was humbled, as pride goes before a fall.

In the same way, other nations that sow war will reap war whereas the neutral states that have not sown war recently will reap no war. This is no coincidence. Logically the individuals that live in these countries fit the nation. Through the universal principle of attraction and repulsion, peace-loving individuals incarnate in neutral countries like Sweden and Switzerland and war-loving individuals incarnate in countries like Serbia and Iraq.

Looking at the situation of the planet today, we can tell that there are some nations that, through an aggressive behavior toward other nations, have a war karma coming to them. While some nations continue to sow the seeds of war, world peace is still far away. Until this sowing, supported by those who manufacture arms, ends, a fully peaceful world remains a utopian dream. We cannot sow war and reap peace.

We have seen how the last century was characterized by a large number of great and small wars and we have defined this passage as the culmination of darkness. We have also seen how Martinus, in spite of the darkness, says, "*everything is very good.*" The things that have happened had to happen so that we could unlearn our animal mentality and learn love and forgiveness. Things are happening according to the master plan. The suffering was there for a reason. Through the look at the law of karma we have seen how this law works and that we reap as we sow. The fact that we reap as we sow also gives us an indication of what will happen in the future. We can see that there are people and consequently states that still sow war. We know that when we sow war we will reap war. This ought to tell us that some states still have a war karma coming to them. Until this war karma has been released, peace on Earth will not be possible. Some countries are still very aggressive and are still building up their stocks of lethal arms. The arms race, although slowed down, has not halted yet. Because there is action, there will be a reaction.

Shaping Our Fate

The main driving force in the shaping of our fate is our own desires, says Martinus. Karma is a very decisive factor in how our life evolves. Our life today is a result of what we have sown before in this and former lives. But in a way karma points backward, as karma is the fruit of what we have sown. However, in our fate there must also be a compass so that we can set our rudder in the right position to enable us to go forward in life in the right direction. Our own desires are this compass. What else could it be? Our desires can only go in the direction of the opposite of the things with which we have become satiated. The fundamental principle of hunger and satiation helps us define our desires.

We will get what we want, sooner or later. In this life or in a future life. Our thoughts and desires are energies that we send out into the universe. Sooner or later our life will shape itself according to these desires because energies are set in motion to make them reality.

There is no experience that the living being is not granted by Providence. If the being wants to be a warlord and wants to feel like a great and important person who fights and kills other beings, so be it. If the being wants to be a high and mighty millionaire who has a large palace to live in, a garage full of smart cars, and a lot of servants to order about, so be it. If the being wants to be an important politician who makes big decisions about the future of the country, so be it. If the person wants to be a rich and famous movie star who is admired by everybody, so be it.

But logically, the being must reap the harvest of what he has thus sown. And if the harvest is a bitter one, then the being must accept this bitter harvest and through this learn that what he once desired was not a good mixture of the cosmic energies, as the result was his own suffering. Through this the being will learn to set his compass in the right direction and to desire only things that do not cause harm for others and consequently for himself.

In order to create a happy fate for ourselves, there is only one rule: "Love your God above all else and your neighbor as yourself." If this is our compass and we sow only good deeds and love, our harvest will be a life in happiness and bliss. We can only be to our own advantage by being to the advantage of others.

So the recipe for happiness is quite simple: Only do to others what you want others to do to yourself, and love your neighbor. Be positive and truthful and let your love shine on everybody. In this way we sow only happiness and we will reap only happiness.

Through this look at the law of karma we have seen that we reap as we sow, that we are the only ones responsible for our own fates and that nobody is a martyr. We have seen that the strictest justice rules the spiritual world and that nobody suffers an unhappy fate that was not his own doing. We have seen that, in a cosmic sense, there is no sin, only acts whose consequences we will have to bear. We have seen that karma is not a punishment, but a loving instruction of what is good and what is bad. We have seen that our fate is shaped by our karma and by our own desires, and what we desire we will eventually have. This may take time, but we will get what we want eventually. If what we want creates an unhappy fate for others, then we must reap the consequences of this and reap an unhappy fate for ourselves. Through our sufferings we will learn what is good and what is bad and in the end we will graduate as real humans, free of all animal tendencies. We will then learn to sow only love.

14

The Transformation of
the Sexual Poles

Two Kinds of Love

In previous chapters it has been explained that the
universe is God's body and that everything that exists is part of
God's body. As God is pure love, the basic tone of the universe is
love. But there also has to be a contrast to love. In order to renew
our experience of life there has to be contrast, as contrast is fundamental for all perception. As the darkness is there only in order to
constitute a contrast to the light, the darkness is a blessing in the
same way as the light is a blessing. Seen from God's own viewpoint
darkness and light are two different manifestations of love, equally
necessary and equally good. In this way there is nothing in the universe that is in essence bad, there is only good, although the good
can be divided into the pleasant good (light) and the unpleasant
good (darkness). The unpleasant good is the animal kingdom.

The universal love which is the basic tone of the universe is the
first kind of love, the basic love that is God. This universal love is
light. The being that nurtures universal love loves all living beings
unconditionally: plants, animals, and humans.

However, the universal love or unconditional love between all
living beings is not present in the passage of darkness. There would
be no darkness if the light of all-encompassing universal love were

to be present in the darkness. God can only create darkness if he takes the light of universal love away. So in order to create darkness God has made a place where the light of universal love has been excluded. This place of darkness is the animal kingdom. The animal kingdom is a place where God paints a picture with a lot of darkness in it. But still, in this black picture there are a few streaks of light. So even in the passage of the animal kingdom, in the passage of cosmic darkness, there is a faint ray of light, a weak kind of love present. This love has nothing to do with universal love, as it does not allow the beings to love all other beings. The weak kind of love or faint ray of light that exists in the animal kingdom is the love that exists between two beings of the opposite sex, or "mating love."

The "mating love" is the second kind of love. This kind of love is a limited love, as it only allows the beings to love one chosen member of the opposite sex. "Mating love" only allows the heart to flow with loving feelings toward one single member of the opposite sex at a time. In this way we see that "mating love" has nothing to do with universal love, as universal love means that the being loves all living creatures.

This "mating love," often referred to as "romantic love," is highly praised and sought after today, indeed it is considered as the most important kind of love. However, it is nothing but a faint shadow of the real thing. But as this romantic love is all we have at this point in time, it is no wonder that we cling to it as a ship-wrecked person clings to a piece of driftwood. Innumerable books, films and songs are dedicated to the praise of this romantic love, which is the highest object of our desires today.

Being "In Love"

Martinus explains that "mating love" is in fact an artificial love. It is artificial in the sense that you do not necessarily really love the being that you are "in love" with, you are only infatuated by the being. If you have ever been "in love" you will know what is meant by this. Being "in love" is really a kind of obsession. When you are "in love," you feel as if you have caught some kind of flu that has taken complete hold of you. Your whole bodily state is changed. Your pulse is higher, you have no appetite, you pine for the "loved" one and think of nothing else. You cannot concentrate on your work, you are very nervous, and in general you are not far from feeling crazy. Martinus explains this state in the following way:

When you are "in love," the loved one represents God for you. When you think of the loved one, you think that this person is somebody very elevated, grand, noble, and august. The mere thought of the loved one fills you with awe and you feel that you are really not worthy to be with him. When you are away from each other and you think of him (which you do almost incessantly) you cannot really remember his face. When you prepare to meet him, you take great pains about your appearance, you try on ten different outfits, you put on makeup and set your hair as if you were to meet the King himself. You are generally too early for the appointment and you nervously have to wait for time to pass in alleyways or behind parked cars. When you finally meet, you are so nervous that you feel that your knees cannot carry you. When you touch the loved one, it is as if flashes of fire run through your whole body. This whole range of feelings that you experience when you are "in love" have in reality nothing to do with the actual person that you are "in love" with. These feelings arise because in the state of being "in love" the beloved one represents God. You feel for this person as you would were you faced with God himself. You are full of awe and admiration. Martinus calls the desire and fire that you experience in this case "the highest fire."

Then when you have been with your "beloved" for a certain time, this feeling of being with someone grand and noble wanes off and after some time you see the person "only" as he really is. God "has left." It is then very often the case that the person cannot live up to the grandness and nobleness that you thought he possessed while you were "in love." The person may show some less flattering or even base qualities, and logically you become very disappointed. If in the meantime, in the frantic state of being "in love," you have gotten married, you have then inadvertently got stuck with some-body that you may not necessarily even like. Logically this causes a lot of unhappiness and misery, especially if there are now children and the marriage has to be dissolved.

The elated feeling of love that we feel toward the beloved dur-ing the period of being "in love" is really a substitute for the uni-versal love to which we have no proper access during our passage of the animal kingdom. This elated, frantic feeling is artificial in the sense that it has very little to do with the person for whom we feel this love. It is an infatuation. If we are lucky, we find that we can love and have warm feelings toward our mate after the honey-moon is over and the infatuation has gone out of the relationship. We may then experience a happy marriage. The infatuation that we experience while "being in love" also secures the propagation of the species, as the experience of "the highest fire" has been linked to reproduction in this section of the cycle.

Let us look at the organic structure that is responsible for the two different kinds of love: the sexual poles of the beings and the transformation of these poles.

The Human Being in the Image and Likeness of God

Have you ever wondered why there was no Mrs. Christ? Have you ever asked yourself why Jesus did not have a wife? Well, whether you have ever thought about this or not, the fact is there: Jesus was single. He was unmarried. He did not have a wife. Nor was there a Mrs. Martinus. Martinus was also single.

Now, why did Jesus not have a wife? Because, although Jesus appeared on Earth in the body of a man, he was not really a man. He was a human being. The human being in the image and like-ness of God is neither a man nor a woman. The human being in the image and likeness of God has his masculine and feminine poles in balance. This means that the female pole has reached the same degree of unfolding as the male pole. The two poles are equal in size. The human being in the image and likeness of God is as much a woman as a man, as much a man as a woman. The human being in the image and likeness of God is Man as in Mankind.

The Two Poles

The concept of the two sexual poles can be explained like this: Imagine that each individual has two imaginary test tubes in his supraconsciousness, each representing either the male or the female pole. Let us say that we can fill the test tubes with mercury. When it is only the male test tube that is full with mercury, and the female test tube is empty, the individual is 100 percent male. When it is only the female test tube that is full with mercury and the male test tube is empty, the individual is 100 percent female. However, the level in the test tubes is never completely constant. It fluctuates. The level is regulated by the mother energy. At a certain point in time one of the test tubes is full and the other is empty. You then have an individual that is 100 percent either male or female. This pure state of either maleness or femaleness is reached in the part of the animal kingdom where the beings are still real animals. How long this stage of 100 percent maleness or femaleness lasts I cannot say, but after a certain time energies are put in motion that will start a process away from the full stage of only one of the tubes. Gradually the level of mercury drops in one test tube, only to be placed in the other test tube. Once the level of mercury drops in the male test tube, the level rises in the female test tube. At a certain point the level of mercury in the two tubes reaches a balance point. At the balance point there is an equal amount of mercury in both test tubes. The individual is then neither a man nor a woman, but double poled.

Once the balance point has been reached, it stays like that for a considerable time, that is from the real human kingdom on the physical plane and all through our passage of the spiritual realms and into the physical plane of the next cycle. When we reenter the physical plane after having lived as spiritual beings for eons of time, we still have our two poles in balance. It is only in the plant kingdom that one pole starts to predominate and the other starts to decline. So whether we are male or female is something that is regulated by the mother energy and consequently it fluctuates. Maleness or femaleness is not a constant characteristic of the being.

Let us take a closer look at this interesting aspect.

The One-Poled Being

The beings that live in the animal kingdom to which we humans still belong are either very much male or female, men or women, masculine or feminine. They are in general completely dominated by either their masculine or their feminine poles. Beings, in which one pole predominates, we call "one-poled" beings.

In a male animal it is only the masculine pole that is developed or predominant. The female pole in the male animal is there, but it is dormant. In the female animal it is only the female pole that is predominant and although the male pole is there, it too is dormant. In fact, one could say that in the animal kingdom the beings are only half. In order to become whole they have to get together with a being from the opposite sex. Only then do they experience wholeness and happiness. The culmination of this happiness takes place during the act of intercourse in which the beings are in reality one flesh. For one fairly brief moment they are a whole being. For one fairly brief moment they experience a ray of light in the darkness.

The fact that the beings in the passage through the animal kingdom depend so much on beings from the opposite sex to fulfill their happiness gives rise to a whole series of related problems.

When a woman's whole happiness depends on being able to secure a man as her own, this means that she looks upon all other members of her own sex as rivals. To the woman, the worst imaginable thing would be if the male object of her desire were to prefer another female to her. The mere thought of this makes her blind with jealousy. This is the worst possible scenario that a one-poled woman can imagine. She does not want to share "her" male with anybody. In a way she nurtures a deep suspicion and jealousy toward all other members of her own sex, in some cases including her own mother or daughter. So deeply rooted is this aversion toward members of one's own sex that the jealousy can include one's own mother or daughter.

The male also feels intensely jealous if a member of his own sex as much as looks at "his" female. If another man touches her, he gets blind with rage and jealousy, and will start beating the rival to keep him away from her. If he were to catch "his female" having intercourse with a rival, it is not unlikely that he would kill this rival. In fact, this jealousy is quite logical as his whole happiness depends on being able to secure "his female" only for himself as long as he is a one-poled being.

It is logical that this one-poled state cannot convey any universal love. It is logical that the being living in a predominantly one-poled state cannot love his neighbor as himself. The one-poled man can only love his neighbor if he is a she. The predominantly one-poled being can only love members of the opposite sex.

With time the one-poled beings learn to tolerate the members of their own sex as they may depend on each other for survival, but the relationship with their own sex is often full of suspicion and jealousy. The jealousy lies just underneath the surface and any small incident may make it flare up and cause the rivals to start a fight. It is like dropping a spark in a barrel of gunpowder. In the predominantly one-poled being, jealousy is raging like a fire through the veins. It is logical that this being cannot show love and kindness to all beings. He simply does not have the organic structure to do this. He does not know how. It is not a question of will if a one-poled man cannot love his neighbor as he loves himself. He simply cannot do it because he does not have the organic structure to do it. His organic structure only allows him to love members of the opposite sex. It is only when the two sexual poles reach a point close to being in balance that Man has the organic structure to feel universal love.

The fact that the being can only love members of the opposite sex gives rise to much of the darkness that is characteristic of the animal kingdom. The selfishness, the possessiveness, the jealousy, the intolerance that the predominantly one-poled state carries in its wake, make life one dark experience. You fight, kill, and seek revenge. You think only of your own needs and not of the needs of others. The only exception to this is the love and protection that you show for your mate and offspring. But the love for the offspring is only a prolongation of the love for your mate (and thus for yourself) and has nothing to do with universal love. You do not love all children; you love only your own. If the situation arose in which you had to choose between feeding your own children or those of your neighbor, you would feed only your own children and leave the others to die of starvation. The love for your offspring has nothing to do with universal love.

The seeds that you sow through your selfishness and jealousy will make you experience more darkness and suffering. The passing of the animal kingdom for the one-poled being is an experience of darkness.

But then, fortunately, the happiness that the man experiences when he is with his chosen female is very great. All his desires go toward her, and when they unite in intercourse it is as if they see a small glimpse of the light of heaven. The culmination of the intercourse, the orgasm, is really cosmic consciousness on an instinctive level. In the orgasm we see a little tiny flash of heaven. But only a tiny one. Martinus paints this wonderful picture: Imagine that the kingdom of heaven, the spiritual world, is a large extravagantly lit ballroom. People are in there in all the light dancing to beautiful music and having a wonderful time. We can hear their laughter and their merry steps. But we are not in there. We are outside in the dark. A very large and heavy door separates us from the ballroom. But underneath the door a tiny little beam of light escapes from the ballroom. This tiny little beam of light is the amount of heaven that we experience during orgasm.

But it is a divine measure that even the passage of the darkest part of the animal kingdom is lit up with a tiny little ray of light from heaven through the coming together of two one-poled beings. God sees to it that the being is not completely deprived from the light of heaven even in his darkest hour. Even in the passage of cosmic darkness, a small amount of heavenly light is granted.

The Sexual Organs and the Sexual Act

The intercourse between two one-poled beings provides a short access to the light of heaven. Through this we see that the sexual organs are organs for the experience of the light of heaven or "the highest fire." In this way the sexual organs represent the "holy of holies." They are the organs through which Man, the Son of God, can touch God with his own body. In the animal kingdom there is no closer contact with God's body than the one that takes place through the act of intercourse of two one-poled beings. Through this we see that the sexual organs are sublime, even holy instruments through which the being can create contact with God during his passage of darkness. The sexual act itself is something beautiful and sublime, and having sex is the healthiest thing a one-poled being can do, both to his body and his mind.[1]

In spite of the fact that the sexual organs are the "holy of holies," these sublime sexual organs are, in general, considered to be base, unmentionable, and dirty by the unfinished human being. It is punishable to show these divine organs in public, it is indecent exposure. Through various religions, sexuality has been proclaimed sinful, something that would lead the being straight to hell if the sexual drive was not curbed through cold baths and flagellation. Thinking about sex has been labeled having "unclean thoughts," and many a young man has been forced by Catholic priests to say innumerable Ave Marias in compensation for having masturbated. It is most likely that the priest, after hearing the juicy confessions of the boys in puberty, had to resort to the lonely act of masturbation himself, as this was the only way in which he could find relief for his own natural sexual drive. Confining healthy one-poled beings to celibacy in the holy name of God is a concept so far away from what is natural that it is only unfinished beings with a very limited dogmatic concept of God who could have thought of this. Being kept away from having a natural sexual relationship is extremely unhealthy for the one-poled being.

The poor priests who in the holy name of God are forced to live in celibacy run the risk of losing their sanity. When their natural appetites arise, they think that they are full of sin, and if they relieve themselves through masturbation the sin is even greater. And if their natural sexual drive finally forces them to seek relief with members of their own sex, the other sexually deprived priests, they think that they will forever pine in hell for this biggest of all sins. The ways the various religions have tried to curb the natural sexual desires of the beings are innumerable and only show that the beings who dictated this sexual abstention had no idea about what sexuality really is.

God, for one, does not begrudge the one-poled beings having sex. He is the one who encourages it. If God did not encourage sex, he would not let his heavenly light shine upon the act. If God begrudged the beings having sex, he would not embellish the act with his "highest fire."

From where, then, does this whole aura of sin that surrounds the sexual act come? It can only come from man himself, or rather from the religious authorities who must have begrudged the men and women their sexuality and consequently tried to curb it. Sexuality has been heavily banned, especially by the Catholic Church, which has never let a chance pass to condemn sex as sinful, base, dirty, and smutty. Officially the Catholic Church accepts sex only as a necessary evil to be suffered in the holy name of procreation. But unofficially, certain top members of the Catholic Church, i.e., certain popes living in the Middle Ages, were renowned for their sexual orgies. More than one pope was known to have fathered several illegitimate children. These double standards of morality must have been hard to explain to the sexually deprived congregation, and they only show how difficult it is to carry out prescriptions that are not natural. Having sex is natural. It is not having it that is unnatural. But why then, did the Catholic Church ban sex and stigmatize it as sinful? The only explanation I can find is ignorance and a wish to exert control over the congregation. If people were busy having sex at home on Sundays, they would not be able to find time to go to church. If nobody came to church, the priests would be unable to exert control over people and they ran the risk of losing their position in society. The priests banned sex for their own sake, not for the sake of their congregations. They banned sex to stay in control.

In fact, many religions approved of sex only if the persons involved were married and intended to have sex for procreational reasons only. You were not allowed to have sex just for the enjoyment of it. So strong was the aura of indecency and sin around this divine act in the Victorian age that our great-grandmothers were told to close their eyes, lie still, and think of the fatherland while their husbands crawled around on top of them. This attitude did not exactly promote sexual pleasure and it is no wonder that some of our great grandmothers were accused of being "frigid." The Church and society in general simply did not allow women of a certain class to enjoy sex. A decent woman did not enjoy sex; she suffered it. Enjoying sex was only for the lower classes.

The Zone of the Happy Marriages

However, little did the labels of indecency and sin help. In general, the beings were still engrossed in how to secure the next heavenly act. It is only logical that all the mental activity of the one-poled being is spent on how to secure the next glimpse of heaven. The one-poled male knows that he can secure more glimpses of heaven if he is strong and muscular and can fight off his rivals. He also knows that he can secure more glimpses of heaven if he is rich and lives in a castle and has a strong horse and a smart sword. He also knows that he can secure more glimpses of heaven if he has power over other beings, if he has a large staff of servants to boss around and citizens who obey him.

The one-poled woman knows that she can secure more glimpses of heaven by being good-looking and sweet-natured. She competes with her rivals, the other one-poled women, about who is the most beautiful, who has the prettiest hair, who has the prettiest dress, who is the best cook, etc. Endless hours are spent filing nails, doing hair, applying makeup, getting dressed, and looking into the mirror in order to improve the looks that nature has given you, so that you can fight off your rivals and secure "your" male.

I imagine that the predominantly one-poled man and the predominantly one-poled woman lived some thousand years ago or more. The man could for instance be a knight and he would ride out on his steed to conquer his enemies and gain more land and power and fame. At home in his castle his chosen female was awaiting him. To pass the time she embroidered and made beautiful dresses so that she could be even more attractive to him when he came home. When he finally did come home, the reunion was so sweet and conveyed so much happiness for the two beings involved that all they needed was each other. When they were together their happiness was complete, they created their own little heaven on Earth. When again they had to separate, the parting was full of sorrow. It is not good for the one-poled being to be alone.

The period in which the beings are predominantly one-poled or close to being predominantly one poled Martinus calls: *"the Zone of the Happy Marriages."*

However, it is not God's plan that we shall go on living as one-poled beings. At a certain point in our development, i.e., when we have experienced a fair amount of suffering through the reaping of the bitter fruit of our selfish deeds, our dormant pole is awakened and begins to grow. This means that the female pole begins to grow in the male, and that the male pole begins to grow in the female.

The goal of this growth is for the two poles to reach a point of balance. But logically, once the two poles have reached a point where they are equally big, the being is no longer a man, nor is he a woman. The being is then a human being, not male, not female, but human. The being that has reached the point in which the two poles are in balance is a human being in the image and likeness of God, a being such as Jesus.

We have seen in the chapter about our present spiral circle that we all stand on different levels in our development. If we look around us in the world today we see that there are still beings that are predominantly one-poled. Change the castle into a five-hundred-square-meter villa with a swimming pool, change the horse into a Mercedes sports car, change the suit of armor into a Giorgio Armani suit, and you have a modern version of a one-poled man. He accumulates riches and power, he flashes money around for all to see, he gives big dinner parties and in general wants to make an impression on his surroundings. But why? To ensure that he gets a few glimpses of heaven. As these glimpses of heaven are best secured through riches and power, we see that he is indeed more fortunate than the man who lives in a council flat, owns a bicycle, and wears blue jeans. The latter's access to glimpses of heaven is much reduced compared to the access that the rich man has.

But the predominantly one-poled human being is almost non-existent today in our modern societies. In all humans the opposite pole has started its growth. This again means that the population of the Earth today is at varying stages of development of the opposite poles.

This fact gives rise to many different manifestations.

Two mainly one-poled beings could live in marital bliss for a whole life. The state of being "in love" lasted all their lives and their only interests lay inside their marriage and their offspring. All their energy was spent in the benefit of their married life. They went to work only to secure enough money to provide for the wife and children. They spent all their spare time with the family. The wife and the offspring were their only interest, their only happiness, their only glimpse of heaven. This is indeed the zone of the happy marriages.

The Zone of the Unhappy Marriages

With the growth of the opposite pole, the being begins to take interest in things other than the mate and family. The being may begin to take an interest in some kind of game, in intellectual pastimes, in sports or hobbies, etc. Every interest that the being has that has nothing to do with the breadwinning and the spouse shows that the opposite pole is making its influence felt.

When the masculine pole grows in a woman, she becomes more intellectual, more independent, and less willing to accept that the role as a wife and mother is her only mission in life. She wants to have a life of her own, she wants to be looked upon as a being in her own right and not just as somebody's wife. She wants to have an education and a job of her own, so that she does not depend on a man for her sustenance. She wants freedom and independence. She gradually becomes unfit for marriage and wants to live alone. With time she assumes the jobs that were traditionally male, such as managing director, top politician, lawyer, doctor, dentist, policeman, even soldier.

The growth of the male pole in the female also means that the curse that God flung at Eve when he threw her out of Paradise *"Your desire shall be for your husband and he shall rule over you"* (Genesis 3:6) has outlived itself. With the growth of the male pole in the woman, she is set free. She is no longer "ruled" by a husband. She has become her own person. It is only when the masculine pole in the woman reaches a certain level that she can free herself from masculine domination such as we see it today.

When the female pole starts to grow in a man his intellect also grows and he becomes less aggressive, kinder, and milder. He starts to participate in looking after the children when they are small, he takes an interest in household chores, he no longer wants to fight, he begins to show empathy and more understanding for others. He begins to take on jobs that were once considered purely female. Today there are male nurses, male kindergarden teachers, male cleaners—in other words, there are males in jobs that were once traditionally female jobs. The development of the female pole in the man means that he will gradually give up his traditional position as "master of the house," as the one who makes all the big decisions and as the one who is in power. He will gradually no longer want power. He will no longer want to be the "master of the house," he no longer wants a woman who is totally dependent upon him, he will gradually want to have an equal companion, a friend and not a subjugated wife. His lust for power will ease and his interests will become more altruistic and less self-centered. He will also gradually outgrow marriage and will want to live alone.

Martinus puts it like this: "*What, then, does the growth of the opposite pole in the man and the woman lead to?—For the moment it develops the intellectuality of the being. The woman gets masculine talents and the man feminine talents, and both develop their intellectuality. With this development the woman and the man become more and more alike, become more and more the same kind of being. As the absolutely perfect marriage in its pure stage is based on the totally masculine male and the totally feminine female in their pure one-poled stages it is clear that marriage degenerates to the same degree as the two parties become more and more alike. It is not the masculine qualities in the woman that the man loves and not the feminine qualities in the man that the woman loves. Because of this the woman becomes a less and less attractive object for the sexual desires and needs of the man to the same degree as the masculine principle develops in her and in the same way the man becomes less and less attractive for the sexual desires and needs of the woman to the same degree as the feminine principle develops and manifests itself in the behavior of the man. Thus it is the feminine principle in the man and the masculine principle in the woman that cause the degeneration of marriage. This again gives rise to the existence of so many degenerating, halting, imperfect and unhappy marriages that I have had to express this as 'the zone of the unhappy marriages.' Is marriage then supposed to cease to exist?—Yes, it proves to be a fact for he who can look deeply into things. When the beings so obviously outgrow the principles that determine a perfect marriage, this clearly cannot continue to exist, but must disappear concurrently with the disappearance of the conditions of its existence.*" (*Kosmos* May/1996, page 84).

I think it is clear that we are witnessing the degeneration of marriage today. In Europe there are many more one-parent families than there have ever been before. Men and women may live together as long as the honeymoon lasts, but once the honeymoon is over, the ties of marriage begin to feel tight and the couple cannot make cohabitation work. This shows that many people have outgrown marriage, that they can no longer accept "belonging" to somebody else. They want freedom and independence; they don't want to be tied down to one specific person. This is a clear sign that the opposite poles are growing.

The growing of the opposite poles in both men and women means that they become more and more whole. The woman no longer <u>needs</u> a man; the man no longer <u>needs</u> a woman. They can both cope on their own. They become independent and free. They gradually feel encumbered by always having another person around. They gradually outgrow the institution of marriage. As more and more people reach this point the institution of marriage will slowly die out. The traditional two-parent family, such as we know it today, will gradually dissolve.

As the opposite pole grows, the person also grows toward being less selfish, less intolerant, less self-important, and more altruistic. It becomes less important to show off and drive around in a flashy car with a blonde at your side. It becomes less important to own a big house and have a staff of servants. It becomes less important to show how clever and smart you are. It becomes less important to flash fancy clothes and jewelry. It now becomes more important to help others, to serve and yield, to contribute to the welfare of everybody, to be humble, kind, and loving toward every living creature.

As we have seen, the growth of the opposite pole in the individual gives rise to what Martinus has called *"the Zone of the Unhappy Marriages."* When the two beings are predominantly one-poled their marriage can be a very happy one. But with the growth of the opposite poles, the beings begin to have interests outside the marriage and also the change in the combination of the energies means that the sexual drive of the beings grows. At a certain point the beings are very easily aroused sexually and their craving for sex becomes stronger and stronger. They can no longer be satisfied with having only one sexual partner. It becomes exceedingly difficult for them to stick to the wife or husband. Their growing sexual drive has to be satiated with various different partners. This is logically not in harmony with the interests of the marriage, and sooner or later the marriage is dissolved. Beings that go through a series of marriages find themselves in the zone of the unhappy marriages.

Many have reached the point at which they are no longer fit for marriage. The lucky ones remain single and thus they have made no solemn vows that they then later have to break. The unlucky ones may have agreed to marry in the ecstasy of being "in love," and before they have time to think, they are settled with a family.

For the beings that end up being married, although they have in fact outlived their ability to live in a marriage, the marriage will be an unhappy one and it will sooner or later be dissolved. This may cause much unhappiness and misery, not only for the unfit being, but also for his wife who may still be in the zone of the happy marriages. Consequently the breaking up of the marriage can cause much bitterness for the part that has thus been let down and also for the children. But neither of the beings can help that they stand at different levels of transformation of their poles. The person who has outgrown marriage cannot help it and neither can the person who is still fit for marriage. This is indeed a difficult phase to pass through.

But again the universal principle of hunger and satiation plays a part here and at a certain point of the degeneration of the ordinary pole and the growth of the opposite pole, a kind of one-poled sexual satiation sets in. With this satiation the attraction of the one-poled sexual orgasm declines. The one-poled sexual act loses its fascination. The being has had enough of the one-poled sexual act. But at the same time as the attraction of the "normal" sexual act declines, the being's desire for a different kind of sexual experience starts to grow. The sexual drive does not decline even though the sexual structure is changed.

Homosexuality

At a certain point the two poles are so much in balance that the being can start to love members of his or her own sex. The humanity of the being has reached a point at which he cannot love only members of the opposite sex. He can love all beings irrespective of their sex. When the two poles reach a point at which they are almost in balance, though still not completely, the being is very much both a man and a woman. He himself is both sexes, although his outer appearance is still either male or female. He may look like a man, but as a matter of fact he is not really a man. So in a way, once a person has reached a point close to the balance point of the poles, there is no opposite sex, because the other beings that have reached the same point in development are also very much both male <u>and</u> female themselves. So to speak, there is no opposite sex to love. There are only other like-minded beings to love. Because the outer appearance of the being is either male or female we say that a person who loves his own sex is homosexual.

Although homosexuality is a natural step in the development of the beings towards the balance point of the poles, some male homosexuals (and probably also lesbians) have been seduced into homosexuality before their feminine pole had reached maturity. They may have been seduced in a former lifetime for instance at a boarding school, in a prison, or in a monastery, where they were forced to have sexual intercourse with members of their own sex, as there were no members of the opposite sex present. Because they were excluded from experiencing a natural sexual act with members of the opposite sex, they had to resort to having sex with members of their own sex even though their pole structure was not "ready" for this. Through a premature homosexual act the feminine pole of the boy or man is forced to grow too soon and instead of a natural development a forced development then takes place. The beings become homosexuals prematurely. This unnatural and forced growth of the opposite pole also affects the beings in their following incarnations. The forced growth of the feminine pole in the man gives rise to the very effeminate homosexual man. In such a man the feminine pole is unnaturally overdimensioned and the movements of his body, his voice, and general appearance is dominated, not by his natural male pole, but by the female pole.

Had the man reached homosexuality through the natural growth of his female pole, he would not have been unnaturally effeminate. But the man who has been seduced and whose feminine pole has been forced to grow prematurely can be grotesquely effeminate, much more so than even the most one-poled woman. In this way we see that the very effeminate man is a result of an unnatural forceful exclusion from natural sexual activities. Had he not been placed in, say, a monastery, he would not have been forced to find release from sexual tension with members of his own sex and his development toward homosexuality would have taken a natural course. In this way we see that many men have become homosexuals because circumstance placed them in situations in which they were deprived from having a sexual relief that corresponded to the level of transformation of their pole structure. Just think of the amount of homosexuals that have been hatched in Catholic monasteries where the monks and nuns were decreed to live in celibacy but who, because of their natural desire to experience "the highest fire" or glimpses of heaven, felt compelled to have sex with members of their own sex. Thus, ironically, the Catholic Church itself helped hatch the homosexuals that it would later condemn as the worst sinners and wrongdoers.

When the development of the opposite pole has been forced, the homosexual man often wants to appear as a woman and dresses, sets his hair, and makes up like a woman. He sometimes becomes a transvestite and tries to seduce men, making believe that he is a woman. Many a one-poled man has had an unpleasant surprise at the start of sexual activities when he realized that his new potential sexual partner was a man and not, as he appeared to be, a woman.

When the poles are allowed to grow harmoniously, the ordinary pole will have the lead until the being reaches the point at which the poles are in balance and he achieves cosmic consciousness. This again means that it is not everybody that will experience homosexuality. All through the natural course of development, the ordinary pole will have the lead and the being will keep his outer appearance, his bodily looks, his posture, walk and pattern of movement, and to a certain degree his voice within the frames of the ordinary pole. It is then only just before the great birth or the opening of cosmic consciousness that the being reaches a stage at which he is bisexual or homosexual. The universal love is then so great that the being is indifferent to whether the person he loves looks like a male or a female. It is the person he loves, not the person's sex. But at this point we can no longer talk about "opposite" sexes. At this point there is no opposite sex. Because the majority of people will then have their two poles close to a balance point, we can no longer talk about men and women. We can then only talk about human beings. Consequently we can no longer talk about homosexuality, as we understand it today, but only of sexuality between equal beings.

Let me just mention that Martinus underlines that nobody leaves a particular type of manifestation until he has become completely satiated with that manifestation. As long as we are still fascinated by the one-poled sexual act, we will have it. It is only when the act has completely lost its attraction that we "move on" to different types of sexual experiences.

The Homosexual and the One-Poled Being

It is a well-known fact that many homosexuals are kinder, friendlier, and much more tolerant and loving than predominantly one-poled beings. Most homosexuals are kind and sweet-natured and not at all aggressive. This is due to the strength of their universal love, which develops in tune with the balancing of the poles. It is also a well-known fact that many homosexuals are persecuted by predominantly one-poled beings for their homosexuality. But this is very unreasonable, as the homosexuals are, in fact, further in their development than the one-poled beings. The capacity for universal love is greater in the homosexual than it is in the one-poled being.

But there is also a reason why the one-poled beings are intolerant toward the homosexuals. This intolerance stems from the animal kingdom in which animals will kill a fellow being that has been injured or wounded or that is sick. In other words, the animal will kill its own kind when these deviate from the flock or when they cannot run along at the pace of the flock. This killing of the wayward fellow being is really a merciful thing to do, as there is no other way that the animal can shorten the sufferings of its fellow being.

It is this instinctive persecution of the being that deviates from the flock that the one-poled being experiences as intolerance toward the homosexual. As the homosexual is different from the majority of the individuals in the flock, he stands out as a sore thumb. The homosexual will be persecuted and despised by the one-poled beings because he does not fit in, he is not part of their flock, he is what they are not, so he must be put down.

Many homosexuals are so unhappy about their state that they dare not bring their sexual tendencies out into the open. They do not dare tell their family or friends about their tendencies and they may live for many years as "closet homosexuals," keeping their homosexual tendencies secret. Some are even married to a member of the opposite sex. These beings are naturally very unhappy, and submitting them to persecution and disdain only shows intolerance and lack of understanding on the persecutors' part. It seems, however, that things are easing up; homosexuality is in general becoming much more accepted, and in various countries marriage between homosexuals has been legalized.

Sexuality in the Real Human Kingdom

As mentioned in chapter 11, development will lead us into the real human kingdom in a little less than three thousand years. But what, you may now logically ask, will happen to the population of the Earth when we reach that kingdom and no longer take an interest in the opposite sex? How will we procreate when we stop having intercourse with members of the opposite sex? How will we procreate when there is no opposite sex?

To answer this question we must again consider the fact that we all stand at different stages of our development. Even though those that are furthest along in development stop procreating, there are still millions and millions who are having intercourse with members of the opposite sex. We see today that there are many homosexuals, but this does not mean that the population of the Earth is dropping. On the contrary, the size of the population of the planet has grown in spite of the fact that there are more homosexuals than ever. Even when a lot more people have reached the point where their two poles are in balance, there will still be people who cherish the sexual act between opposite sexes and thus reincarnation through the womb will continue. But once the majority has reached the real human kingdom and our two poles have reached a perfect balance our sexuality will have changed and so will our way of procreation.

In this connection we must remember that our bodily structure is under development just like our mental structure. Our mental structure is developing away from the animal thought climates towards human thought climates, and when our mentality changes the body follows. Our physical body is shaped according to the energies reigning in our mentality. Our ray-formed body is the primary body, which creates the physical body. As we become milder and more humane our bodily structure develops away from the coarse animal body toward a much finer human body. The body that we will have, once we reach the real human kingdom, will be of a much lighter and finer structure. To the being in the real human kingdom our present body will be as the body of a gorilla is to us today.

With the fine body of the real human being, the person will seek sexual culmination with a like-minded being in a suitable intimate act. This act is exceedingly unselfish and does not demand cohabitation, marriage, or joint possession of goods. There is no desire to possess the other being; there is no jealousy. The act only produces happiness, well-being, inspiration, and bliss for the parties involved without any kind of demand on the other being. After an act of love between two cosmic born, free beings, they go on happy, invigorated, and fulfilled to new wonderful experiences with other partners and so on. In the real human kingdom only culminating love exists and everybody loves everybody.

In a society of real human beings you do not marry, and through this we see the truth in Jesus' words, *"For in the resurrection they neither marry nor are given in marriage"* (Matthew 22:30).

In the real human kingdom the ability to procreate has been taken away from the sexual act, so beings can enjoy a sexual type act or "the highest fire" without the fear of consequences that we know from the animal kingdom.

But if reincarnation in the real human kingdom no longer takes place through the uterus of the female, as only few bisexual acts of intercourse take place, how then will the beings manifest themselves in physical matter?

Materialization and Dematerialization

In the real human kingdom, beings will manifest themselves through the act of materialization and they will cease to manifest themselves on the physical plane through the act of dematerialization. Through the Bible we are already familiar with this process, although we may not be used to calling the process materialization and dematerialization.

When Jesus fed five thousand people with fish and bread at the shore of the Lake of Galilee, he materialized the fish and bread. When Jesus' dead body had disappeared from the cave in which it had been laid to rest after the crucifixion and the stone had been rolled away, it had been dematerialized. When Jesus showed himself for his disciples when they gathered after he had been crucified, he materialized himself and later, after a brief intercommunication with the disciples, he dematerialized himself.

Let us look at how this process works.

In the real human kingdom the body of the beings will be of

a much finer structure, of a much more ethereal matter than our present animal-like body. It is the decrease of the energy of gravity that is responsible for this development toward finer and more ethereal bodies. As has been explained earlier, all matter, both physical as well as spiritual, is a result of vibrations of energy at different wavelengths. The more condensed the energy, the more physical the matter. In the physical world all matter has a relatively coarse wavelength and the matter is fairly dense. As we develop toward the real human kingdom our bodies become finer and more ethereal because they will be created of finer energies. This means that the wavelengths on which our bodies vibrate become finer and finer. This again means that the material of our bodies will be less heavy, less dense, and it becomes more and more spiritual in its nature.

In the period in which a being lives in the physical part of the real human kingdom, i.e., in the period just before it stops reincarnating altogether, its body is of such an ethereal nature that it can be built up of the mental energies or ray-formed matter of the bodies of other living beings. Martinus calls this mental matter "A-matter." This matter is present in the aura of all living beings, as has already been explained. Now, when a discarnate being who has reached the two-poled stage wants to manifest himself on the physical plane, his talent kernels for the building of a physical body create contact with the "A-matter" present in the aura of other living beings. The talent kernels that are in action in this case are the same talent kernels that were responsible for the creation of the embryo in the womb of the woman. During the passing of the animal kingdom the process of reincarnation is very slow, as it takes nine months. But when the being has reached the two-poled state the process of reincarnation takes place in a matter of minutes or even seconds. When the being feels the need to manifest himself on the physical plane, his talent kernels for building a physical body go into contact with the "A-matter" that is present in the aura of other human beings and thus the discarnate being is able to materialize his body in a matter of seconds. He "simply" borrows ray-formed matter from the aura of others, which he then condenses to create a body according to his own talents. When the being has finished doing what he came to do on the physical plane, he then dematerializes his body as quickly as he materialized it, thus giving the "A-matter" back to the beings from which he had borrowed it. The process of materialization and dematerialization will substitute the processes of birth and death in a matter of two to three thousand years, says Martinus.

The being that has reached this stage can, so to speak, walk in and out of the physical and spiritual planes according to his wishes and desires. Through this we see that the distinction that we have now between "the living" and "the dead" does not exist once we have reached the two-poled state.

At a certain point in the passing of the cycle the being has no more to learn, as he has completely outgrown his animal tendencies and his manifestations of universal love are complete. At this point even the need to manifest himself briefly on the physical plane through materialization is outlived. The being then stops reincarnating altogether and lives on in the spiritual world through eons of time in which he passes through the spiritual realms as described in the chapter about our present cycle.

Sex Change

With its two poles in balance the being now wanders through the spiritual part of the real human kingdom, through the three spiritual kingdoms: the kingdom of wisdom, the divine world and the kingdom of bliss (or memory), and into the plant kingdom on the physical plane of the next cycle. This means that the being is two-poled all through the passage of the spiritual worlds and even into the physical plane of the next cycle. From the conclusion of its sojourn in physical matter of the "old" cycle till the beginning of its sojourn in physical matter of the new cycle, the being maintains its two-poled state. So when the being first manifests itself in the new cycle as a physical being, it is still two-poled. The first physical kingdom that the being enters after its passing of the spiritual realms is the plant kingdom (apart from a sojourn in mineral matter). This explains why some plants are self-fertilizing or autogamous. They are still two-poled and do not need a being of the opposite sex to fertilize them. In fact there is no opposite sex for them. But through the passing of the plant kingdom the splitting of the sexes begins. One of the poles begins to stagnate, the other pole begins to grow and gradually the being becomes either male or female. The pole that was predominant in the physical realms of the last cyclic passage now begins to stagnate, and the being will manifest itself with the opposite sex as the one it had in its last cyclic passage. So a being that was male in its last passage of the physical realms will be female in its next passage of the physical realms. This again means that a being has the same sex all through the passing of the physical realms of a cycle. Once a being is female it is female all through the plant kingdom, the animal kingdom, and into the real human kingdom, where the poles reach a balance point. It is only after the completion of a whole cycle that the being changes sex.

In this connection it is interesting to note that many regression therapists find that the being can change his sex from one incarnation to the other. In one life the person seems to be male and in the next female. This is not possible according to Martinus and it is very logical that it is not possible. We have seen that it is the talent kernels of the being that are responsible for the creation of the different bodies that the being has. A talent is something that we develop through practice. Through many incarnations the female develops the ability to create a female body. The creation of the body as female depends on the talent kernels but also on the state of development of the predominant female pole. The development of the poles from stagnant to predominant takes millions of years. The ability to create a female body with all the female organs is an ability that is developed through millions of years. It is impossible that the talent kernels and stage of development of the pole should be able to change from one incarnation to the next. It would be the same as believing that we could change our system of breathing, our system of digestion or our system of blood circulation from one life to the next. It would be the same as believing that we could be a fish in one life and a bird in the next. The female and male organs of procreation are very complicated, and if our talent kernels have evolved the ability to create ovaries and uterus through millions of years, they cannot suddenly create testicles and a penis from one life to the next. Where should this ability come from? We slowly develop our bodily structure from one life to the next. Development is a slow evolutionary process. We do not jump from one level to the next. We crawl. So changing sex from one life to the next is not possible. One cannot be a woman in one life and a man in the next. One simply does not have the ability to create a man's body if one's talent kernels and pole structure are female. It cannot be done.

I think that there is a large untouched field of research here, as it would be interesting to see why it is that some people experience themselves as female in one life and male in the next through regression therapy. In my opinion it could have something to do with the fact that both the therapist and the patient believe this is possible and consequently neither is able to correctly interpret what it is the patient experiences under hypnosis. If a woman experiences herself as a man during a regression, it may be that she sees a man with whom she identifies and she thinks that this man was herself, but it could, in fact, just as well have been a man with whom she sympathized or felt close. Martinus explains that during hypnosis a certain possession takes place of the hypnotic subject by the therapist. The "I" of the therapist "overshadows" the "I" of the patient or subject to a certain degree. So it could be that a former life of the therapist suddenly "appears" as having been lived by the patient. In Ian Stevenson's very thorough work he found that "only" 5 percent of the cases were of sex change. These cases of "sex change" could be due to misinterpretations or possessions. As I see it, sex change from one incarnation to the next cannot be logically accounted for.

I find that the study of the transformation of the poles is extremely interesting as it gives many answers to why we behave as we do today. Many of our manifestations are a result of the level of growth of our opposite pole. If our opposite pole is still weak we will manifest ourselves as selfish, self-centered, vain, jealous, aggressive, and possessive beings. If our opposite pole has reached a fairly high level of development we will be more intellectual but also more altruistic, kinder, humbler, and more loving beings. When our poles approach a point of balance, our organic structure for the manifestation of universal love has been created.

15

Death and the Afterlife

Death Is an Illusion

The vast majority of people living on Earth today live in ignorance about the process that all physical beings must undergo, the process of dying and its result—death. They believe that life ceases at death, that death is final, and that we have only one life. They desperately cling to this one life and many are very afraid of dying. But as we have read earlier, death as such, or death as a cessation of consciousness, does not exist. What we call death is only an exchange of bodies. In the chapter about the structure of the living being we saw that the "I" (or X 1) and its ability to create (X 2) survive physical death, and that it is only the physical body or the part of X 3 that corresponds to the energy of gravity that becomes inanimate at death. Our other bodies, one corresponding to each of the basic energies, i.e., our body of feeling, our body of intelligence, our body of intuition, our body of memory, and our body of instinct, all of which can be seen in our aura, live on after the death of the physical body. These bodies constitute an electrical field or a field of energy, and this field of energy is eternally connected to X 1 and X 2.

As we have a body for each basic energy, each of which is at a particular level of unfolding depending on the strength of the basic

269

energy in question at the time, our day-consciousness is taken over at the time of death by the next body in line, in our case the body corresponding to the energy of feeling.

People who have had near-death experiences unanimously claim that losing their physical bodies did not mean losing their consciousness. They relate how they hovered above their physical bodies. Many saw that their physical body was dead, but they were very much alive, in fact they were feeling fine and actually much better than when they were in their physical body. They had no pain, they felt light, unencumbered, and free. As the spiritual bodies consist of matter that is thousands of times lighter than physical matter, it is no wonder that a feeling of great freedom invades the beings at the moment of severance from the physical vehicle. Especially when the physical body has been rendered more or less useless through old age or injury it is obvious that being severed from this must convey a feeling of great joy.

Death: A New Birth

What is very clear from accounts from near-death experiencers is that consciousness does not cease at the time of physical death. But then what happens? Martinus gives us a very full explanation of this in his book: *The Way to Paradise* and in the leaflet *Through the Gate of Death—Sleep and Death*. In these two writings Martinus reveals what happens when we shed our physical body. Death is a new birth in exactly the same way as our physical birth is a birth into this level of existence. Our birth on the physical level is a birth to an existence in the heavy physical matter, and our death is a birth to an existence on the much lighter spiritual level.

Millions of Deaths

We have all experienced dying millions of times before, so this process is something that we are very used to, although we cannot remember our former deaths with our present level of unfolding of the energy of memory. We saw earlier that the energy of memory has a very weak degree of unfolding at our present stage in the animal/human kingdom. This energy is so weak at this point that we cannot even remember all the details from our present physical incarnation, we cannot remember all episodes from our childhood—indeed some people cannot even remember what they did yesterday. So in view of this it is no wonder that we cannot remember our previous deaths, not to mention our previous lives.

However, regression therapists have shown that this memory can be accessed through hypnosis, thus enabling the individual to relive some of their previous deaths. In these cases the experience of death was always a very pleasant one, so there is absolutely no reason to fear death, as we shall soon see.

All those who have had a near-death experience lose all fear of death and unanimously say that being "dead" was very pleasant. They also become convinced that there is life after "death." So if we listen to those who "have been there," it becomes clear that there is nothing to be afraid of.

Our Two Levels of Experience: Physical and Spiritual

When we looked at the physical plane of existence, we saw that all man-made physical manifestations, indeed also the physical manifestations of nature, are reflections of creations in spiritual matter. Our thoughts and ideas are creations in spiritual matter and nothing exists in the physical world that was not a thought or an idea first. First we get an idea and then we make a drawing of this idea. When we are satisfied with the drawing, we then proceed to transfer the idea to physical matter. There is no exception to this rule. Every man-made physical thing on the planet was an idea before it became a physical reality. All our physical creations are copies of thoughts or ideas that we have already created in spiritual matter in our heads. Everything exists in spiritual matter first.

This again means that we have two different experiences of life, a physical experience and a spiritual experience. Our physical experience is what we experience through our physical senses. Our spiritual experience is our world of thoughts or inner world. We are not so used to being aware of our spiritual experience, but when we start thinking about it, it is clear that we, also in our physical existence, have a spiritual level of experience through our thoughts, dreams, and daydreams.

All our thoughts consist of spiritual matter. In our thoughts we make constructions of spiritual matter. Let us take an example. When we plan a holiday we decide where to go, which hotel or house to stay in, how to get there, etc. We immediately form a picture in our mind about how things will look in this place. We cannot help this. As soon as we start gathering details about an unknown place, we immediately start forming mental pictures of how things look there. These mental pictures are constructions in spiritual matter and from these we could, given the possibilities, create a whole world. Unfortunately, when we arrive at the holiday resort, the place very seldom coincides with our mental or spiritual creation and we sometimes feel quite disappointed when reality does not coincide with our dreams. This is, however, logical, as creations in spiritual matter are more beautiful and perfect than creations in physical matter. We all create pictures, ideas, thoughts, and dreams in spiritual matter.

The same thing happens when we read a book. The people and places of the book become mental pictures in our mind; we create them in spiritual matter. Again when the book is filmed we are often disappointed because the pictures on the screen do not coincide with our mental constructions. Our mental constructions are more perfect and more beautiful than the pictures constructed in physical matter. It is through these spiritual manifestations in our mind that we experience having an inner world.

This inner world is not visible to our fellow beings, but its non-visibility does not mean that it does not exist. What we can experience with our physical senses is only the part of this inner world that has been transformed into physical matter through words, drawings, pictures, or films.

When we look at a house, this is a reflection of the architect's spiritual creation, copied in physical matter. When we express our thoughts and dreams to others, we manifest these thoughts through vibrations of our vocal cords and thus give them physical expression, which can then be picked up by the physical hearing apparatus of our interlocutor. In this way or through writing we can communicate our ideas, thoughts, and dreams to others. In rare cases we can communicate fragments of our thoughts through telepathy, but this is not the norm on the physical plane, although it is the only means of communication on the spiritual plane, as I shall soon explain.

The inner world of our thoughts and dreams is our spiritual world on the physical plane. This means that we have a spiritual experience also while we are in a physical body. Our experience of a spiritual world never completely ceases. In our thoughts we can travel in this nonphysical world, we can conjure up any image we want to. In this way we see that spiritual matter obeys our wishes, but the images in spiritual matter stay inside our heads. Inside our heads we have a spiritual level of experience and we can conjure up whatever image we want to. Spiritual matter obeys our wishes. We can think of whatever image we want to and this image will appear on our inner "screen." This again means that spiritual matter is very moldable. Spiritual matter is the first and primary type of matter, and the spiritual world is the primary world.

The fact that the spiritual world is the primary world and the physical world is the secondary world also means that we have to revise our view of death. We think that this is life and that the other side is death, but it is in fact just the other way around. The spiritual world is the world where we live eternally and blissfully in our spiritual bodies, and the physical world is where we "go to school." What we traditionally look upon as "life" is really a sojourn in the less pleasant of the two worlds. Life on the physical plane can be full of unpleasantness whereas life on the spiritual plane is always pleasant. Why this is so we shall soon see.

Sleep

When we sleep, we have no consciousness on the physical plane. Our experience of what happens around us is nil. Indeed, during sleep our "I," which is described in chapter 6 as being a strong electrical field, has left the physical body and is in contact with it only through the so-called silver cord. The silver cord is like a "cable" that connects the physical body to the spiritual body during sleep. If the sleeping body is disturbed during sleep, the "I" has to return to the body via the silver cord. This return of the "I" can be quick or it can be slow. We all know that some people are easy to wake up, while others take a long time to regain physical consciousness.

What we unknowingly experience during sleep is actually an "out of body" experience, which a number of people have also experienced while awake or through near-death experiences.

The reason why the "I" has to leave the physical body during sleep is that, during the day, we inflict a lot of wear and tear on our nervous system. Throughout the day the nervous system is inflicted with small wounds and injuries that have to be repaired sooner or later. When we feel sleepy or tired this is a sign that the wear and tear of the nervous system has reached a level at which repair work has to be carried out. Usually we start to yawn. The yawning is a collective prayer for help from our microcosmos or cells telling us that rest is needed. The repair that has to be carried out is a repair on a fine, microcosmic electrical level. In order to carry out this repair, the strong electrical field of the mesocosmic "I" has to be taken out of the body so that the repair on the fine microcosmic level can take place. The electrical field of the "I" is simply too strong and disturbs the repair work on a microcosmic level, so the current has to be "switched off," so to speak. In order for the repair work of the nervous system to take place, the strong electrical field forming the "I" has to leave the body. When the repair is done, the "I" can return to the physical body and this is felt when we wake up on our own accord. If we have to be awoken by an alarm clock or otherwise pulled out of sleep, the repair work may not be completely terminated and we consequently still feel tired.

Let us look at what happens to the "I" when it leaves the body during sleep, as this is a process very similar to what happens at death. The only difference is that during sleep the silver cord is still intact, allowing the "I" to return to the body, whereas at death the silver cord has been severed thus making it impossible for the "I" to return to the physical body.

When the "I" leaves the body at the onset of sleep, the consciousness goes with it, as the "I" and the consciousness are one. During sleep the "I" dwells on the spiritual plane. On this plane the "I" experiences a large variety of happenings and it is remnants of these happenings that we experience as dreams. Many people cannot remember their dreams, but those who can often experience the dreams as something very real, which indeed they are as they are experiences in spiritual matter, which is as real as physical matter. If what they dream is classified as a so-called nightmare, they may wake up sweating and with an accelerated heartbeat. Through the silver cord the agitation that the being experiences on the spiritual plane is transferred to the physical body. The nightmare feels very real and it is very real, as it is something that the "I" experiences in spiritual matter. So although our experience through the physical senses has been put out of action during sleep, we can still experience on the spiritual plane. On this plane, while our physical body is under repair, we can communicate with other beings that are also asleep and whose "I"s are on a wavelength similar to our own. If we dream about a specific person, this is probably because we have had contact with this person's "I" on the spiritual level while our physical body was sleeping. If we dream about our lover it is probably because our "I" has been in contact with his "I" on the spiritual plane during sleep.

We can also be in contact with dear deceased beings while our "I" is temporarily on the spiritual plane. People who are mourning the death of a beloved person will often be in contact with this person's "I" during sleep and can thus communicate longings and regrets in this way. After such a meeting on the spiritual plane, the bereaved will often wake up with the feeling that he has had contact with the beloved person and in many ways feels comforted and relieved. This is not "just a dream," but something that has really happened on the spiritual level while we were sleeping. In this way it becomes clear that a deceased beloved person is never "lost" to the people who love him. Contact can be established during sleep with this person as long as we may need it. Martinus says that this is the only natural contact between the living and the "dead."

Martinus puts it like this: "*The natural connection between the spiritual and the so called physical beings takes place when the latter are asleep. When you seem to have dreamt about a person who has passed away, it is in most cases because you have been together with this person on the spiritual plane. This happens because you are 'on wavelength' you have something to give each other spiritually, you have something on your mind, which can help or please the other in exactly the same way as you could while you lived together in the physical world*" (*Kosmos*, October/1990, page 203).

So during sleep we experience life on the spiritual plane. When we wake up certain details may linger in our memory and these we call dreams. Just after we wake up we may still remember some dreams, but once our day-consciousness has taken a complete hold of us, we can no longer remember our dreams. It is mostly in the "twilight zone" between sleep and being awake that we remember our dreams. It is also just when we wake up that we may experience inspiration or new ideas. This is probably because we have been inspired during our sojourn on the spiritual plane and just when we wake up we remember this inspiration. If we want to retain our dreams or inspiration, we can write them down immediately after waking up, as they may otherwise be forgotten once our day-consciousness takes over. The day consciousness is generally so strong that it overshadows the night consciousness completely, once it has got a proper foothold.

Eternal Life on the Spiritual Plane

The experience of life on the spiritual plane never ceases. This experience is eternal, as it is not based on a renewable organism such as the physical body. We can only interact with the physical plane through our physical vehicle. Once our physical vehicle needs replacing through either injury, illness, or old age, it is in general so that our ability to experience on the physical plane ceases. But our spiritual bodies are under a constant renewal according to the unfolding of the basic energies of which they consist and thus our experience of life on the spiritual level can never cease, it is eternal.

Our experience of life on the physical plane is cut off in the periods when we are without a physical body (between "lives"), whereas our spiritual experience of life is eternal and constant as we also have spiritual experiences in a physical body during sleep and through our world of thoughts, as we have seen. Through this it again becomes clear that our physical existence is secondary, as it is inconstant, and our spiritual existence is primary, as it is constant and eternal. We are eternal beings. Our existence has never begun, nor will it ever end. Eternal life is not something that we will get eventually, but is it something that we have already.

As our existence as spiritual beings is constant, this means that the so-called dead are anything but dead, they are only unmanifested on the physical plane, they are discarnate. As we saw earlier, the spiritual plane consists of various realms or kingdoms on a whole range of different wavelengths where life unfolds in innumerable ways, and it is in these realms that the "dead" experience life when they are unmanifested in physical matter. It is in the "empty" space between the sun and the planets (or the neutron and the electrons) that the spiritual realms are to be found. So the "empty space" is anything but empty, it is "full" of spiritual matter, which can be picked up by us here on Earth as cosmic radiation.

The Necessity of the Physical Plane

But when life is unfolding eternally on the spiritual planes, why then do we need to enter the cumbersome and heavy physical plane? We have already discussed the necessity of contrast, but there is another reason: spiritual matter is too light to learn to think logically in. On the spiritual plane all matter is extremely light and it automatically shapes itself according to the energy impulses of the being. As soon as we think of something, it manifests before us in spiritual matter. What we think about will present itself as our outer reality. Spiritual matter is so light that it shapes itself according to our thoughts. We just have to think about a meadow of flowers, and we are there. We just have to think about a palm-clad desert island, and it is there in front of our eyes. The spiritual energies obey our thoughts and they will manifest at our beck and call.

When we think about it, this is no different than on the physical plane. If we close our eyes and think of a palm-clad island, we can conjure up a mental picture of such an island. Also on the physical plane do the mental energies obey our wishes. In the world of our thoughts we can conjure up any vision we want to. The difference is that on the physical plane the vision stays inside our heads, but on the spiritual plane the vision becomes our outer reality. However, the principle is the same—spiritual matter obeys our thought impulses—also on the physical plane. We can conjure up any image we want to inside our heads. On the spiritual plane there is no heavy physical matter to prevent the creations in thought matter from manifesting themselves as an outer reality. On the spiritual plane the energies move completely unhindered and they shape themselves after our wishes. Also we communicate only through telepathy—no words are necessary as our thoughts travel unhindered between the beings. On the spiritual plane all beings are mind readers.

As spiritual matter thus shapes itself according to our own energy impulses, it is not possible to learn to think correctly on the spiritual plane, because the spiritual plane offers no resistance. When there is no resistance, we do not know when we have acted correctly or incorrectly. But the physical plane offers the needed resistance and here it hurts to act wrongly. If we act "wrongly" by killing our neighbor, the karma that we have thus released against ourselves will eventually teach us the difference between right and wrong. Through our sufferings we will learn to act correctly, i.e., in a charitable and loving way. The experience of what is right and what is wrong can only be obtained on the physical plane. Therefore the physical plane is necessary and therefore the being is equipped with a physical body at intervals when he needs to enhance his knowledge of good and bad. Once the being has learned all there is to learn and has updated his knowledge of darkness he has become "man in the image and likeness of God" and the need to enter the heavy physical matter is no longer there. The being then stops reincarnating for a long period of time until he ends the passing of the spiral cycle revealed in chapter 11. After a long sojourn in the spiritual realms and when he has become completely satiated with light, he then enters the next cycle, where he will again have to enter the physical plane to renew his experience of life, as the physical plane offers the needed darkness and resistance as contrast to the spiritual kingdoms of light and lightness.

Death Is a Period of Rest

As is becoming clear, death is really the entrance to or the beginning of a break or a holiday away from heavy physical matter. We can compare our lives on Earth to a long walk that we have to make from east to west. The walk is tedious and tiring and it sometimes takes us through stony and mountainous terrain, sometimes it takes us through flowering meadows, and sometimes it takes us through lush and shady forests. Sometimes our walk goes through hot and hostile deserts with no water and sometimes through fertile valleys where cattle graze. The walk may be hard, it may be tedious, it may be pleasant but at the end of each day we reach a five-star hotel, where everything has been prepared for us and where we will be able to rest in the surroundings that we like most. We may have to wait a bit in the reception, though, in order to have the dust from the day's trip removed, but that is only a minor inconvenience. The afterlife is such a five-star hotel and paradise is no illusion. The reception area is what is traditionally known as purgatory. Let us discover how and why.

On the Spiritual Plane All Thoughts Are Visible

After severance of our "I" and consciousness from the physical body we are purely spiritual beings. As spiritual matter shapes itself according to the desires of the being, the thoughts of the now discarnate being appear as visible details around him. Our thoughts manifest themselves around us and can be seen by all other beings on the same wavelength.

When we pass over we are automatically attracted to a wavelength that is similar to that of our own consciousness or thought matter. When we no longer have a physical body, our day-consciousness is taken over by our spiritual body and this body consists of thought matter. Our thought matter is electrical in its nature and it moves at a particular wavelength. It is the specific wavelength of our thought matter that determines where we go when we pass over because like wavelengths attract each other. It is the law of attraction and repulsion at play. This means that we will enter the spiritual plane on a wavelength similar to our own. The wavelength we thus enter is made up of the thought matter of all the beings whose energy fields or "I"s vibrate on a wavelength similar to our own. This joint thought matter creates the outer world of this particular wavelength.

As our thoughts appear as an outer feature, nobody can hide or disguise his true character on the spiritual plane. If we are dishonest or cruel this will show around our spiritual body. So on the spiritual plane we cannot hide our inner self.

The higher spiritual realms exist on fine wavelengths. These fine wavelengths convey joy and happiness. But "below" the higher spiritual realms there are coarser wavelengths also in spiritual matter where we can find animal thought climates such as intolerance, anger, greed, envy, hatred, irritability, etc. Thoughts on these low wavelengths are simply too coarse to be able to enter the higher spiritual planes, where the thought climates of love and forgiveness reign. The mental matter of the animal vibrates on wavelengths that are so coarse that they are repelled by the fine wavelengths of light and love. Again this happens in an automatic way through the workings of the law of attraction and repulsion. Thoughts of love and forgiveness form part of the higher spiritual world and this world exists on a very fine level of vibration. Into this fine level of vibration we cannot bring the coarse vibrations of animal thought climates in exactly the same way, as we cannot bring our muddy boots into the king's chambers. The low animal thoughts have to be removed first, and once removed we have "only" positive and loving thoughts left. With what we have left we are now able to enter the higher spiritual wavelengths. This again means that our existence on the spiritual plane can only be one of happiness and bliss, because all low thought climates simply cannot enter the spiritual realms—their vibration is incompatible with the fine vibrations of the higher spiritual realms. The low animal thought climates have to be left behind and they are deleted in purgatory, which is a kind of reception area for the spiritual realms. Once deleted, it is logical that the experience in the spiritual realms can only be one of happiness and joy. There is simply no animal thought climates there because of the incompatibility of the wavelengths on which the two types of mental matter vibrate.

As all primitive or low tendencies in a being are revealed for all to see, the transition to the spiritual plane can be painful for beings whose disposition is not very loving. If a being feels bitterness or hatred toward a fellow being and dies while nurturing these feelings, these negative feelings will appear on the spiritual plane as a visible, outer state. When the being passes over, he automatically goes to a wavelength that corresponds to the wavelength of his thought matter, through the workings of the law of attraction and repulsion. The being is automatically attracted to wavelengths similar to those of his thoughts. So if the being is bitter and hateful at the time of death, he will, at his transition to the spiritual plane, enter a low wavelength where spiritual matter of bitterness and hatred reigns. On this wavelength there will be other beings that are likewise full of bitterness and hatred and it is the joint thought matter of these negative and hateful beings that constitutes the outer reality of this dark wavelength. The thought matter of the beings on the same wavelength constitutes an outer world. As the thought matter consists of bitterness and hatred, this is a very somber and unpleasant world. There is no longer a physical world to see with its blue sky and green grass, which would normally alleviate the being's grim state of mind on the physical plane; there is only a world of dark shadows on this particular wavelength. Here on the spiritual plane there is no outer nature other than that which beings on the same wavelength can create or imagine. As long as they feel bitterness and anger, they cannot get out of this dark state. They are trapped.

The fact that the beings are miserable and isolated from all mental sunshine soon brings them into a state of unhappiness. With the feeling of unhappiness there automatically comes a wish to get help. As soon as the being expresses a wish to get help, the vibration of its thought matter changes and this change means that the guardian angels can contact the being. The plea for help opens a wavelength accessible to the fine vibrations of the thought matter of the guardian angels. They can then free the being from its dark reality. This process of freeing the beings from their dark thoughts is known as purgatory.

Purgatory

Purgatory is a place where beings are purged or cleansed from dark and bitter thought climates that operate only on the lower wavelengths. Purgatory can be envisaged as nothing but a period of preparation during which the senses through which a being can experience disappointments, anguish, sorrow, worries, bitterness, anger, hatred, etc. are deactivated.

After this deactivation, the being can think only happy and light thoughts. It can then no longer access wavelengths that can

create enmity, dislike, anger, jealousy, envy, sorrows, disappointments, and worries. As all the animal thought climates have been
deleted at the entrance to the spiritual plane, the being is freed
from experiencing all the unhappiness that these thought climates bring in their wake. The complete set of senses of the being
through which it can experience the low animal thought climates
is simply deactivated in purgatory.

This explanation makes it clear that the spiritual "rest" between
physical lives becomes a perfect mental experience of light, a state
of happiness and joy. In this way the being is liberated from all its
unfinished field of consciousness. On the spiritual plane the being
can think only positive and loving thoughts, as the wavelengths
on this plane do not allow for the lower wavelengths of animal
thought climates to enter its range.

So purgatory is a period of transition in which the being is
purged of its animal thought climates. We know from earlier pages
that all beings on our planet stand on different levels in their development. Some are very close to the animal in their mentality and
others have a very humanitarian and loving mentality. Between the
very animal and the very humanitarian mentalities there is a vast
range of stages. Beings that can no longer kill, steal, deceive, lie,
cheat, gossip, brag, etc., are obviously on a higher stage and more
advanced than those who can still do these things.

The passage through purgatory for each one of us will be a
reflection of our stage of development. If we have reached a high
level of development and we are forgiving and loving persons, we
will experience little or no purgatory, as there are very few animal
thought climates to purge. If we are still in the grip of our animal
mentality, the passage through purgatory will be more cumbersome, as there is more purging to be done.

If a person dies full of bitterness and hatred, this person will,
when he leaves his physical body, enter a wavelength that is characterized by these dark thoughts. Here he will experience other beings
on the same dark wavelength and this may not be a pleasant experience. If a person is addicted to alcohol, drugs, or other "earthly"

things, it is likely that he is unwilling to pass on to the higher spiritual realms and will stay on wavelengths close to the physical plane.

The darker the experience, the sooner the being will become unhappy and once the being asks for help, he accesses wavelengths with which the guardian angels can come into contact. As soon as the guardian angels can come in contact with the unhappy being, they rush in to help, and the being is purged of his bitter and hateful thoughts and is helped into the higher and pleasant spiritual realms by the guardian angels.

Usurpers and "Ghosts"

A number of people that pass over are afraid of hell. They have heard about hell in church and they fear that they will go straight into eternal flames because of things they have done, their so-called sins. These unfortunate beings are simply afraid to "pass on" into the spiritual realms because they do not know what awaits them. They are so afraid that they feel it is safer to remain close to the physical plane, even without a physical body. So they prefer to "stay." They then linger on wavelengths close to the physical plane. As they do not have a physical body, they feel homeless on the physical plane. They will then sometimes try to usurp the bodies of living beings and this is what happens when a person becomes possessed. I have mentioned how possession can take place when a person is drunk because the alcohol causes the aura to debilitate. But possessions can also take place in hospitals. Patients are often quite weak after, say, an operation, and in such a case the aura is also debilitated. It is fairly easy for a discarnate being to possess a body when the aura is "down." Persons that have been operated on are often weak with a debilitated aura, and they then become easy targets for the "usurpers" who can enter the body of the weak person and take possession.

Obviously, when there is more than one "I" inhabiting a body, a conflict of interests arises. In certain situations the possessing spirit or spirits are in control, and the original "I" of the body does not understand his or her own behavior. Fortunately, making the usurpers go away is not all that difficult. A medium or a specialized therapist has to speak directly to the usurper and tell him that he has been detected. By telling the usurper that there is no hell and that beloved beings await him, he will normally leave quite happily. One can ask or pray that the guardian angels of the being come to assist. We should remember that usurpers are ordinary people who have just been misinformed about the afterlife. They are afraid and miserable. They are not devils or anything like that.

How can we protect ourselves from being possessed? We can protect ourselves by being positive and loving and sending out loving thoughts. The aura of a loving and positive being is strong and impossible to penetrate. Martinus says, *"By sending loving thoughts to a possible dead enemy, you are protected from being possessed by him. It is not only love, friendship and common interests that can "bind" people together in the physical world, but also the mental manifestation that we call hatred. When a person hates another person he manifests a spiritual force, which binds the two together in a common "hell" if the person whom the hatred is directed against is also hateful. This hell exists as long as the persons hate each other and it can span several incarnations. The parties can liberate themselves from their hell once they conquer their hatred, but if they die while still nurturing the hatred in their consciousness, it will inevitably follow them onto the spiritual plane, because it is a spiritual reality. The one of the two hateful parties that is dead has indeed in certain cases the possibility to persecute and "possess" his enemy, if the latter is not protected by his own thoughts. And he certainly is not if his thoughts are bitter and hateful. If he has conquered his hatred and forgiven his enemy, this enemy cannot in any way have any power over him. There is no need to think that there is any reason to be afraid of being the victim of such a possession. If people to whom you have not had the best relationship have died, you should think lovingly of them and maybe pray that they may find peace...."* (Kosmos, Oct./1990, page 204).

It is also beings "trapped" on the lower wavelengths that sometimes manifest themselves in their spiritual body as "ghosts." They are also very unhappy beings that are afraid to pass into the spiritual realms because they fear hell. They may then stay in the houses or surroundings that they know from when they had a physical body and appear at intervals to scare the living daylights out of the physical beings now living there. They may also manifest their presence through mysterious sounds, they may turn electrical devices on or off, they may move things or do various mischievous acts. But again a "ghost" is nothing to be afraid of. He is a miserable and lonely prisoner in a dungeon of his own invention. If he would only ask for help, he would not be there. Should we encounter such a miserable being or hear or otherwise experience his manifestations, we should pray that he be helped on to the spiritual plane and that his guardian angels come to take him away. This may be all it takes.

Practicing Death

Seen in this light it is a good idea that the person living on the physical plane starts to familiarize himself with the thought that he is one day going to leave the physical plane. It is also a very good idea to find out what lies beyond, as knowledge about the spiritual plane will eliminate all fear of dying.

We all know that we have to die one day, but this knowledge is often ignored and mentally put aside. It is something that we do not want to think about, so we pretend that it does not exist. But it is better to prepare oneself than to pretend that death does not exist. Once the thought of one's own death has been internalized in our mentality, we can start to mentally prepare ourselves for this passage. If at the same time we seek to cleanse our mentality of dark thoughts, death will be a beautiful experience, just as the many people who have had near-death experiences describe it. Again we might remember that death is just a change of bodies and as it is an entrance to a light and joyful level of existence, indeed to a wonderful period of rest, we should look forward to it.

One can, in fact, practice how to die in the right frame of mind. We saw earlier that sleep and death are very closely related. We know that when we are haunted by negative thoughts or worries or regrets or anger it can be hard to fall asleep, even when we are very tired. We start thinking about the problems of the day, of what we could have said or done in a specific situation and our mind races. We twist and turn on the sheet and no rest is possible.

If instead of this we concentrate our thoughts in prayer to God and thank him for the lessons that the day has taught us and we ask God to bless the people we know and ask him to help us to develop our humane sides and in general concentrate on being positive and grateful, we will fall asleep before our payer is finished. It is in this positive and grateful frame of mind that we should also endeavor to pass over, because then we will bypass purgatory and go directly to the loving light, which is God's primary consciousness.

Not all beings have to experience purgatory. Beings who are in no mental conflict with anybody and who die in a positive and peaceful frame of mind will immediately after the passage be on a wavelength accessible to the guardian angels who will thus be able to contact the newly arrived being and help him adjust to the new situation. A part of the adjustment to this new situation is an adjustment to the principles and laws that govern the spiritual world. We now have to get used to operating in a much lighter matter than the heavy physical matter, we can move around without being pulled by gravity, we can communicate telepathically with other beings and the things we want to experience automatically manifest themselves before our very eyes just by thinking about them because spiritual matter obeys our will. Our guardian angels will be there to help us adjust to this new life.

The Guardian Angels

The principle of guardian angels is a universal principle. Every physical being has guardian angels and these are his or her personal guards. A whole "army" of spiritual beings is in a permanent state of alert in order to help all beings in need on the physical plane. Just as there are midwives and helpers present at our birth onto the physical plane, there are helpers in the shape of guardian angels present at our rebirth back onto the spiritual plane. And just as our birth onto the spiritual plane is a death from the physical plane, so is our physical birth a death from day-conscious experience on the spiritual plane. Each birth involves a "death" and vice versa.

The helpers or guardian angels are beings that have special interests in the field of helping others. Through the forces of attraction and repulsion of the universe, these beings come to help precisely the beings that they are best able to help. This works in exactly the same way as when we are born onto the physical plane, when we are attracted to the parents whose mentality is on a wavelength similar to our own. The parents will be our guardian angels on the physical plane and in exactly the same way we are met by guardian angels, who will "parent" us when we are born onto the spiritual plane.

Then what do these guardian angels look like? Do they look like the angels on Rafael's paintings with plump bodies and white feathery wings? Well, they do, if the person who has just died expects them to. As spiritual matter shapes itself according to our wishes, we will see our guardian angels in exactly the shape we want to or expect. If the "dead" person has died unexpectedly, for instance in a car accident, and does not expect to be met by anybody, the guardian angels will take the form and shape that can be most helpful under the circumstance. Maybe the guardian angel is a being who has known the newly deceased while they were both on the physical plane and he or she will then appear in the known form in order to be best able to comfort and guide the "newly arrived."

There is also the possibility that the newly deceased will be best comforted in hospital surroundings and in this case the guardian angels will appear as doctors or nurses or similar professional helpers and as such they will little by little reveal to the newly deceased what has happened and help him adjust to the spiritual plane.

If a soldier dies very suddenly on the battlefield full of fear he may not immediately know that he is dead. He may think that he has just been wounded and will expect to see helpers from the Red Cross take him away to a field hospital where nurses and doctors will take care of him. He will then "wake up" in surroundings like these and little by little he will get used to the idea that he is "dead" but that there is nothing wrong with him and he only has to accept this fact. The guardian angels will then gradually be able to convince the soldier that he has passed over to the spiritual plane and that there is nothing to worry about anymore.

On the subject of soldiers dying in combat let me just in passing mention that Martinus underlines that the first to die in a war are the soldiers who do not have a war karma coming to them. The soldiers who have already outlived their desires to kill and who have paid their karmic debts in this respect will be the first to fall in combat. In this case their deaths are a release from the sufferings of war. Through this early death they are freed from the whole horrible experience of combat with its gruesome impact on both the body and the mind of the soldier. The soldier who survives many battles and is wounded and ends up with a mutilated body is paying off his karmic debts and through his sufferings he will develop his ability to feel love and compassion for his fellow being instead of killing him. So there is indeed truth in the saying that in a war or a similar tragic condition the living envy the dead.

The guardian angels also protect and help people who are still on the physical plane. The guardian angels are instrumental in answering the prayers of people on the physical plane and they can interact in the fate of the physical beings according to the karma of that being. The guardian angels are present everywhere and can in apparently miraculous ways interfere in the fate of beings and in many cases save them from harm.

The Religious Person's Purgatory

We now know that on the spiritual plane all matter shapes itself after the thoughts and wishes of the being, so it is very important to try to die in a positive frame of mind.

If we, through religion, have been imbued with dogmas and ideas about hell, about eternal flames because of our sins and a hoofed devil with horns, this is in fact what we will experience as the spiritual matter shapes itself according to what we conjure up mentally. If we conjure up thoughts of hell, we will find hell, as such a hell will exist as a spiritual reality created by the thoughts of all those who believe in hell. Death for these people can be an unpleasant experience, as they will actually live through a situation in which they "burn" in the flames of hell. These religious people will have a reinforced experience of purgatory.

So in this case it would be a good idea to cleanse the mind of all pictures and images of hell. Don't think of hell. Simply forget about hell. There is no hell on the spiritual plane, only if we conjure it up ourselves. Real hell is here, on the physical plane, during our passing of the animal kingdom, the passage of darkness. There is no other hell. On the spiritual plane it is up to us, whether or not we experience hell after we have passed over. If we do not think of hell, we get no hell. If we want hell, we get it!

The real hell exists on the physical plane in the passing of the kingdom of darkness, the animal kingdom with its wars, killings, diseases, sorrows, tragedies, torture, accidents, mutilated bodies, etc. There is no other hell.

Paradise

Once the purging is over, the being can then enter the spiritual realms guided by his guardian angels and he will experience exactly the kind of paradise that corresponds to his desires and wishes and according to the wavelength of his thought climates or mentality.

If you are a scholar and your wishes and desires go toward science and research, this is what you will experience beyond "death." You will find yourself with other like-minded beings in a world of knowledge and research.

If you are a hunter you will experience wonderful forests and fields full of animals for you to hunt, and if you are an artist you will experience the afterlife as a long creative process full of inspiration and fulfillment. Every being gets a paradise experience completely according to his own wishes and desires.

Let us give some examples of what it means when matter automatically shapes itself after the desires of the living being such as it does on the spiritual plane.

Let us say that you were an architect in your physical life and that you still have great desires to create beautiful buildings after you have passed over. On the spiritual plane the architect can build castles, palaces, and conference centers just as he pleases. He does not have to worry about making money or winning competitions. On the spiritual plane there is no breadwinning to think about, so we don't have to worry about making money. When the architect wants to create a building, he does not need bricklayers and carpenters and fitters to complete his work. Nor does he have any problems getting materials as the spiritual substance or "building materials" in spiritual matter are present everywhere. He just has to think of a particular building and the building will materialize before him in the state of perfection that he has been able to conjure up. On the spiritual plane he can construct all the buildings he never had the chance to complete on the physical plane. Here thinking is the same as creating, and a work of art will materialize as soon as its creator has thought it out.

People who are not so advanced in their development will also experience exactly the paradise that they most desire. The pygmy will experience a paradise in which there is plenty of access to game and water and where his tribe is triumphant over its enemies and where his village is well protected and in a good state.

The poor man who has been living a life of misery on the physical plane, hungry and freezing with only rags on his body and no roof over his head, will experience a paradise with a nice house, good clothes, and plenty of food and money for his sustenance.

In the same way there are no limits to the degree in which the vain person's dreams can come true. The vain person will here experience himself as the center of everybody's attention, surrounded and adorned by silk, silver, and gold. He himself will be dressed in purple robes with ermine, and on his chest all sorts of medals and decorations will underline his grandness. He may even sit on a golden throne and from there address his subjects. The vain person may also want to be a millionaire and to live in a grand palace with lots of servants, a garage full of expensive cars, a luxury yacht, and his own stable full of racing horses.

The religious person will want to experience himself sitting at the foot of God's throne surrounded by hosts of angels. He will see Christ sitting at the right hand side of the Father and the Holy Spirit will hover above them in the shape of a radiant dove. He will experience being selected by Jesus when he separates the sheep from the goats and thus he will belong to the great white flock of the blessed that play harps and swing palm leaves to the sound of the singing of psalms and rejoicing.

People who have developed a high degree of humanity and love for their neighbor can on the spiritual plane be able to assume the role of guardian angels and thus look after and help people on the physical plane and during their passing from the physical to the spiritual plane.

There is no need to go on mentioning the millions of different paradise experiences that the person can have on the spiritual plane. Each person will experience a paradise or the highest state of happiness that his level of development enables him to imagine. This state will be shaped by the experiences, knowledge and humanity he has been able to practice in his physical existence. This means that the more advanced his humanity and altruism is, the higher will the spiritual realms be that he can access after passing. There is a multitude of different wavelengths in the spiritual realms and this is in fact what Jesus referred to when he said, " *In my Father's house are many rooms*" (John 14:2).

During each stay on the spiritual plane the being experiences a paradise just to his liking. But as the universal principle of hunger and satiation also applies in paradise, it is only logical that, after a certain time in paradise, we will wish to see a different show. The guardian angels then lead us on to other parts of the spiritual worlds, as we have to pass all the spiritual realms described in chapter 11 during each stay. These visits to the kingdom of intelligence and to the divine world may be brief or they may be long according to our desires, but eventually we will find ourselves in the kingdom of memory or bliss from where all beings return to the physical plane. In the kingdom of memory we will remember many of our previous incarnations, and as we experience these as "gold" copies, we will start to long to get back to the physical plane. We know that we need to get on with our development and that this can only take place on the physical plane, so we start wanting to return.

Our memories of bliss are energies on the same wavelength as the energies of ecstasy that emanate from two lovers in the act of intercourse on the physical plane and through the universal law of attraction and repulsion, we will be attracted to exactly the right lovemaking couple and be their next child such as it has been described in chapter 12. We then recommence the process of reincarnation into physical matter.

The Gates of Death

We have seen how the guardian angels are there to help us in our passing from the physical to the spiritual level. Let us try to look at what Martinus says about beings that pass over at four different ages in their physical existence: the child, the young person, the middle-aged person, and the old person.

The Death of a Child

There can be many reasons why a being has to leave his physical organism while he is still a child. One reason can be that he has destroyed his ability to create a healthy body in his former incarnations through for instance excessive intake of alcohol or drugs. In this case his talent kernels for creating a healthy body have been destroyed and his new body is born with many defects and will not be able to withstand the same diseases as a healthy body. In this case the child's body may succumb to many different kinds of illness such as tuberculosis, leukemia, or other kinds of cancer.

The being can also have created a fate in which he is unprotected against accidents and he may consequently be the victim of an accident. He may also once in a former incarnation have caused the death of children and he now has to reap the karma that this implies.

Whatever the reason for the early death, the unpleasantness that the child has created for itself in former lives will not manifest itself in the process of dying. Of course, the child may experience fear if it is suddenly killed, but this fear will be quickly removed by the guardian angels. The process of death for a child is without darkness. There is normally no passing of purgatory, as very few children have dark thought climates and if they have, these will be quickly removed by the guardian angels. The guardian angels designated to the reception of children on the spiritual plane are beings who have a strong love for children and who have special abilities to help and guide these beings. The world of the child is a world of games and adventure and this is what the child will experience when it has left its physical body. It will enter a type of kindergarten where loving beings will take care of it and entertain it and tell it fairy tales. On the spiritual plane the fairy tales will not have to be read aloud, they will manifest themselves in spiritual matter and appear as real sceneries with real people. The teller of the fairy tale only has to think of his story and it will unfold in front of the eyes of the spectators. Among the guardian angels that take care of children there can be beings that were great fairy tale writers and poets in their physical existence. The fairy tales "told" in spiritual matter can sometimes "spill over" and be "caught" by persons on the physical plane as flashes of inspiration and may thus give rise to cartoons or written fairy tales.

Once the child has received all the attention and loving care and entertainment that it needs, there comes a time in which the child is satiated with the experiences in this world of games and adventure. The guardian angels will then take the child through the other spiritual realms of intelligence and intuition and this will also be an experience of light for the child, although its sojourn here is relatively short. Before long the child finds itself in the kingdom of bliss and from there it starts preparing its return to the physical plane. The memories of earlier incarnations make the child long to return to the physical plane, and these energies of longing and bliss are now attracted to the emanation of bliss from two physical bodies who are experiencing the culmination of their mutual love through the act of intercourse. Of course, it is no chance who becomes the parents of the being now ready to reenter the physical plane. As we have seen before, the forces of attraction and repulsion that govern the universe are in action in this case and thus the discarnate being gets the parents that best fit his dispositions and the karma he has in store through what he has sowed in former incarnations. His new parents will be beings who can give him exactly the experiences that he needs to continue his development on the physical plane and may in fact have been his parents or other relatives in one of his previous incarnations.

The Death of a Young Person

If a person dies in his youth, the process of death will be different from that of the child. The young person's mentality is filled with thoughts and feelings that are quite different from those of the child. Youth can often be a period of many difficulties, where the young person is filled with criticism and protest. At the same time the young person is very concentrated on the physical world, interested in school, in friends, in a career, and probably in the opposite sex. If this is the case, the sudden death of a young person can cause certain problems, as the person is totally unprepared. If death comes through illness the person has time to prepare himself for death, and although the person is not aware of it, this preparation still takes place as it happens during the night while the "I" is away from its physical body. Thus on the spiritual plane the young person is being prepared for his death.

But if death is very sudden, for instance through an accident, some time may pass before the young person realizes that he is dead. And here the same rules apply as always at the gates of death. The guardian angels can only get in contact with someone who asks for help. If the person is so full of anger and denial of what has happened, it may take some time before the guardian angels are able to help. If the young person is so concentrated on his physical life and has no belief in life after death, he may not realize that he is dead and his thoughts may continue to circle around the last events that happened before he died. He can then be surrounded by his own world of thoughts, which will be like a mental prison from where it is difficult to escape. In his thoughts he may drive again and again toward the place of the accident in order to reconstruct and realize what actually happened. The young person will eventually realize that something has happened that he cannot understand, but as soon as he asks for help, this will be provided by the guardian angels.

But young people are very different. Some are very mature when it comes to the question of spirituality, and for these the transition will be quick, as they will soon ask for help and the guardian angels will then appear to the young person in the shape and form that is best fitting for the situation.

The person who dies young will, as in the case of the child, reincarnate again fairly quickly after having had a paradise experience and then after having passed the various realms of the spiritual world.

The Death of the Middle-Aged Person

As in the case of the young person, a person who dies in the prime of life is often very concentrated and engaged in his physical existence. Both men and women can be very busy with their careers, with their families, with building up a business, or with scientific work, etc. If a person dies suddenly and has had no time to prepare for death, the transition can be difficult, as the thoughts of the dead person keep revolving around his physical existence. His head is full of plans for the future, and this future has now suddenly been taken away from him. It is in principle the same as when a carpenter loses both his hands. It is a disaster. If the person who has died has no knowledge about the afterlife, he may not realize that he is dead and may be very confused and uncertain about what has happened. In this case the dead person may need some time to adjust to the new situation and as soon as he asks for help, the guardian angels will be there to provide the help needed.

If it is a mother who dies, she will logically be full of worries for her children, but again the guardian angels will show her that the children are being taken care of and she many even herself take on the "job" as guardian angel for her children and look after them and protect them from the spiritual plane.

The Death of the Old Person

The most beautiful death that a human being on Earth can experience is the natural death of old age. The person has then matured to the spiritual existence and there is no longer anything that binds him to his physical life. In general, old age makes people milder and more tolerant and they are able to accept the coming of death. Life itself has prepared them for this and they may look forward to leaving the mortal frame, which has been rendered more or less useless through wear and tear and old age. It is often a relief to be freed from the burden of an old and frail body, whose functioning is not what it used to be.

The old person will often quietly just slip into the so-called death during sleep and he will suddenly experience himself in a wonderful state of freedom and weightlessness. He sees a radiant gate, which he now remembers having seen many times before during sleep, but then it was not possible to get near it, although he could see how the gate opened to let other beings in, who were free from their physical bodies.

This time it is his own turn to be able to approach the gate and he sees how a brilliant light comes towards him. He sees that he no longer has an old, worn out body but a new, young one from which rays shimmer in a pearly gleam.

At the gate there are more beings of light waiting to welcome him, and the whole scenery is bathed in the colors of the sunrise. The newly arrived now notices that the beings waiting at the gate, who at the first glance looked like angels, are really old friends and relatives whom he has known, maybe through many incarnations. These well-known beings are there to welcome the newly arrived to the heavenly spheres and naturally the reunion is one of pure joy.

During all this, beautiful music has been played, and beyond the gate there are wonderful landscapes as far as the eye can see. There are lakes and forests with all kinds of plants and the air is full of the voices of many birds, which mix with the sound of music. But this revelation is only the gates of death. It is an initiation to a life in the realms of light, and from there the roads lead to wonderful, divine worlds where the being will experience the highest form of happiness, bliss, and peace. He will experience the presence of God more strongly than he has ever done before.

Then after a rest in these wonderful worlds of light and bliss the being will eventually want to return to the physical plane to continue his development and progress and he will reincarnate in a new physical body. Again, he will be a child to two physical beings.

The Dying Person

As we have seen, death can come as a friend if you are an old person whose physical body is no longer fully serving its purpose as a vehicle for the experience of life on the physical plane. A person who is about to die of old age is generally ready to die, and the thought of death does not create any great anguish or worry.

Logically the person who has to die of a disease in the prime of life suffers much more at the thought of death. This person may think that it is very unfair that he has to die now, in the middle of life when the whole world is out there waiting to be experienced.

But the knowledge that reincarnation is a fact and that many pleasures await us on the other side of death should be a great comfort. With this knowledge we know that there is no real death and that we will come back to the physical plane again in a new physical body. We know that we will not lose the people we love. Through the law of karma, our existence is intrinsically interwoven with that of our loved ones and we are certain to meet again, both on the spiritual and on the physical levels. There may be a time of separation, but this separation is only limited and we will certainly meet again.

There is a very interesting observation in Elisabeth Kübler Ross' book *On Death and Dying*. Dr. Kübler Ross observes that the people who are best able to cope with their own death are those who believe that there is a God and who are able to accept their impending death and say, *"Thy will be done."* In this way they accept the inevitable and commit their spirit into the hands of God.

This is exactly what Martinus points out in a very interesting article entitled "The Garden of Gethsemane," published in book number 15, *Out of Darkness*. In this article Martinus explains what happened to Jesus the night he spent in the garden of Gethsemane, the night before he was arrested. Jesus separates himself from his disciples and goes into the garden to pray alone. He knows what fate awaits him, but thinking of the suffering that he and his microcosmos have to go through, he prays to God saying, *"Father, if thou art willing, remove this cup from me; nevertheless, not my will, but thine be done." "And there appeared to him an angel from heaven, strengthening him."* (Luke 22:42–43). Although Jesus was a being from a higher realm, he was so much also a being of flesh and blood that this fear had to come. Jesus expressed his fear like this: *"Watch and pray that you may not enter into temptation; the spirit indeed is willing, but the flesh is weak"* (Matthew 26:41). Jesus was also a being of flesh and blood from the effect of his physical parents' unfinished states. This meant that he could not completely subdue this fear (the flesh is weak) although he himself, had he not been under the influence of the unfinished sides of this physical parents, was completely above all fear of death (the spirit is willing). And we see how Jesus quickly conquered this darkness through the strength of his own soul and through prayer. He prayed intensely to God to support him, and an angel of light then appeared before him. And with the words, *"Lord, not my will, but thine be done"* this crisis was over.

This is a model for all beings of how to conquer a crisis. When a person is in the middle of his own "crucifixion," in the middle of a crisis, or facing a great loss, a death, a divorce, or a separation, this person has to mobilize all his intellectual power in order to find out what can be God's meaning for the pain and suffering. If a person does this he will, like Jesus, conquer darkness.

To the person who is able to give up his own will for the benefit of God's will there will always be sent an angel in the hour of need. And God's will is best done when we renounce the things that have caused the crisis. This may be the loss of a child, the death of a beloved husband, the revelation of infidelity from our partner, or being let down by the person we love the most. The crisis of Gethsemane has many ways of showing itself, but for all of us it is valid that it can best be conquered by adjusting ourselves to the inevitable. What has happened cannot be undone. The hopes that we nurtured about what has been lost have to be let go.

We have to muster all our strength to uncover the possibilities that the new situation offers. And the moment we place all the pain in the hands of God and release ourselves from fear and the demolishing forces of hatred and bitterness and accept that God's will be done, a radiant angel will enter our aura and we will feel the nearness of God so intensely that fear and sorrow will leave us.

The joy of life will then slowly work its way back to our blood and nerves, and we will be able to live our life fully again even after facing a great loss.

This, I think, is the best advice to give to people who are suffering, mourning, or dying, and Dr. Kübler Ross's experiences confirm that this works.

Suicide

"Thou shall not kill," says the Fifth Commandment. This means that you must not kill anybody, including yourself. Suicide is not a good idea. Suicide should be avoided at all costs. Now why is this?

If a person commits suicide, chances are that his frame of mind at the time of dying is very somber indeed. If he were not very low, he would not commit suicide. We have seen before what happens when we enter the spiritual world in a very dark frame of mind. We get trapped on the dark wavelength on which we entered the spiritual plane and we are stuck there. If a person has committed suicide, he has probably not been able to ask for help from others.

If he had asked for help on the physical plane before he committed suicide, somebody would certainly have helped him and he would still be on the physical plane. But he did not want to ask for help and he committed suicide instead. So when he arrives on the spiritual plane, it is also very unlikely that he will ask for help there. He may, in fact, not even realize that he is dead. By committing suicide the person had hoped for oblivion, but after "death" he is just as unhappy and miserable as he was before. He does not know where he is or what has happened, and asking for help is not the first thing on his mind. Asking for help is, as has been explained, the only way the guardian angels can come into contact with beings on the lower wavelengths. The guardian angels have no access to the lower wavelengths unless the beings there ask for help.

So probably the suicider will find himself stuck for some time in the frame of mind in which he killed himself. He will "wake up" from the suicide being exactly as miserable and unhappy as he was when he killed himself. He may not even realize that he is dead. All he sees is the darkness of his own miserable state and that of other equally miserable beings that are on the same somber wavelength. Here on these dark wavelengths there is no sunshine, no nature to seek refuge in, no birds that sing, no parents or friends to call, nothing but a dark reality. Until the suicider finally gets so miserable that he asks for help, he will be stuck in these dark surroundings. As soon as he asks for help, help will be provided by the guardian angels and he will be able to experience a paradise just to his liking, like everybody else.

But in his next incarnation he will eventually find himself in exactly the same situation in which he committed suicide in his last incarnation. Suicide is going back to square one. The situation that caused the suicide has to be solved by the person in a positive and constructive way. If he, in his next incarnation, commits suicide again in the same situation, it is back to square one once again.

Martinus clearly points out that suicide is a very cowardly thing to do. Instead of solving the problems that you have created for yourself, you leave others to sort out the problems for you. By committing suicide you often put a lot of people, your closest family and friends, in a very painful situation. They have to clean up after you. They have to face and find solutions to many practical problems, and they furthermore have to cope with the terrible guilt that your suicide has inflicted upon them.

Suicide is not a good idea. It brings you nowhere. It is better to ask for help and find solutions to the problems on the physical plane than to press the "escape button." There is no escape. The only real escape is to find proper solutions to the problems and work them through.

The Dead Body

Once the "I" has left the body, the body becomes a corpse. The main electrical field, the one that made the body move and talk and laugh, etc., has departed and it is now the mortal frame that remains. This mortal frame has to be disposed of somehow, as it cannot go on lying around. But how is this best disposed of?

In our body there are billions of cells. These cells carry out a wide range of different jobs in our body, as we all know. We saw that under sleep, when the strong electrical field of the "I" had temporarily left the body, these cells were busy carrying out their various tasks. The cells were not dead or asleep. They were at work.

When at death the "I" has left the body, the majority of the cells in our body are still alive. Their living conditions now change, there is less to do and they will also eventually die, but they don't die right away. Even three months after the death of the body there are still cells that are alive in the body.

The cells have served us well, so it is our duty to consider what is the best way to treat our cells after "we" have departed. There are billions of individuals there to consider, and it is our responsibility that they are treated in the best possible way. The best way is to give the cells time to die a natural death so that they can live their full normal life span. The best way is to let the body slowly dry out, for in this way the cells will have time to die a natural death. As the average life span of a cell is about three months, the cells can live on until their natural time of death and there is still enough liquid in the body to allow them to do this. In this way they have come to no major harm. The burial that is carried out in most of southern Europe, where the body is placed on a sort of shelf aboveground in an oblong box in a cemetery, is ideal. Here the body is exposed to the air and it will slowly dry out, thus allowing the cells to die a natural death.

The second best way is to be interred or buried in the ground. In this way the cells may also have time to die a natural death, but in the ground the body does not dry out so easily and there are more bacteria in the earth that can get in contact with the cells and attack them. Because of the humidity in the earth foreign bacteria have better living conditions and they may attack the cells and eat them. So this way is not as good as the one practiced in southern Europe.

The worst possible way of disposing of a dead body is cremation. During cremation the healthy cells that are still very much alive in the body are exposed to a horrible death. Imagine that we place the whole of the planet Earth in a wooden box. Then we place it on burning coals and let the whole thing go up in flames. Our cells experience the cremation of our body in exactly the same way as we would if the whole Earth burned. This is not only a very unkind way to treat our cells, but it is also bad for our karma. Cremation is a kind of torture for our cells, and this torture may become our own fate one day.

The fact that cremation is a widely practiced way of disposing of the dead body again shows that at our present stage of development we are very little aware of the well-being of our microcosmos. We are ignorant about how our microcosmos experiences life, and we think that once the body is dead, there is no more life in it. But this is not so, the body is still teeming with life. And this life has to be respected just like all other life has to be respected. A life is a life. God makes no distinction between big and small. Size really doesn't matter.

Organ Transplants

On the subject of death it seems relevant to say a few words about organ transplants. Today we are told to make "organ testaments" that allow doctors to take out our organs and transplant them into other bodies in case we die in an accident. As there is a shortage of organs a considerable amount of pressure is put on people to "donate" their organs. We are told that this is a loving thing to do as we can help save the life of a fellow being by donating our organs after our own death. But is this really a loving thing to do? Let us look at this aspect.

First we should remember that life is eternal, so what can be "saved" is only somebody's temporary existence on the physical plane. And we should remember that life on the physical plane is an existence in the zone of suffering and darkness. When we donate our organs we help prolong the receiver's sojourn in this zone of darkness. We should remember that the alternative is paradise. I am not saying that we should not try to help where help is logical, but the question is if transplanting an organ from one being to another is logical. Indeed, the whole idea of organ transplants is the ultimate consequence of the Cartesian/Newtonian view of man as a machine whose individual parts can be exchanged when they no longer function in the same way that we can replace a worn ball bearing in a tractor.

When Martinus died in 1981 the practice of transplanting organs from one human to another was not yet widely used, and he does not mention the subject in *The Third Testament*, but at a meeting in the council of the Martinus Institute in 1971, Martinus said the following about the death criterion:

1. Man must die, when there are no longer any natural ways to keep him alive.

2. It is unfortunate for life in the spiritual world to keep a body alive beyond its possibilities to regain a fairly natural life condition.

3. The present practice of keeping for instance a completely brain damaged person alive is used exceedingly.

4. Some kind of authority has to be established to decide when life should no longer be maintained artificially.

5. Organ transplantation is an unnatural process and should not take place without the express consent of the person in question.

This is what Martinus has said. He does not condemn organ transplants nor does he recommend them. It is up to the individual person to decide and to take the karmic consequences of such a decision. Again we have free will, and as in all other choices we make there are consequences to face.

It is not a goal in itself to prolong life on the physical plane, but if a person strongly desires to receive an organ from another person's body and this person agrees, then this possibility is there. Let us, however, look at the possible consequences of such a decision.

If we are born with say, a deficient liver, this illness has its roots in a former life and is a consequence of debauchery and a former life lived in excesses. In other words the liver disease is karma. Karma is a loving instruction from Providence about how to behave. We need the liver disease to learn how to treat our cells in the correct way. If we can "just" get another person's liver instead of our own, we may not learn the lesson to the full.

In addition to this, we have to more or less kill our own immune system so that it does not reject the liver. One in 100 cells of our body belongs to the immune system. This again means that our immune system consists of billions of cells. Debilitating or even killing these cells is not only bad for our general health as we won't be able to fight off even a common cold, but it will be bad for our health in future incarnations. In our next life we may be born with an immune deficiency disease. The medicine that we have to take to prevent our body from rejecting the transplanted organ is the same as starting chemical warfare in our body, and this has karmic consequences.

The whole idea of organ transplants is rooted in the belief that life exists only on the physical plane and that we have only one life. But as we certainly do not only live once, but eternally, it seems pointless to spend a lot of time and money to swap organs around trying to prolong one physical life for a few years. Seen in a cosmic perspective, the idea of organ transplant is illogical, as the transplantee harms his immune system, interferes with his karma (to the extent that this can be done), prolongs his stay in the zone of suffering, and postpones his reincarnation in a new body.

Death Is like Coming Home

As Martinus points out, there is no reason whatsoever to fear death. Death is a birth to a new level of existence and as this level of existence is a level of light and love, death is something that we can look forward to with comfort. In fact, real life is after death. It is the spiritual world that is the primary world, the world where our life unfolds eternally and where we are one with God's primary consciousness. It is the physical world that is the world of hardship and suffering. If we think that the physical world is life and the spiritual world is death, we have got the whole thing wrong. It is the other way round. The physical world is trials, tribulations, sufferings, and hell. These do not exist on the spiritual plane. Death is like coming home after a long trying journey full of hardship and trials. On the spiritual plane we experience only a world of all encompassing love and light, so the really pleasant part of life begins beyond death.

16

The Power of Prayer

Praying is a Hot Line to God

Many people today find that praying is a strange thing to do, something that does not harmonize with modern man, something that does not harmonize with sophisticated, open-minded people living in an advanced society characterized by a scientific attitude to life. It is generally considered that praying is only done by little, old Italian widows dressed in black.

However, Martinus points out that it is a very good idea to pray to God or Providence on a daily basis. Let us see why this is so.

We have seen in previous chapters that everything that exists is part of God and that we are intrinsically linked to God whether we are aware of this or not. God or Providence looks after us and every step we take is supervised by guardian angels that see to it that we are kept out of harm's way or otherwise according to our karma. Every day God teaches us things through the various incidents in our daily lives. God communicates with us every day. But as long as we are not aware of this and as long as we do not answer God, this is a one-way communication. Once we realize that God is in constant contact with us and once we realize that we can also be in contact with God through prayer, the communication can change from being a one-way communication to being a two-way communication. Prayer is a hot line to God.

The Most Basic Form of Prayer

Whether we are aware of it or not, we have probably all prayed to God even though we did not know that we were praying. The principle of prayer in its most basic form is what we witness when an animal is attacked by a predator.

The animal that is attacked by a predator sends out a loud scream to the heavens. This scream is a cry for help, but it is not addressed to the predator, who could not care less if its victim screams or not. Nor is the scream addressed to the fellow beings of the same species as the victim, because they cannot help the victim. The scream can then only be addressed to Providence or God. The scream expresses that the being is in trouble, and this is the most basic form of communication with God that the being can express. The scream is a simple form of prayer. But whether it is simple or not, does not matter. Providence through a host of guardian angels hears the scream and comes to the rescue of the being in need. This rescue may not mean that the physical life of the being can be spared, but it then means that the guardian angels are there and are ready to help the being with its passing to "the other side."

Most people also scream automatically when they are afraid or if a sudden danger arises. They do not know why they scream and can come up with no explanation for the screaming. They just scream. Screaming is a "built in" reaction and is a basic form of prayer.

The Laws of Praying

All our prayers are heard, but not all can be fulfilled. The principle of prayer has its own laws, its own structure. Learning to pray in the right way is a science of its own. Let us look at why this is so.

Jesus said, *"Everything you ask for in my name will be granted you by God."* This has led innumerable priests to believe that all we had to do was to say "in the name of Jesus" and then the prayer would be fulfilled. But this is clearly not so, because then there would be no illnesses, no deaths, no wars, no natural catastrophes, etc. If everybody would pray in the name of Jesus for these things not to happen and these prayers would be fulfilled, then there could be no suffering and consequently no development of the mentality of the being away from the animal tendencies. No, we cannot pray to avert our karma and expect this to happen, neither can we expect to obtain long life and happiness for our children or for ourselves as our fate has already been outlined before we are born. Nor can we pray for the climate of our local region to become Mediterranean and expect this to be fulfilled by Providence. Nor can we pray for our children or ourselves to be very intelligent or gifted, as these things can only be obtained through hard work and practice during various incarnations. Nor does it make any sense to pray for ourselves to become millionaires or for any special favors to be bestowed upon us by Providence, just as it makes little sense to pray for the course of the Earth around the Sun to change.

But what, then, can we pray for, and what did Jesus mean when he said that everything we ask for in his name will be fulfilled?

Martinus explains that by "the name of Jesus" we have to understand the spirit of Jesus or with the attitude of Jesus. To pray for something in the spirit of Jesus or with the attitude of Jesus is the same as praying for something that is in contact with universal love, which again means something that is unselfish and consequently in contact with the will of God. It is no wonder that Jesus could promise that everything that we ask for which is unselfish and in contact with the will of God will be fulfilled.

A prayer can be manifested in two ways: either in the name of Jesus, where we pray that God's will be done; or in the name of selfishness, in which we want our own wishes to be fulfilled no matter if these wishes mean harm and suffering to others. The first kind of prayer will be fulfilled, whereas the last kind of prayer will not be fulfilled.

Of course, the question is how to learn to pray in "the name of Jesus" or pray for things that are in harmony with the spirit of universal love, which means that the prayer is intended to create joy and blessing for everybody and harm and suffering for nobody.

All desires that are fundamental for the sustenance of life such as hunger, thirst, etc., are not selfish, as the daily life of the being could not be maintained if these desires were not fulfilled. So praying for our fundamental needs to be met is not selfish, and these prayers will be heard and met in cases where the fulfillment of these is in danger.

Jesus points out this aspect of providential supplies when he says, *"Look at the birds of the air, they neither sow nor reap nor gather into barns, and yet your heavenly Father feeds them. Are you not of more value than they?"* (Matthew, 6:26).

So praying for our basic needs to be met is perfectly in tune with the will of God and those prayers will be heard and fulfilled.

Martinus says that we should pray even though we do not believe in praying. It works anyway. The more we "talk" to Providence, the more confident we become. Once we have started praying we become more and more familiar with it, and just as we get to know a person with whom we talk every day, we "get to know" Providence better and better when we pray. We become more observant as to what Providence teaches us, and after some time we speak to Providence all day, just as if we were talking to a dear friend who was right beside us. Martinus says that after practicing we reach a point at which we talk to God as we would talk to a neighbor. There is no need to go into a church to pray or to kneel down or anything like that. God is not so petty that he demands any particular ceremonial observed. As soon as we address our thoughts to God, they will be heard because a prayer is an energy on a specific wavelength that enters the spheres of the spiritual world where it is picked up by invisible spiritual beings or our guardian angels.

Our Lord's Prayer

Again on the question of prayer Martinus explains and enlarges on what Jesus said. The prayer that Jesus taught his disciples, Our Lord's Prayer, is still the best way to pray. But again Martinus reveals the cosmic meaning of this prayer.

Let us look at what it is that we ask for through this prayer (Matthew 6:7):

Our father who art in heaven

Through this opening the praying person opens a canal upwards to God through which the following wishes can enter the consciousness of the divine being through the intervention of invisible angels that are present everywhere in nature and who act as God's special listening organs.

Hallowed be thy name

The fact that God's name "be hallowed" shows that the praying person accepts that "everything is very good," that is, he accepts that the world is as it should be, given our present stage of development. If he didn't accept this he would not "hallow" God's name. In this way he expresses a cosmic insight and accepts that God has created a perfect world.

Thy kingdom come

God's kingdom is the same as the real human kingdom, or the kingdom in which the animal mentality has been outlived. To pray that this may come is completely in line with God's will and the aim of all development. In this way the praying person asks for help to outlive his animal tendencies so that his humane side can be nourished and so that he can learn to love his neighbor.

Thy will be done,
On earth as it is in heaven

This line is in reality a repetition of the previous line. The praying person prays that God's will be done, so that the development may lead us out of the animal kingdom and into the "Kingdom of God," the real human kingdom. In this way we pray that all selfishness and greed may be eradicated so that love and forgiveness can be the rule of conduct.

Give us this day our daily bread

In this we pray for our basic needs to be met, as already described on the previous pages. Thus we also pray that every man be given access to the life sustenance necessary for him, so that starvation, poverty, and misery cease to exist. Poverty can only be eradicated through a more equal distribution of the Earth's riches, so in this way we also pray that large concentrations of money be dissolved, so that a more just access to the Earth's riches will be the result.

And forgive us our debts, As we also have forgiven our debtors

This prayer is meant to eradicate feelings of guilt or bad conscience in the praying person. Feelings of guilt or bad conscience are very bad for our cells, as these thoughts create a very negative-atmosphere for our cells to be alive in. Consequently these feelings are also very bad for our health. As no person can be any better today than he is, there is no need to go around feeling sad, depressed, or guilty, because one isn't always as good or perfect as one would like to be. It is God's will that all living beings shall find happiness according to their level of development. Being depressed or sad because of the state of the world or of one's own lacking abilities of love is not God's will. This prayer helps us to find the point of balance between forgiving ourselves and forgiving others for not being perfect either.

And lead us not into temptation

Here we pray that we may in all situations be able to draw on our experiences to the full so that we do not commit unnecessary mistakes. We pray for all our memories of previous similar situations or of knowledge acquired through study to be mobilized, so that we do not let negligence or mental laziness determine important issues in our lives. Through this we pray for help to mobilize all our experiences to further our development. The "temptation" that is mentioned is the temptation to disregard previous experiences or not to heed warnings, the temptation to ignore knowledge about possible dangers. In this way we pray that we may in all situation in life be able to muster all our experience and all our knowledge, so that unnecessary mistakes may be avoided.

But deliver us from evil

This again can be seen as a repetition of the previous prayer. Again we pray that we be able to avoid sufferings in areas where we have enough experience to avoid them if only we could muster all our mental potential.

For thine is the Kingdom, the Power and the Glory for ever and ever. Amen.

With this prayer we commit ourselves completely to God. The Kingdom refers to the universe and the Power to the governing of the universe, which is the same as the will of God. When referring to the Glory we accept that God's will is brilliant and perfect. We accept that everything is God's Kingdom (God's body) and that the Glory also belongs to God. In this way we also renounce any glory for ourselves for anything that we have created and accept that everything is a result of God's creation.

This prayer is the most perfect prayer that can be expressed and it is completely in tune with the divine will. There are no selfish wishes in this prayer and it fully covers the needs of the praying person. Should there be additional wishes of an unselfish nature these can be added after the completion of Our Lord's Prayer. If our own desires and hopes are in line with the divine will, if they are unselfish and do not cause harm to others, they will be fulfilled.

Praying is a means through which man can ask for help—not help to be exempt from suffering or for dark experiences, because these are necessary, but help to be strengthened and inspired to participate in God's remodeling of himself to become "man in the image and likeness of God." Through praying man can achieve optimism in his unhappiness and be able to see it as an "unpleasant good." Praying is an open door to God.

Martinus recommends that even the person who has lost his ability to believe in God should pray, because praying helps. Nobody who is in need should abstain from praying. God will see that the atheist needs his help even more than the pious believer. God is not so petty that he helps only those who believe in him.

17

Conclusion

For Whom Has the Third Testament Been Written?

What you have just read is an outline of some of the most important aspects of Martinus' work, which he calls *The Third Testament*. As we have seen, *The Third Testament* reveals the invisible or spiritual forces that lie behind the physical world. It reveals how the whole universe is constructed of living beings inside living beings and how the spiritual level and our fate are governed by laws just as the physical level is. *The Third Testament* unveils the mystery of life and explains what is the meaning of our sufferings; it explains from where we are coming and to where we are going. *The Third Testament* explains why we reincarnate and why there is no death. It reveals that "everything is very good" and that life is one long revelation of divine light and love, even though darkness exists. As darkness is a necessary contrast to light, its existence can be accounted for. *The Third Testament* reveals that everything is exactly as it should be, that things are taken care of and that there is absolutely nothing to worry about as God is in his heaven and justice and peace reign in the universe. *The Third Testament* explains the meaning of life. It is a sequel to *The New Testament* and it has been disclosed to mankind at a time when man's intelligence has developed to the extent that his religious instinct has degenerated, making him unable to accept religious dogmas that are not founded in logic and that cannot withstand intelligent analysis.

Because we have reached this stage in our development through the growing influence of the energy of intelligence and the consequential advances in our sciences, we are now ripe for new directions. *The Third Testament* reveals the new directions in a form that fits our present level of development and our present level of intelligence. But logically not everybody is ready to understand or to accept the new revelations.

There will probably be quite a number of readers who will think that this is all a lot of nonsense and that what Martinus says cannot be proven. But in this connection we have to understand that Martinus did not really write for his contemporaries. Martinus mostly wrote his books for future generations. He came when he did to offer a logical explanation to those who through their sufferings have reached a point at which they are hungry for an explanation to what life is all about. There are people who have reached the point in their development at which they are in dire need of new directions. Many people today are crying out in despair for an explanation to what life is all about, they raise their fists to heaven and cry "WHY?"

Among the needy we find many homosexuals. Homosexuals have been prosecuted, ridiculed, and cast out of society for decades and are badly in need of an explanation to their special sexual tendencies. Martinus explains that being homosexual is perfectly normal and a consequence of the transformation of our pole structure. Indeed, the homosexuals are further along in development and more advanced than the majority of the population on Earth.

Some people are beginning to experience cosmic glimpses and they also need Martinus' teachings right now, so that they can know what is happening to them.

Those who study the process of death and reincarnation are in need of Martinus' work as it offers the theoretical foundation to what their research reveals.

Even though the majority of people on Earth may reject Martinus' work, there are people living here right now who are in dire need of his teachings. We should not for one second think that

Providence has miscalculated its timing.

However, all those people who are happy with their religion or with their belief systems should not bother about Martinus' works. They should just ignore it, because *"Those who are well have no need of a physician, but those who are sick"* (Matthew 8:12). Martinus is not trying to convince anybody and he would never enter into an argument about the veracity of his work. He simply reveals the natural laws of life. Time will prove that he is right. Martinus is not concerned with arguing or defending his points of view. You either accept his analysis or you don't. Whether you do or not is not a question of will, but a question of the combination of the basic energies in your mentality.

Martinus' work will have no appeal to people whose energy of instinct is still fairly strong, as these people still believe in the religions. All those who are still able to believe in a religion should go on doing this as long as they can. Martinus is not trying to win supporters or proselytes for his teachings. He says, "Take what you can use and leave the rest."

Also Martinus' work will have no appeal to those who believe in the materialistic sciences and who think that the materialistic sciences will save the day. These are the people who demand experimental proof for everything. These people cannot believe in anything that cannot be proved experimentally. A logical explanation and living proof is not enough for the really hard-core materialist who is unable to accept the existence of the spiritual world, because its existence cannot be proved in the "right" way. However, the hard-core materialist cannot prove that the spiritual world does not exist. So he is also a believer, as he believes in the non-existence of something that he cannot prove. Science has already established that many things exist even though they are invisible and intangible, such as electricity, sound waves, television waves, microwaves, X-rays, time, our thoughts, etc. As the existence of the rays and waves of ray-formed matter is irrefutable, it is just a question of how we define it. Materialistic scientists may claim that the rays and waves of the electromagnetic spectrum are physical, but is it actually logical to call matter that is both invisible and intangible physical? Isn't it more logical to say that matter that is both invisible and intangible is spiritual? Once we agree to this definition and say that ray-formed matter is spiritual matter it has already been established that a spiritual world can exist. With this definition we have discovered the first evidence of the existence of a new world, a metaphysical world, and we can now start exploring the details of this world. We can become explorers of a new reality. We don't know what secrets this reality holds, but acknowledging its existence is the first step in the process of exploration.

The Overall Picture and the Details

Martinus outlines the overall world picture. He does not offer a lot of details. We, the humans of this planet, will have to fill in the details ourselves. Through our materialistic sciences we have been filling in the details of the physical world for many centuries. We have measured, weighed, and carried out experiments. Through this accumulation of facts our sciences have obtained great insight. But our sciences have now reached a point where little more can be learned through traditional scientific research. Our sciences have to be taken up to a new level of cognition. We can only reach this level when we start accepting the existence of the metaphysical or spiritual world. We have to include the spiritual level in order to know more. We have to pass the threshold to the metaphysical level to reach new insight.

To me it is clear that we have reached this point today. The works of the people to whom I dedicate this book show that we have to start accepting that our materialistic science has limits. We are aware of an increasing number of phenomena that we cannot explain with our existing level of science. We now have to take our sciences up to the metaphysical level and start filling in the details of this level in exactly the same way as we have been filling in the details of the physical level through centuries. This filling in of details of the metaphysical or spiritual level has already begun through the work of the people to whom I dedicate this book.

Ian Stevenson fills in many details that confirm that reincarnation is a fact. His very thorough work of gathering cases of children who remember a past life establishes very valuable evidence of reincarnation and can be seen as the first step to the foundation of a spiritual science. His work shows how character traits, talents and scars on the physical body are carried on from one physical body to the next. This is completely in harmony with what Martinus has written, as he explains that the character traits and talents are carried on from one life to the next through the position of the talent kernels in the supraconsciousness, which is an eternal spiritual entity united with the eternal "I."

Brian Weiss, Roger Woolger, Helen Wambach, and Edith Fiore have through their regression therapy revealed a treasure of details of the former lives of their patients. From this very interesting material we can see how both physical and mental traumas are carried on from one life to the next and how we are a result of all the things, good and bad, that have happened to us in former incarnations. Through this we not only get insight and begin to understand the origins of many traumas but we also get a glimpse of the workings of the law of karma. Most of all the work of these therapists reveals that reincarnation has to be a fact, as regression therapy would otherwise not be able to have the curing effect that it has. A fantasy about a former life cannot cure deeply rooted traumas. A trauma that can be cured has to have roots in reality. The lives that the patients relive during hypnosis or trance have to be real. Otherwise the traumas could not be cured when "relived." The work of the therapists mentioned also confirms that talents and character traits are carried on from one incarnation to the next. Furthermore their work gives us valuable glimpses of the "afterlife" or, more correctly expressed, the "interlife," which can also be accessed during hypnosis or altered states of consciousness.

In addition, Edith Fiore's research shows how many unhappy discarnate beings from the spiritual wavelengths close to the physical level can usurp the bodies of physical beings when their aura has been debilitated through the intake of excessive amounts of alcohol or through illness. She thus fills in details about possession and usurpation by discarnate beings "trapped" on the lower wavelengths.

Carol Bowman's research points to the fact that many children are affected by former traumatic deaths and through this she reveals details of how former lives and traumas can have repercussions in the lives of our children. But most important her research also shows how we can help them.

The many cases of near-death experiences collected by Raymond Moody and Kenneth Ring show what happens at the moment of death, and they are in harmony with what Martinus says about the passage from the physical to the spiritual level and the afterlife. The study of the near-death experience can be said to be the first study of the spiritual world carried out by our materialistic sciences.

Elizabeth Kübler Ross has been a pioneer in the field of death studies. She is one of the first people within the established medical profession who has had the courage to face death openly and squarely. Through her compassion and love she not only helped many people, but she was also able to come to the conclusion that death was not final and that there was more beyond death. Thus she confirms many aspects of Martinus' work, not only about death, but also about living happily through self-sacrifice and love for our neighbor. She also shows that accepting the inevitable and allowing God's will to be done helps the dying person on to the spiritual plane in the right frame of mind.

James Lovelock fills in some very interesting details of why the Earth has to be a living being. Martinus states that everything is life inside life and that this is the only way that life can exist. We are all micro and macrobeings at the same time. Lovelock's observations confirm that the Earth is a living being and he fills in certain details that point to this fact. Temperature control and constant oxygen levels of the atmosphere and saline stability of the seas are things that point to the fact that somebody regulates these things.

Lovelock calls this somebody "Gaia."

Joel L. Whitton reveals details of the *Life Between Life* through taking his patients and subjects to the interlife during hypnosis. Thus his patients reveal a number of characteristics of the spiritual world and as far as I can see all these details harmonize with what Martinus says about the spiritual world.

Hopefully, when Martinus' teachings have become known to more scientists researching the afterlife, more details will be revealed. I hope Martinus' work will be an inspiration to scientists and give them more hints about what to look for.

The details that the above-mentioned people have revealed are only the tiny little tip of the iceberg, the first fumbling steps in the direction of establishing a spiritual science. The exploration of the spiritual world is only just about to begin. It will be the job of future scientific investigation to fill in the complete picture.

Is Martinus a False Prophet?

The people mentioned above who have researched death and reincarnation confirm the truth in Martinus' teachings through their work. So their work points to Martinus being right. But are there other things that point to the fact that what Martinus says is the truth? How do we know that Martinus is not a false prophet?

Let us see what Jesus says about false prophets. Jesus tells us what to look for in Matthew 7:15 where he says, *"Beware of false prophets, who come to you in sheep's clothing but inwardly are ravenous wolves. You will know them by their fruits. Are grapes gathered from thorns, or figs from thistles? So, every sound tree bears good fruit, but the bad tree bears evil fruit. A sound tree cannot bear evil fruit, nor can a bad tree bear good fruit. Every tree that does not bear good fruit is cut down and thrown into the fire. Thus you will know them by their fruit."*

Martinus' work has only one fruit: love. Love is the conclusion and the solution to everything. Love is the basic tone of the universe and both light and darkness are expressions of love. God is pure love—he does not judge and condemn—he teaches us the way things work so that we can eat from the Tree of Knowledge. We may think that God has forgotten about us, but he has not. He constantly reminds us that we are part of him and that he loves us.

It took Martinus sixty years of his life to write *The Third Testament*. In those sixty years he had to contend with hardship, poverty, and privations. He was incredibly diligent. He worked from four o'clock in the morning till late afternoon every day. He often went out to give lectures in the evening. He had practically no money. Nothing of what he did, he did for himself. He did not want to achieve fame and prosperity. He did not want to be admired and he was very self-effacing. There was never a sect or cult around Martinus' work or his person. Martinus wanted no attention. He only wanted to be able to concentrate on his work. He clearly pointed out that he was no guru. It was the writings that were important. His person was not to be made the center of any attention. Martinus called his mission "the Cause," but there is no membership and no cult or sect. Everybody who wants to is free to study his work. The access to his thoughts is as free as it is to the sun in the sky. Martinus clearly wanted no special attention or special privileges because of who he was.

Another aspect of the veracity of Martinus' work is that I do not believe that anybody through fantasy or imagination would be able to reveal a complete holistic world picture where the structure of life is revealed. Martinus' insight could certainly not come from the study of our earthly sciences, and even a wild fantasy or a very lively imagination would not come up with the revelations that Martinus presents. His insight is such that it has to come from a metaphysical source. Mere imagination may supply visions of Martians or extraterrestrials or all sorts of bizarre creatures from space, but mere imagination cannot offer a complete world picture based on logic. If Martinus had not had a divine source, he simply could not have been able to reveal a holistic world picture, nor do I think that anybody would have had the audacity to call their writings *The Third Testament*, if they were in fact not that.

Martinus clearly points out that he does ask anybody to believe in what he says. He says that everybody who takes an interest in his work must test it against reality. It is in life itself that the truth of his teachings is revealed. It is only through comparing Martinus' work with our reality that his work can finally be proven true. Nobody should "believe" in Martinus' work or make a new religion out of it. In Martinus' words, *"Of course there will be people who believe in this spiritual science and make it into a new religion, but this shows that they have not had the ability to understand it. I do not want my cosmic analyses to be an authority that people believe in. The spiritual scientist who takes an interest in the cosmic analyses must carefully test and study my work. He must confront it with his own experiences and perceptions. Only then can it be of value to him."* (*Kosmos,* Oct./1990, page 206).

The Parable of the Prodigal Son

Who, then, is ready for these new teachings? As already mentioned, *The Third Testament* has been written for the intellectual person, the person who has outlived the ability to believe in the religions. In order to accept the new teachings you may have to have passed a point at which you are an atheist. You have to reach a point at which your intellect tells you not to believe in the religions and that if believing in God is accepting what the religions say, then you don't believe there is a God. You then become an atheist or agnostic. Another realization to be reached is that although we know a lot, we still don't know it all. You have to have reached a certain level of humility.

Jesus' parable of the prodigal son is a symbolical representation of the situation of modern man who has left the house of the Father (become an atheist), has squandered his inheritance (lived many lives in excesses), has learned humility and come back. Let us look at what Jesus says in Luke 15:11–32.

He said, *"There was a man who had two sons; and the younger of them said to his father, "Father, give me the share of property that* falls to me." And he divided his living between them. Not many days later, the younger son gathered all he had and took his journey into a far country, and there he squandered his property in loose living. And when he had spent everything, a great famine arose in that country, and he began to be in want. So he went and joined himself to one of the citizens of that country, who sent him into his fields to feed swine. And he would gladly have fed on the pods that the swine ate; and no one gave him anything. But when he came to himself he said, 'How many of my father's hired servants have bread enough and to spare, but I perish here with hunger! I will arise and go to my father, and I will say to him, "Father, I have sinned against heaven and before you; I am no longer worthy to be called your son; treat me as one of your hired servants."'"

And he arose and came to his father. But while he was yet at a distance, his father saw him and had compassion, and ran and embraced him and kissed him. And the son said to him, "Father I have sinned against heaven and before you; I am no longer worthy to be called your son." But the father said to his servants, "Bring quickly the best robe, and put it on him; and put a ring on his hand, and shoes on his feet; and bring the fattened calf and kill it, and let us eat and make merry; for this my son was dead, and is alive again; he was lost and was found. And they began to make merry.

"Now his elder son was in the field; and as he came and drew near to the house, he heard music and dancing. And he called one of the servants and asked what this meant. And he said to him, 'Your brother has come, and your father has killed the fatted calf, because he has received him safe and sound.' But he was angry and refused to go in. His father came out and entreated him, but he answered his father, 'Lo, these many years I have served you, and I never disobeyed your command; yet you never gave me a kid, that I might make merry with my friends. But when this son of yours came, who has devoured your living with harlots, you killed for him the fatted calf!' And he said to him, 'Son, you are always with me, and all that is mine is yours. It was fitting to make merry and be glad, for this your brother was dead, and is alive; he was lost, and is found.'"

In this parable Jesus lets us know how the father gladly lets his younger son squander away the family inheritance on prostitutes and loose living because the father knows that in this way and through the sufferings the son reaps from his squandering, he will eat from the fruit of the Tree of Knowledge, he will accumulate experience, and he will consequently learn humility. After the son has eaten with the swine, he wants to return to his father's house, not as a son, but as one of the hired servants. The son has suffered away from his father's house and now he wants to return as a servant. He has learned humility. He has learned that it is better to be a servant in his father's house than to live away from it. The father is more than happy to have the son back and bears no grudge against him whatsoever; on the contrary he arranges a party to celebrate his return.

The older son on the other hand is jealous of the attention his brother gets and wants to be celebrated because he has never left the house of the father. But the father says that because he has never been lost, there is nothing to celebrate. The older son has not yet eaten from the Tree of Knowledge, he has not learned humility, he still wants to have the privileges of a son, and he does not express any desire to become a servant. So now it is the older son's turn to leave the house of the father so that he, too, can learn humility.

The younger son symbolizes the atheist who has left the house of the father with his inheritance. Through loose living during many incarnations he has squandered away his inheritance (his belief in God) until there was nothing left. In his poverty and misery he learns that it is better to be a servant in his father's house than to eat with the swine. And with this knowledge and with the desire to serve, he returns. He returns with the knowledge that it is better to give than to take. He has eaten of the fruit of the tree of knowledge and is ready to accept to be a servant, to help others. The father happily celebrates the return of the son and bears no grudge against him whatsoever, because the father knows that the act of leaving his house is what brings the son knowledge. If the son had not left, he would not have become wiser.

The older son symbolizes the believers, those that have not yet left the house of the father. But also the older son has to leave the house of the father sooner or later, so that he too can learn humility, can stop feeling superior and privileged, so that he too can learn that it is better to give than to take.

Those who have lost the ability to believe, those who have learned humility through their sufferings, those who know that we know nothing, are the people for whom *The Third Testament* has been written.

Jesus also says, *"But many that are first will be last, and the last first"* (Matthew 19:30). Now what does this mean? Martinus explains that "the last" will be the first to accept the new teachings. "The last" are the godless, the atheists, the not-so-decent, those that are nothing in the eyes of the established church or in the eyes of society, those who are the black sheep. "The first" are the representatives of the established religions, the pope, the cardinals, the priests, and the established scientists who think they have swallowed all the wisdom of the world. They will be the last to accept the new teachings.

Martinus Speaks

To conclude this introductory book about Martinus' world picture I will let Martinus speak for himself. A speech given at the Martinus Center at Klint on July 17, 1967, was one of the few occasions Martinus spoke about himself in public. This speech was recorded and later published in the magazine *Kosmos* in March 1991:

About Myself, My Mission, and Its Significance

TONIGHT I WANT TO TALK ABOUT MYSELF

It isn't always nice to have to talk about oneself, but in accordance with the mission I have, with what I have written and the knowledge I have manifested, I have felt it right. There are many people who have said to me that I must have read and studied, but I have not. I am a living proof that you can obtain the highest knowledge through your own consciousness, and this is a state, which all people will eventually reach. I have not been particularly favored by Providence. All those who come after me will have the consciousness that I have, just as all those who are in front of me have. Therefore I think that it could be of interest to you to hear how I have experienced this state.

THE TEACHINGS OF MY CHILDHOOD

I was born in the country, outside marriage, as a so-called illegitimate child and I was brought up by my uncle and aunt. They were then old people and only had very limited means, so there was no question about my studying or achieving a knowledge apart from what you could get in an ordinary country school which only had two classes, one for bigger children who were from ten to fourteen years old, and one for those who were under ten. There I was taught Danish, biblical knowledge, psalms, Danish history, geography and a bit of arithmetic. I was very fond of biblical knowledge. This is all the teaching that I have had from without.

I had a very intense relationship to God. I cannot remember living a single day without praying to God. I prayed to God every day. I prayed that I might be able to know my homework and many other things. Another peculiarity was that when I was in doubt about something, I asked myself if Jesus would do this or not. If he would not carry out an act, then I didn't do it, but if I felt that he would do it, then I did it. It became a kind of guidance for me through life.

THE PREPARATION FOR CONFIRMATION

Once, when we were taught by the vicar, we were sitting in a lovely room opening on to a garden at the vicarage on a summer's day. The vicar was telling different things and then suddenly he said how terrible it was, if a small child died before its parents had had it baptized, then it would go straight to hell. I thought: "This cannot be true. God cannot let a small child burn forever because of the whims of two parents." During the same lesson he also said that illegitimate children were doomed. I felt: "This cannot be true." I could not believe that God would be angry with me, just because I was born outside marriage. In this way I felt that there was something wrong with what the church taught. I then had my own belief, which was very loving, because I could not accept that anybody should burn in hell or that God could be so brutal.

WORK AT THE DAIRY

First I was a worker, then I became a dairyman and later a clerk at the dairy Enigheden in Copenhagen. I had to do something to earn a living. I had no particular interest in these things, but I did my duty. At the same time I had a great longing to do something better. As a clerk I wrote 10,000 numbers a day. There had to be a better life, I thought, than this to go out to write 10,000 numbers, go home, eat and go to the movies, go to bed and go out to write 10,000 numbers again, etc. I would like to become a missionary, but I was not in contact with the church and I did not believe in eternal hell, so I realized that that was out of the question. As a child I had a great desire to become a schoolteacher, and my mother promised me that I would become a teacher, when I grew up, but she died when I was 11 years old, so nothing came of that. But still I became a kind of teacher.

THE MEETING WITH LARS NIBELVANG IN MARCH 1921

At the office there was a colleague who was reading in a theosophical book, and he told me that we had lived before and that the life we live now is not the only one. I found that very logical, and I asked if I could borrow this book. He had borrowed the book himself, and he had to ask the owner if I could borrow it. The result was that I was allowed to borrow it, but the owner wanted to see me and one day I visited this man, whose name was Lars Nibelvang. He was not a member of any theosophical or anthroposophical society, but he had read all kinds of philosophy. He asked questions, and I also asked questions. Among other things I asked if these new movements of theosophy and anthroposophy had anything to do with praying. Yes, they had. Now, if he had said, "No, they don't" then I had been through with him. I listened to him very much and was given the book to take home. I was very eager to read in it, I had a strong desire to know more. I read in the book until I came to a place where it said that you had to meditate, you had to sit down comfortably in a chair and blindfold yourself in order to concentrate better.

THE WHITE BAPTISM OF FIRE

Now I had to try this. I had a new wicker chair, which was very nice and comfortable to sit in. It was very much alive, quite magnetic and it creaked all the time. I sat down in this chair and blindfolded myself, so that it was dark. Suddenly I saw a figure resembling Christ. It was Thorvaldsen's statue of Christ that says: "Come to me." This figure was small and stood some distance away. Then it became dark, then light again and then the figure had come alive and was in a natural human size. It was dressed in a robe of small sparkling stars, almost like a robe of diamonds. It was giving off an enormous amount of light, the light was white as snow, the shadows were blue and the figure came slowly toward me. I sat in the chair and could not move. It became dark again and then light and then the figure went up through the ceiling and down through the floor. It went straight toward me, walked into me and stopped. The light from this figure inside me beamed out over the world, I could see continents and seas with sailing ships, etc. It was as if I witnessed that the globe turned and turned, and I could see one continent after the other, still within this beam of light. When I had seen this, I took the blindfold away and I could move again.

THE SIGN

What all this meant, I could not understand, but later it became clear to me. It meant that I was to preach the consciousness of Christ for Mankind. This beam from Christ shone over the world, over continents and seas. This was the sign, but I didn't know how to do it, as I had no knowledge about anything.

THE GOLDEN BAPTISM OF FIRE

On the following morning I sat down again in the wicker chair and blindfolded myself. Then it went dark again. A piece of sky appeared and across this sky a shadow passed. When the shadow has passed, the sky became lighter and so it went on. The shadow passed across the sky and it became more and more light, at the end this sky shone with an immense radiance in the color of gold. Everything disappeared, my organism, my room, house, everything, I was only sitting in some golden rays. I felt a colossal pressure on my consciousness and I felt: "This is God's consciousness. This is how the highest part of us is, without attachment to anything else, and thus we have this divine radiance, this divine force inside us."

THE CONSEQUENCES OF THE GREAT BIRTH

It would not have been of great consequence that I had experienced this, if I had not afterward discovered, that when I thought of a higher problem to which I had no idea about its solution, this solution came to me as an explication, which presented itself to me in total clarity. I could control this and with my intelligence I could deduct the answer.

But I also realized that I was not supposed to read anything. When I wanted to go and pick up a book, there was something that held me back. For three years I could not read a book with philosophical or spiritual accounts. I was not supposed to receive any knowledge from without. I discovered that I received all the knowledge that I wanted from within. I had many questions, many desires and one answer after the other popped up in my consciousness. It was a hard time, because it hurt a lot in my consciousness and I did not immediately understand this change in me.

THE ANALYSES ARE STRENGTHENED THROUGH CONVERSATIONS WITH LARS NIBELVANG

I had to return the book, which I no longer needed, to Lars Nibelvang. I told him what I had experienced, and he became very, very fascinated. From his study of spiritual books he knew that such experiences existed, he had read almost all the philosophy in the world, you see. He was full of questions and this meant that I had to focus my consciousness on all higher subjects. But this also meant that I became good at creating unwavering analyses, because he was exceedingly skeptical. When I presented an analysis, he would say: "No, it cannot be so, because this or that author says this and that." I had not learned to create analyses, so my analyses could be over-turned. But the principle, the final answer in my analyses, could not be overturned. I became so good at creating analyses that in the end he could not overturn anything and he was willing to give in, when he saw that I was right. "Yes, you are right, nobody else has been able to see this," he said. In this way my analyses became enormously strong. Even today nobody will be able to overturn my analyses, they stand unshakably firm. He who tries to overturn an analysis will start to fumble and can make no sense of it all.

THE FIRST WRITINGS AND THE LONG SENTENCES

I worked on creating analyses, but I also had my job to do. But in this respect I was helped, so that I could quit having a job and dedicate myself to the spiritual side. The idea was that I was to explain, and Nibelvang was to write, as I did not think that I had the ability to do this. But one day I tried to write anyway and this turned out to be the epilogue of my main work, LIVETS BOG. That is the first thing I ever wrote. This, then, showed that I was supposed to write myself. He said: "No, I don't have to write, you must write yourself."

So it was, and for seven years I wrote on a book. My writing was not so correct, because I had sentences of half pages, among other things. I thought that people could understand things better, when the sentences were not interrupted. Later, when I began writing LIVETS BOG, I had to rephrase the sentences and make them shorter. In LIVETS BOG there are still many long sentences, but there are things that force you to write long sentences.

Mental States During the First Seven Years

So seven years passed before I could begin to write in the right way. But there were also other things that I had to go through during these seven years, among other things various mental states. I could feel other people's illnesses in my own organism. When I rode in the tram, I could feel if somebody behind me had a problem with his lungs or kidneys. It was a very hard time.

In the movies I could not stand watching films that had shootings, murder or killings in them. I was extremely sensitive. For seven years I had to fight all this with a colossal mental strength. It was fought and today I am very strong toward these things.

The Main Symbol Was Finished after Three Years

When I saw these cosmic analyses or cosmic answers, I discovered that I could transform them into symbols, which made them easier to explain. During those three years, in which I was not allowed to read, I drew symbols and reached the point at which I had finished the world picture. When I had finished the main symbol, the symbol of the whole universe, where the basic energies and all the many details form a whole, I felt that I had the support of the whole spiritual world. I felt a happiness and a blessing, which I can hardy describe. Then I had been given the basis for the analyses that I was to write later. With this symbol I was safe against creating contradictions in the big task. No one will be able to find contradictions in my analyses, precisely because the whole world picture was finished in this symbol.

Seven Symbols Were Ready to Be Presented after Seven Years

I drew more symbols, so that I could show the major principles of the universe. During this period I was helped and supported partly from Lars Nibelvang and partly from other friends. When I had drawn seven symbols and was able to show the basic principle and structure of the whole universe, I felt that I had to reach out toward more people. During those seven years there were only close friends, very few people, who were informed about these things, but now I felt that

I was ready to go public, that I could show it to more people.

In my youth my hobby was photography, painting and drawing and therefore I was able to make colored slides of my symbols. Now I could show the world picture in its first elementary form and I took contact to a man who had a great interest in the occult. I wrote to him and sent him the foreword to LIVETS BOG and he wrote back saying that he was very interested and amazed by it and he referred me to a producer called LØW who was, he said, a sage who would be able to understand what I was doing.

The Meeting with Bernhard Løw in 1928

It was then agreed that I had to present myself at Bernhard Løw's place one Sunday afternoon and bring my pictures. This elderly gentleman welcomed me and it was as if we had known each other always. I showed my pictures to him, his disciples and some guests and for the first time I presented the whole spiral cycle. They were very impressed and Løw, who was an old anthroposopher and mathematician, was very enthusiastic.

The First Public Speech in 1930

I gave my first public speech at Forhåbningsholms Allé in a little hall, which was all filled up. Later I had to move to Borup Højskole, which was also filled with people. I don't understand how they could stand it, because I spoke for two to three hours without stopping. Later we have experienced that we are only supposed to speak for three quarters of an hour, maximum an hour. But they came.

The Magazine KOSMOS 1933

A magazine called OM was started to which I supplied articles, but then we thought that we might as well write articles in our own magazine, so we established the magazine KOSMOS.

The Vacation Colony Kosmos Is Founded in 1935

We could work and give lectures in winter, but in summer people don't attend lectures. But in order to continue the work during summer we founded the Vacation Colony Kosmos. One day one of our friends came with a newspaper advert about the sale of a large area, which was exactly right for a vacation colony, and it cost only 5 øre per square yard. Therefore it seemed that we would be able to buy it. We did, and since then it has grown. We built the first lecture hall and later an even bigger one and now we have an even bigger hall from where we teach, as you know.

An International School at Klint

As I have mentioned, we have the vacation colony in order to continue work during summer, but the idea is also that we shall one day establish a major school here. Here we have to establish a school, where we can educate people from abroad to give lectures in their own countries. We cannot travel to all countries, but we can educate people to give lectures in other countries. The plan is that this vacation colony is to become an international school of spiritual science. One day there will be a large town here with hotels etc., but this will be in the future. Right now we are just beginning.

The World Picture for the First Time in the History of the Earth

The cosmic analyses turned out to be a picture of the whole universe. Never before in the history of the earth has there been created a world picture. All wise men have bits and pieces of the world picture, and what you learn is bits and pieces of it, but in the world picture that I have been allowed to present everything is there, everything fits and tallies.

There are people who have said to me: "How can you know that yours is correct? They all say that they have the truth." I can say this because I have the total picture. The world picture, I have made, shows eternity. A world picture has to be a picture of eternity. If it is not, it is just a time and space dimensional thing, then it is a created *thing and then it has nothing to do with a world picture.*

That is why I can know that my world picture is correct. Everything fits and tallies and its conclusion is this: "That you must love your neighbor as yourself and God above all things." My analyses show this all the time and everywhere. You cannot find one single point, one single analysis, which does not show this.

DARKNESS AS PART OF LOVE

The world picture also has a task which is completely new: to show that darkness is not the work of the Devil, with which God has nothing to do or which comes from a devil who has been expelled by God and who persecutes Mankind and keeps it in the darkness. This is old superstition. Later, in the new world culture, for which my analyses will create the foundation, darkness will be seen as a divine blessing, as something that is absolutely necessary. Without having seen darkness, one will never be able to see the light. To the same degree that one has experienced darkness, one will be able to see the divine light. The world has been so cleverly constructed that people are allowed to experience exactly what they do to their neighbor. Our whole way of behavior is directed toward our neighbor and we get this back through our neighbor. It is our own acts that we get back. That is to "eat from the tree of knowledge." This makes us realize what is good, and what is evil, what is right and what is wrong. My world picture shows the giant mission of darkness, it shows that this is also a part of love. If there were no opposite to love, we could not know what love was. You cannot paint a landscape with white colors on a white canvas, that will be fairly invisible. You have to have contrast. Through my analyses you get a living experience of this. All the way through I show the importance of darkness, why it exists, and I show that there is no eternal hell. A human being lives one earthly life here, and it has been said that if its sins are not forgiven, it shall burn in an eternal hell. But it cannot, in its short life, even if it lives to be 90 or 100, sin so much that an eternal punishment can be just. It is illogical, but all the former religious guidance of Mankind has been illogical. It is not logical, it is symbolical. It is not adjusted to intelligent analysis. It is adjusted to people with instinct, people who believe in authorities and who need commands: You must not do this and you have to do that. These people only have this instinct that the ways of the Lord are past understanding.

THE MISSION OF CHRIST

Against the background of this instinct Christ could not complete his mission, but had to leave part of it to posterity. In his mission he had to show that love can exist. At the cross he showed that you can forgive your worst executioners and pray for them, pray that they are not punished. He says: "Father forgive them, for they know not what they are doing." That was his mission.

THE SPOKESMAN THE HOLY SPIRIT

It has been my task to clarify a part of the explanations of Christ in the world picture. It is a continuation of the teachings of Christ, which he himself also calls "The Spokesman, the Holy Spirit." He said to his disciples: "You cannot understand it, you cannot bear it, but to future generations the Father shall send the Spokesman, the Holy Spirit. It shall teach them what they do not understand, it shall take of mine and give to them." Here he says that an illumination shall come, not a person, not a new world redeemer, but "The Spokesman, the Holy Spirit." But what is "The Spokesman"? It is not a man. As far as I know, the Jews call their holy books the Spokesman. Spirit is the same as thoughts and knowledge. So "The Holy Spirit" is holy thoughts and holy knowledge. What, then, is holy thoughts and holy knowledge? It is thoughts that express the absolute truth. He does, in fact, say that the absolute truth shall come to Mankind, the absolute knowledge about the mystery of life shall be given to them; he does not say that a new Christ shall come. Now it is not the person who is in focus, it is not a dictator, a world redemption in the shape of dictatorship. Now it is a science, which has to be linked up to the materialistic science and become a divine science. On the basis of this the world shall be led forward, and this is all happening. The materialistic science is advancing rapidly and the spiritual science has been revealed through the solution to the mystery of life. He who wants to, can now study the world picture and achieve knowledge about the laws of life, what is right and what is wrong, and come to learn to see it all from God's own viewpoint.

THE ELECTION TO REVEAL THE SOLUTION TO THE MYSTERY OF LIFE

To reveal the solution to the mystery of life and the laws of life and to see it all from God's own viewpoint is what I was elected to do through the before mentioned experiences with the figure of Christ who walked into me. It is still there, it still shines for he who can see it. It shone over the seas, countries and continents, over humanities, etc. It could not have been shown more fundamentally.

I had my brain opened and was able to see a world which is as gigantic in comparison to what I saw before, as the physical world is for the small child that comes out of its mother's womb. It was like this with my ordinary physical consciousness, which was like the consciousness of all other people, just as ignorant. Suddenly an area of my brain was opened which meant that I could now see better spiritually than physically. The entire giant spiritual world lay open for me. I can go on writing. Even if I live for a 100 years, I can never get to the bottom. What became my task was to show the essence, to show the basis of this world picture. The details can come later. But in the short time a life is, I had to limit myself to precisely what Mankind had to have to come to understand life as a reality, to live in truth. I was not supposed to teach Mankind occult forces, to make miracles. It is not my task to make miracles, but there was one miracle that I had to make, so to speak: to reveal the world picture for Mankind.

SPIRITUAL SCIENCE AND MATERIALISTIC SCIENCE

So in this way the world picture is now ready to be adjusted to science when science is ready. It is still fairly new, but it is growing with enormous steps. Scientists are not going to continue being only materialists, because there are other people than materialists who can become scientists. The spiritually developed people can also become doctors and professors on the material plane. In years to come, when the world war and the world catastrophes that are approaching have passed, there will be made ways to combine the materialistic science with the spiritual science, i.e., the analysis of the world picture.

You may think that I am boasting, but try to see if there is anybody like me. Is there another world picture? No, there is not. There is no other, there will be no other, you are not going to get other analyses. It has been presented to you as science and this is what is "The Spokesman, the Holy Spirit." My analyses are "holy knowledge and holy thoughts" and it is these that will be the foundation for the salvation of Mankind and for the development of Mankind to be "man in the image of God."

THE BRIGHT FUTURE OF MANKIND

Without these analyses Mankind would not be able to advance. And advancing is very important because you are in the process of developing away from being an animal. The constellation of your poles is developing enormously and in a few generations you will not be able to live in the same way as today. Then you will want to live in a different way, and the life that you will then enjoy will lie ready for you. It will be a divine life in light and joy, science and art, and not a life in unhappy marriages, faithlessness, perversities, misery and poverty, war and exile. It is of such a character, that you are not able to comprehend it today and it may sound as if I am exaggerating, but I am not. I cannot exaggerate life's structure of love. Even if I use all my intelligence, I cannot exaggerate the divine love and wisdom within the whole system. I have been allowed to show this to a certain extent—in a form in which it can be understood by man. If I were to give it a higher form, you would not be able to understand it. If I were to continue, I had to glide into a new form, which you would not be able to understand. Through the study of the cosmic analyses of the world picture and the solution to the mystery of life, you will grow into experiencing what I have experienced. You will become sovereign just as I am sovereign.

MY UNFINISHED BODY WAS SHAPED THROUGH SEVEN YEARS TO OBEY MY SPIRITUAL STATE

I don't have to ask others, how it is in the spiritual worlds. What we do when we die. I have the open, complete day-conscious access to see and to describe this in my awake, physical state. At this material plane I am able to live in a divinely transfigured state of life, even though I have to have a camouflage. I have to look like other people, because I have been given a body that is equal to that of other people. But this is not my own body; it is not the body I am used to having in my own world. It is a body I had to have here, because there were no others to get. But as already mentioned, I have adjusted this body through the first seven years so that it obeys my "I." It obeys my spiritual state, so that I have been able to live so much in it, that my faculty of intuition, which is the organ for cosmic experience, is permanent, is under the control of my will in the same way as my physical eyesight is under the control of my will. With my intuitive faculty under full control, I have been able to create the world picture.

PROVIDENCE DIRECTS AND GUIDES THE DEVELOPMENT ON EARTH TOWARD A DIVINE STATE

Naturally I am protected by the collaborators of world redemption, by Providence. There is an organic society of highly initiated beings on the spiritual plane. They are united, but not through membership and not through an association, but through having the same divine will, the same development, and the same view of what is right and what is wrong. Through this they are a unity. This unity directs and guides the world and it also decides what I have to give the world and what I must not give. Providence is my protection, my foundation. It is this unit that can hear your prayers, that hears my prayers; it hears all the sighs and screams of the animals. It is this unit that directs and guides the world, it instates different governments and politicians and takes them away when they no longer have to be there. It directs the entire divine plan that Mankind is looking for. Mankind is not left to be governed by chance, it is governed firmly toward a divine state.

This you can also learn through my analyses. There you will be able to see the entire divine world plan and see how everything fits and tallies. And you will be able to see that "everything is very good," just as God sees it. At this moment everything is as perfect as it can be based on its past and in view of what it will be in the future. A speck of dust cannot fall accidentally, if it could, the whole universe would be out of order. There is no miscalculation in the universe; then it would never have been able to exist eternally. Something that has to last eternally must be made so that it can last eternally.

THE SHEEP WILL BE SEPARATED FROM THE GOATS THROUGH FUTURE COLLECTIVE RELEASES OF KARMA

Now I have told you something about my mission and what it will mean for the future. The lovely state of affairs, this prosperity which reigns here, will not last forever, waves of karma will also roll over the welfare states and people will experience misery and pain. It is the sufferings that will make people humane, that develop the ability that means that you cannot find it in your heart to do evil. Therefore the sufferings are something good, and I have called it an "unpleasant good." It is not pleasant, but it is a good thing.

With this ability you will come to the side, which Christ calls "of the sheep." Christ separates the sheep form the goats, and it happens so that as the collective releases of karma, i.e., wars and natural disasters, take place, a lot of people will suffer greatly, become invalids, etc. When they then die and are reborn, they are against war and all brutality, against harming others. They advance towards light and pleasantness and these are the ones that Christ calls the sheep. The goats are those that have not suffered so much and that have still not received their karma. They say, "We have to have war, we have to have the military, we have to defend ourselves, there is no other way, etc. It is now the goats' turn to go through karma, through wars and the natural disasters in order to come over to the other side and become the sheep. In this way we have the sheep and the goats open before us and we belong either to the sheep or the goats ourselves.

The whole world picture shows that you have to learn to love and that love comes because of the sufferings. But the intellect also has to be included; it is not so good that the feelings rule on their own. It is good and wonderful that we can love each other, that we can caress each other, that we can be fond of each other, but it is also wonderful that we can be geniuses in art, that we can reach the highest genius in creating works of art in every way, music, painting and many other forms of art which is the occupation of the spiritual world. That is what will come about when mankind has passed its violent karma. What we today call "to work in the sweat of one's face" shall not go on, it is not the plan that Mankind shall be slaves. The plan is that work or being employed shall end up as artistic abilities. In the higher worlds there are no workers, there everybody is an artist. Everything that is created is art and everybody is free from financial worries and politics and everything that we find in this world, which is not finished.

THE FORGIVENESS OF SINS

The real Christianity is not over, even though the old Christianity is on the retreat. We no longer believe in "eternal hell," "grace" and the forgiveness of sins. We will get "forgiveness of sins" but not in the way it has been said in the churches. When we perform a bad deed and go on performing this bad deed, we get the same deed back. When you have performed a bad deed toward a human being and you realize that this was wrong and you repent it and you are not able to do it anymore, then you don't get the karma back, you get "forgiveness of sins."

All the many people who eat meat today are accomplices in the killing of all these animals. They break the fifth commandment. They never get to repay this completely, because when they become vegetarians, because they can no longer find it in their hearts to kill animals, then their sins will be forgiven. In this way you can get out of the evil, come out of your karma, because you have so much karma, that you would otherwise never get out of it.

TO BE A JOY AND BLESSING FOR EVERYBODY AND EVERYTHING

The main thing is not that you know the analyses and the complex issues to a high degree. The main thing is really that you can forgive your neighbor. This is where Christ says, not only seven times, but until seventy times seven times you must forgive your neighbor. This is the main problem for man in his daily life. Most people have somebody who they do not like and do not think well of. But you have to be in the same way as the sun. The sun is the foundation of the physical life here. In the same way we have to be the foundation for our surroundings. We must send light and heat into the terrain of ice in the mentality of other people. Maybe we can illuminate the mentality of "dark people" if we are strong enough, or we can train to do it. It is all about saying to ourselves: "Today I want to be a joy and a blessing to everything I get in contact with." Then you are in complete harmony and you are helping recreate yourself and Mankind to be in the image of God."

Ole Therkelsen has edited the article. The editing has been approved by the Council of the Martinus Institute.

God's Plan

Because the universe is God's body it is ruled by order. Eternal laws determine the reactions of all matter. There are no coincidences and no chance occurrences. The universe rests in a perfect balance. This again means that everything happens according to a plan. When we looked at our present spiral cycle we saw how the fluctuations of the basic energies gave rise to all the different life forms we know on Earth. We saw that on the physical level the development of the beings goes through manifestations in mineral matter, in plant bodies, in animal bodies, and in human bodies. All beings go through this development and this dressing of oneself in various different bodies conveys a renewal of the life experience of the being and consequently a renewal of God's life experience. Through this passage of the various realms of the cycle, the living beings experience contrast. We eternally move between the two extremes of light and darkness. Our whole development of enfolding and unfolding takes place according to a master plan—God's plan. We are microbeings in God's body and consequently our whole existence is ruled by logic and intelligence.

As our existence is a part of God's existence and as his existence is ruled by laws that are based in a plan for his eternal existence, there is no chance that God's plan with the living beings will fail. There is not even the remotest chance that God's plan will fail. We will with absolute certainty arrive at the gates of the real human kingdom in approximately three thousand years. This again means that life is a game we cannot lose.

When we look at the situation of the world today, it may not be very uplifting. We still have wars, killings, and terrorism. We are still living in darkness. But just as we can be absolutely certain that daylight will follow the darkness of night, we can be absolutely certain that the darkness we are now living in will be substituted by light. There does not exist even the remotest chance that the light will fail to dawn. And don't we know that the darkest hour is just before the dawn? The world may not be a perfect place right now, but that is because the perfect stage has not been reached yet. The perfect stage is being developed and just as we should not judge the apple by its sour stage, we should not judge the world by its present unripe stage. Over the next centuries we will outgrow our animal mentality and gradually we will be able to create a peaceful world. This peaceful world will come with absolute certainty, because its coming is part of God's plan.

At our present stage we have a certain amount of free will. If we want to we can use our free will to help create a peaceful world. As individuals we cannot change the world. We can only change ourselves. But through changing ourselves we will contribute to changing the world. When we have eradicated the deeply rooted animal thought climates from our own mentality, there is one animal less and one supporter more for love and peace living on this planet. We can only start creating world peace by first creating peace in our own mentality. World peace begins with every one of us.

Martinus gives the following seven instructions on how to strengthen our humanitarian side:

- Eradicate the concept of "enemies" from your consciousness.
- Never talk back when faced with anger, slander, or other forms of unpleasantness directed toward you.
- Never say anything evil about anybody or anything.
- Be completely truthful or honest in all situations of life.
- Be completely unaffected by flattery, praise, or reproach.
- Never participate in killing, hurting, or crippling.
- Never let your thoughts stop thinking of how you best can serve your fellow man; then you will perform the highest form of yoga or the perfect training within the part of development that has been placed within reach of your will and that in connection with the other part of life's own shaping of your nature will lead you to become a moral genius or the perfect being or a 'man of God'.

—The Structure for Cooperation

Martinus calls these points *"The Ideal Attitude to Life."* If we want to we can try to live according to these guidelines. This may be easier said than done, but there is only one way to improve and that is to practice. If we have enemies we could start looking for positive sides to their character (everybody has some positive sides) and focusing on these. The more we focus on the positive sides, the better will our image of our "enemy" become. After some time we may stop thinking about the person as an enemy. Once we have reached that point we can start to forgive him and bless him. When we have blessed the person for many consecutive nights in our prayers, we no longer see the person as an enemy but as a fellow man. This could be one way of starting. We can also start by changing our diet to be less based on meat. We can start by doing charity work and helping others. We can start by concentrating on being positive and forgiving. It is up to us to promote our exit from the animal kingdom.

Eradicating our animal thought climates and tendencies may be a colossal job, but the sooner we start and the more mental energy we spend on eradicating it, the sooner will we achieve our goal. We are all responsible for the development of this planet. We can help development by "unlearning" our animal mentality and learning to serve our fellow man. Luckily we are helped and supported by Providence in this process, but if we also help and support Providence, development on the planet will accelerate toward peace, prosperity, and love.

According to Martinus the love and light that await us in the real human kingdom and beyond is so indescribably great and all-encompassing that we cannot even begin to imagine it. As our future is so bright and full of love, there is no need to linger any longer here in the animal kingdom than is absolutely necessary. Let us practice humanity. The development of our humane ability is a condition for the evolution of our intuition. The more humane our manifestations become, the more will we be susceptible to the inflow of intuitive energies. It is only when our humanity has reached a certain level that we will be candidates for cosmic glimpses.

Martinus clearly states that the most important thing is not to know his analyses and the complicated explanations. The most important thing is to practice humanity and forgiveness.

As there is no death it might be a good idea to consider what we can take with us from here to the other side. Can we take real estate, jewelry, gold, fur coats, cars, shares, stock options, and money? Well, no. Jesus says, *"Do not lay up for yourselves treasures on earth, where moth and rust consume and where thieves break in and steal, but lay up for yourselves treasure in heaven, where neither moth nor rust consumes and where thieves do not break in and steal. For where your treasure is, there will your heart be"* (Matthew 6:19–21).

Our kindness, help, love, and good deeds are our "treasure in heaven." These are the only treasures that we can take with us to the other side and into our future lives.

To learn more about Martinus' work and to get an update on which titles are available in English you can visit the website of the Martinus Institute at www.martinus.dk

I hope that this introduction has made you want to read Martinus' original works. If it has, I hope that you will enjoy reading Martinus' own words. His works are very interesting reading, they are uplifting, exciting, and full of humor and love. There is never a dull moment.

When you have read his works, you will have achieved cosmic consciousness yourself, but on an intellectual level, not through your own experience. This experience will come later, first through cosmic glimpses and later through the great birth.

Through the insight you get from reading Martinus' works, you cannot help becoming an optimist as you will see that "everything is very good" and just as it should be. The final Armageddon has been canceled. The Earth with its humanity is not doomed and all life will never be eradicated. Everything is fine, and if our world is not perfect right now it is because it is not finished yet. As long as there are wars and killings of animals it is not yet a perfect world and as long as we sow war we shall reap war, but one day the creation of the perfect stage will be finished and we will all become "man in the image and likeness of God." Let us take comfort and rejoice that we are not alone and unprotected, but that we are taken care of by the highest and most loving being, God.

Notes

NOTES TO DEDICATION

1. Please see the bibliography for a list of titles by the persons mentioned.

2. In his classic tragedy *Faust* from 1808, Johann Wolfgang von Goethe (1749 -1832) lets the aging Faust make a deal with Mefistoles, the devil, in which Faust will regain his lost youth and the services of Mefistoles while on Earth in return for giving up his soul to Mefistoles after death. After swallowing the elixir of youth and being transformed into a handsome young man, Faust is ready to set forth with Mefistoles as his guide and he asks:

"Where are we going?"

And Mefistoles answers,

"Where ever you want,
First we see the small,
And then the big world."

CHAPTER 1

1. John Skynner and John Cleese, *Life and How to Survive It*, Mandarin, London, 1993.

2. This project was headed by cardiologist Pim van Lommel, Hospital Rijnstate, Arnhem, Holland.

3. John Engelbrecht, *Den intuitive tanke*, vols. I–IV, Borgen, Copenhagen 1982.

4. Martinus: Please refer to the bibliography to find a full list of his publications.

5. Martinus wanted his main work *Livets Bog* to be published with its original Danish title in all languages.

CHAPTER 2

1. Copernicus, Nicolaus (1473–1543). Polish astronomer. His astronomical observations constituted a showdown with the traditional geocentric world picture of the Greeks. According to Copernicus' observations, the Earth rotates once around its own axis in twenty-four hours at the same time as it circles the

sun together with the other planets. His main work *De Revolutionibus Orbium Coelestium Libri I–IV* was for political reasons published only immediately before his death in 1543.

2. Galilei, Galileo (1564–1642). Italian physicist, astronomer, and philosopher. He discovered the laws for movements and acceleration and invented a thermometer. In 1609 he built the first telescope and his observations supported the findings of Copernicus. Galileo made innumerable observations of the solar system and the galaxy, and although his contemporaries did not accept his findings, posterity has proved that most of his revelations are true. Galileo is considered the founder of experimental physics.

3. Isaac Newton (1642–1727). English physicist, astronomer, and mathematician. Professor at the University of Cambridge 1660–1703. One of Newton's most important discoveries was the law of gravity. Newton also developed the basic principles of theoretic mechanics. Based on the law of general gravitation, Newton was able to establish that the Earth was a sphere. His calculations of the movements of the planets confirmed astrological observations. His main work *Principia* (1687) was to be fundamental for physics and astronomy for several centuries.

Johannes Kepler (1571–1630). German astronomer. Discovered three laws, the so-called Kepler's laws, which define the paths of the planets around the Sun.

4. "The Universe," *National Geographic,* October 1999. Official journal of The National Geographic Society, Washington DC.

5. René Descartes, French philosopher and mathematician 1596–1650. Descartes' philosophy is based on a methodological doubt about everything, be it perceptions through the senses, the outer reality, thoughts, etc. The only indubitable is doubt itself and consequently the person who doubts. To doubt is to think and consequently Descartes formulated the phrase "Cogito, ergo sum" [I think, therefore I am]. Together with Newton, Descartes viewed the material world as purely mechanical. All processes and events in this world are movements of its parts. All organisms are viewed as machines, as constituted of parts, and the universe is viewed as a huge clockwork, the result of the coming together of all its parts. According to Descartes the body and the soul belonged to two different realms and one could be studied without reference to the other. Only man has a soul. Animals have no soul and function as pure automatons. Descartes' philosophy has had an enormous influence on most sciences to this day.

6. Cosmic consciousness. I have taken the following definition of cosmic consciousness from Dr. Richard Bucke's book *Cosmic Consciousness* from 1901: "*The prime characteristic of cosmic consciousness is, as the name implies, a consciousness*

of the cosmos—that is of the life and order of the universe.... Along with the consciousness of the cosmos there occurs an intellectual enlightenment or illumination which alone would place the individual on a new plane of existence—would make him almost a member of a new species. To this is added a state of moral exaltation, an indescribable feeling of elevation and joyousness, and a quickening of the moral sense, which is fully as striking and more important both to the individual and to the race than is the enhanced intellectual power. With these come what may be called a sense of immortality, a consciousness of eternal life, not a conviction that he shall have this, but the consciousness that he has it already."

7. The following of Martinus' books have been published in English by the Martinus Institute. The list is from the latest updated information published in Kosmos, August 2001.

> *Livets Bog (The Book of Life)*, volumes 1 and 2
>
> *The Eternal World Picture*, volumes 1, 2, 3 and 4
>
> *Logic*
>
> *The Fate of Mankind*
>
> *Easter*
>
> *On the Birth of My Mission*
>
> *The Ideal Food*
>
> *Cosmic Consciousness*
>
> *The Mystery of Prayer*
>
> *The Road to Initiation*
>
> *The Principle of Reincarnation*
>
> *World Religion and World Politics*
>
> *Meditation*
>
> *The Road of Life*
>
> *The Immortality of the Living Beings*

The following titles have been translated into English, but not yet published:

> *Livets Bog (The Book of Life)*, volumes III–VII
>
> *Mankind and the World Picture*
>
> *The Road to Paradise*
>
> *Through the Gates of Death* (leaflet)

CHAPTER 3

1. Quoted from *Martinus Erindringer*, Zinglersen's Forlag, Copenhagen 1987, page 64.

2. Ibid., page 70.

3. Steiner, Rudolf (1861–1925). Austrian philosopher, artist, scientist, and educator whose "spiritual science" movement is a blend of Rosicrucian, Theosophical, and Christian traditions. Steiner had a clairvoyant awareness of the unseen and with time he accumulated a great deal of experience in the nonphysical realms. In 1913, Steiner formed the Anthroposophical Society and thus broke away from the Theosophical Society. Steiner traveled widely and gave more than six thousand lectures, mostly in Europe. He has published more than 350 titles, most of which are collections of lectures, as well as books, articles, reviews and dramas. One of Steiner's greatest legacies is probably the Waldorf School Movement, which has more than five-hundred schools in most parts of the world. The approach to the education of children has been developed from Steiner's spiritual-scientific research concerning child development. The schools also address the educational needs of retarded children.

4. Nostradamus (1503–1566). French physician, prophet, and gifted clairvoyant whose far-reaching prophesies go as far as the year 3797. More than half of his prophecies have been claimed to come true. Among the many great events of history Nostradamus is credited with having foreseen are: The Napoleonic Wars, the history of British monarchs from Elizabeth I to Elizabeth II, The American Civil War, the rise and fall of Hitler, the assassinations of Abraham Lincoln, John F. Kennedy, and Robert Kennedy, and the rise of Iran's Ayatollah Khomeini. He also foresaw air and space travel, manned rockets to the Moon, submarines, and the atomic bomb.

5. *Martinus Erindringer*, page 86.

6. All quotations from Martinus in this book are presented in my own translation from Danish into English.

7. Martinus' books have been translated into the following languages (as of August 2001): English, Esperanto, French, Dutch, Icelandic, Japanese, Chinese, Russian, Serbian, Spanish, Swedish, Czech, German, Hungarian. However, not all the titles have been translated into all the mentioned languages. The Martinus Institute can inform the status of publication and translation into any language.

8. The Danish version of the Bible says: "Men talsmanden [the spokesman], Helligånden, som Faderen vil sende i mit navn, han skal lære jer alt, og huske jer på alt, hvad jeg har sagt." (John 14:26–27). However, in the English version the word "Counselor" has been used instead of "spokesman." The English version

goes like this: "But the Counselor, the Holy Spirit, whom the Father will send in my name, he will teach you all things, and bring to your remembrance all that I have said to you."

9. *Martinus Erindringer*, page 187.

10. Ibid., page 187.

Chapter 4

1. All quotations from the Bible in this book are from the Revised Standard Version, 1952.

2. "Biodiversity," *National Geographic*, February 1999.

3. "The Universe," *National Geographic*, October 1999.

4. Throughout this book I have used the Martinus Institute's official numbers of the symbols. A total of forty-four different symbols have been published to date.

5. In Danish, Martinus uses the word *naturfolk*, which literally translated means "nature people." However, this expression does not exist in proper English, which seems to prefer the term "primitive people." However, there is a derogative touch to "primitive" which does not exist in the Danish expression. The reader is kindly requested to disregard any derogative meaning conveyed by the word "primitive."

6. Pantheism is a metaphysical concept of God being present immanently in the world, i.e., present everywhere in nature and even in the smallest units.

7. Providence. By Providence is understood the host of spiritual beings that help God carry out all the various tasks in the universe. The term Providence is often used synonymously with God, as Providence carries out God's will.

8. Akashic Records. In Theosophy the master records of everything that has ever occurred since the beginning of the universe. The records are said to exist as impressions in the astral plane. The term "Akashic" comes from the Sanskrit word *akasha*, defined as the fundamental etheric substance in the universe. The *akasha* is an eternal record of the vibrations of every action, thought, emotion, light, and sound. According to the American medium Edgar Cayce, anyone can gain access to these records with proper psychic training and attunement.

CHAPTER 5

1. The names of those who have experienced cosmic glimpses are from Svend Åge Rossen's book *Livets Mening*, Borgen, Copenhagen, 1993.

2. The Swedish woman was Ruth Dahlén and she has described her experience in her book *Visionär i tjugonde århundradet*, Stockholm, 1976. The Danish woman was Lis Høyer Mortensen and she has described her cosmic glimpse in her book *Når jeg ser din himmel*, Borgen, Copenhagen, 1979. The story about the American woman who had a cosmic glimpse while picking flowers has been related by Dr. Kenneth Ring.

3. Carol Bowman, *Children's Past Lives*, Bantam Books, New York, 1997, pp. 33–34.

4. The age of the Old Testament is debatable.

CHAPTER 6

1. At the onset of death the electrical field and consequently the aura leaves the body, but a recently dead body will still be surrounded by a weak sheen from the electrical fields of its billions of cells. As cells also have auras as long as they are alive, these may show as a faint shimmer around the dead body. Once the body is dead, the cells will also gradually die, so the shimmer will weaken the longer the body has been dead.

2. See for instance Moody and Ring.

CHAPTER 7

1. James Lovelock: "Gaia." Oxford University Press, 1979.

CHAPTER 11

1. Martinus tells a few instances of this in his memoirs, *Martinus' Erindringer*, Zinglersens Forlag, Copenhagen, 1987.

CHAPTER 12

1. The Human Genome Project. Project supported by the US government to map the human genome. More at: www.ornl.gov/hgmis/

2. In a cosmic sense the Holy Spirit in the shape of the "highest fire" is present in all lovemaking between willing partners, so it is correct to say that The Holy Spirit was present at the fertilization. More about this in chapter 14.

CHAPTER 13

1. A color version of the symbols nos. 19 and 23 can be seen at www.martinus.dk.

2. Ian Stevenson, *Twenty Cases of Suggestive Reincarnation*, p. 92.

3. Roger Woolger, *Other Lives, Other Selves*, page 220.

CHAPTER 14

1. Martinus was once asked which way was the best to relieve our sexual appetites and he answered, not surprisingly, that it was best with a partner. If there was no partner available, masturbation was the next best thing. So it is perfectly natural to take things in our own hands, so to speak.

Bibliography

Bowman, Carol. *Children's Past Lives: How Past Life Memories Affect Your Child.* New York: Bantam Books,1997.

Bruus-Jensen. Per, *Martinus kosmologi.* Copenhagen: Nordisk Impuls,1994.

Dahlén, Ruth. *Visionär i tjugonde århundradet.* Stockholm, 1976.

Engelbrecht, John. *Den intuitive tanke.* Copenhagen: Borgen, Vols. I–IV, 1982.

Fiore, Edith. *You Have Been Here Before.* New York: Ballantine Books, 1978.

———*The Unquiet Dead.* New York: Ballantine Books, 1987.

Kalén, Nils. *Vi och våra gener.* Linköping: Världsbild Forlag, 1998.

Kübler Ross, Elisabeth. *On Death and Dying.* New York: Touchstone, 1969.

———*Questions and Answers on Death and Dying.* New York: Touchstone, 1974.

———*Death: The Final Stage of Growth.* New York: Touchstone, 1975.

———*To Live Until We Say Goodbye.* New York: Touchstone, 1978.

———*Living with Death and Dying.* New York: Touchstone, 1981.

———*The Wheel of Life.* New York: Touchstone, 1997.

———*On Life After Death.* Berkeley, California: Celestial Arts, 1991.

Lovelock, James. *Gaia.* New York: Oxford University Press, 1979.

Martinus:

> *Livets Bog (The Book of Life),* vols. I–VII. Borgen, Copenhagen, 1932–1960.
>
> *Det evige verdensbillede (The Eternal World Picture),* vols. I–IV.

Borgen, Copenhagen 1987–1994.

Bisættelse (Funeral Rites). Borgen, Copenhagen, 1951.

Logik (Logic). Borgen, Copenhagen, new edition, 1987.

Small books:

1. *Menneskehedens skæbne. (The Fate of Mankind)*

2. *Påske. (Easter).*

3. *Hvad er sandhed? (What is Truth?).*

4. *Omkring min missions fødsel. (On the Birth of My Mission).*

5. *Den ideelle føde. (The Ideal Food).*

6. *Blade af Guds billedbog. (Pages of God's Picture Book).*

7. *Den længst levende afgud. (The Longest Living Idol).*

8. *Menneskeheden og verdensbilledet. (Mankind and the World Picture).*

9. *Mellem to verdensepoker. (Between two World Epochs).*

10. *Kosmisk bevidsthed. (Cosmic Consciousness).*

11. *Bønnens mysterium. (The Mystery of Prayer).*

12. *Vejen til indvielse. (The Road to Initiation).*

13. *Juleevangeliet. (The Gospel of Christmas).*

14. *Bevidsthedens skabelse. (The Creation of Consciousness).*

15. *Ud af mørket. (Out of Darkness).*

16. *Reinkarnationsprincippet. (The Principle of Reincarnation).*

17. *Verdensreligion og verdenspolitik. (World Religion and World Politics).*

18. *Livets skæbnespil. (The Fate Drama of Life).*

19. *Kosmiske glimt. (Cosmic Glimpses).*

20. *Meditation. (Meditation).*

21. *Hinsides dødsfrygten. (Beyond the Fear of Death).*

22. *Livets vej. (The Road of Life).*

23. *De levende væseners udødelighed. (The Immortality of the Living Beings).*

24. *Kulturens skabelse. (The Creation of Culture).*

25. *Vejen til Paradis. (The Road to Paradise).*

26. *Djævlebevidsthed og kristusbevidsthed. (Devil Mentality and Christ Mentality).*

27. *Verdensfredens skabelse. (The Creation of World Peace).*

28. *To slags kærlighed. (Two Kinds of Love).*

All small books published by either Borgen or Martinus Institute.

Gennem dødens port. (Through the Gates of Death), leaflet. Martinus Institute.

Vejen til den sande lykke (The Road to True Happiness), leaflet, Martinus Institute.

Samarbejdsstrukturen. (The Structure for Cooperation), Martinus Institute, 1992.

Kosmos—the magazine *Kosmos*. Published monthly by the Martinus Institute since 1933. Six English versions published per year.

Martinus' Erindringer, Zinglersens Forlag, Copenhagen, 1987.

Martinus—som vi husker ham, Zinglersens Forlag, Copenhagen, 1989.

Moody, Raymond Jr. *Life after Life.* Georgia: Mockingbird Books, 1975.

———*Reflections on Life after Life.* Georgia: Mockingbird Books, 1977.

———*The Light Beyond.* New York: Bantam Books, 1988.

Mortensen, Lis Høyer. *Når jeg ser din himmel.* Copenhagen: Borgen, 1979.

Ring, Kenneth. *Life at Death.* New York: Coward McCann, 1980.

———*Lessons from the Light.* Portsmouth, NH: Moment Point Press, 1998.

Rossen, Svend Åage. *Livets mening.* Copenhagen: Borgen, 1993.

Skynner, John, and John Cleese. *Life and How to Survive It.* London: Mandarin, 1993.

Stevenson, Ian. *Twenty Cases Suggestive of Reincarnation.* Charlottesville: Universy Press of Virginia, 1974.

————*Where Reincarnation and Biology Intersect.* Westport: Praeger Publishers, 1997.

Wambach, Helen. *Reliving Past Lives.* New York: Harper & Row, 1978.

Weiss, Brian L. *Many Lives, Many Masters.* New York: Fireside; Simon & Schuster, 1988.

————*Through Time into Healing.* New York: Fireside; Simon and Schuster, 1992.

————*Only Love is Real.* New York: Warner Books, 1996.

Whitton, Joel L. *Life Between Life.* New York: Warner Books, 1986.

Woolger, Roger J. *Other Lives, Other Selves.* London: Aquarian, 1994.